D1096028

TEN YEARS OF PRELUDE

*The Story of Integration Since the
Supreme Court's 1954 Decision*

by Benjamin Muse

The March on Washington in August 1963 was the first peaceful wave of a revolution that is permanently altering the social structure of this country. The Negro at last openly asserted his rights—and the majority of his fellow countrymen rose to support him. From then on, facing the future struggle, he knew he was not alone.

The prelude to this revolution, a prelude that began on May 17, 1954, with the Supreme Court's decision declaring segregation in the public schools unconstitutional, is set forth here in its historical perspective. Beginning with the decision itself and the forces that helped shape it, Mr. Muse reviews its impact, and traces its consequences in the nation at large, in the border states, and finally in the eleven former Confederate states, where grave problems had to be faced. Step by step and year by year, he sets down the record of what happened in each of these areas: his book is not only a permanent source for historical information, but a story of mounting drama.

As the diehard anti-Negro sentiment in the South became solidified, interracial relations deteriorated, state-rights and anti-Supreme-Court zealots arose, the Ku Klux Klan was revived, and the stage was set for violence. It flared in shocking and dramatic fashion in Little Rock in 1957 and 1958; it smoldered in Virginia and reached a crescendo in Mississippi and Louisiana. Opposition to integration was bitter and bloody, but obedience to the law began to make headway. This is the story Mr. Muse, himself a Virginian, has to tell—in all its depth of sectional and personal prejudice, political implication and maneuver, and moral courage.

column and feature articles to *The Washington Post.*

ALSO BY BENJAMIN MUSE

Virginia's Massive Resistance

Tarheel Tommy Atkins

Ten Years of Prelude

THE STORY
OF INTEGRATION
SINCE THE
SUPREME COURT'S
1954
DECISION

BY BENJAMIN MUSE

New York: The Viking Press

1. School integration

Copyright © 1964 by Southern Regional Council, Inc.

All rights reserved

First published in 1964 by The Viking Press, Inc.
625 Madison Avenue, New York, N.Y. 10022

Published simultaneously in Canada by
The Macmillan Company of Canada Limited

Library of Congress catalog card number: 64-13298

Printed in U.S.A. by the Vail-Ballou Press, Inc.
M B G

To the memory of

JOHN FITZGERALD KENNEDY

FOREWORD

The central undertaking in this book is to review the impact of the Supreme Court decision of May 17, 1954, declaring race segregation in the public schools unconstitutional. Until 1960 this was mainly a story of the South and the border region, where public-school segregation previously had been required. The elimination of race barriers in public education has since become only one objective in a broad attack upon all forms of race discrimination, and Negro unrest has spread across the land. While completing the ten-year story of public-school desegregation in the South, an attempt has been made in these pages also to trace the beginnings of this broader movement and to raise the curtain on the civil rights crisis which now confronts the nation.

The production of the book was a project of the Southern Regional Council. A year of research followed three years of travel in the South, and consultation with many deeply concerned individuals, including some of the principal actors in the desegregation crisis. I talked with sixty knowledgeable and hospitable editors of Southern newspapers, to whom I owe much. I was helped in this fashion by hundreds of people.

I had the constant cooperation and help of Staige D. Blackford, the Southern Regional Council's Director of Research, and his assistants, notably Miss Janet Smith and Mrs. Barbara Patterson. Dr. Leslie W. Dunbar, Executive Director of the Council, was my mentor and valued critic; to him should go a large part of the credit for whatever merit the book may have.

The manuscript was read in its entirety and at all stages by Dr. Dunbar and Mr. Blackford; also, with the exception of the concluding chapter, by Harold C. Fleming, Executive Vice President of the Potomac Institute. Mr. Fleming also offered helpful criticism and corrections. Others read critically portions of the manuscript related to episodes and conditions which they had had exceptional opportunities to observe. Among these were the Reverend Will D. Campbell, of the

National Council of Churches; Honorable Brooks Hays, Special Assistant to the President; Alfred O. Hero, Executive Director of the World Peace Foundation; Mrs. Leo Mervis, of New Orleans; Dr. James W. Silver, Professor of History at the University of Mississippi; Robert Smith, associate editor of the Norfolk *Virginian Pilot;* and J. Everett Tucker, Jr., President of the Little Rock School Board.

My debt to all of these is warmly acknowledged.

BENJAMIN MUSE

Manassas, Virginia

CONTENTS

TEN YEARS OF PRELUDE

Chapter 1

THE BROWN DECISION

The decision which the Supreme Court handed down on May 17, 1954, outlawing segregation by race in public schools, was one of the great milestones in the history of the United States. For our Negro minority, now widely diffused but still residing preponderantly in that southeastern region which we call "the South," it was a pronouncement second in importance only to President Lincoln's Emancipation Proclamation. In the evolution of the Great Republic it may well be remembered as "the point at which the South cleared the last turning in the road to reunion. . . ." [1]* But, first, in the area which unforgettably was once the Confederate States of America, it inaugurated a period of painful awakening, of impulsive resistance, and of tension and hysteria to the point in many instances of violent convulsion.

The race problem—or the problem arising from the presence of Negroes, in the proportion earlier of as much as one-fifth, and in the twentieth century about one-tenth, of the country's population—has been for a century and a quarter the most disruptive domestic problem with which our statesmen and our people have had to deal. It fired the controversy which tore the nation asunder from 1861 to 1865. In the South after the Civil War it dominated a generation of confusion and unrest. In that still prostrate region three million illiterate Negroes had been suddenly separated both from the slaveholder's dominion and from his provision for their daily bread, and had even been thrust into the political arena. As the nineteenth century drew to a close and the twentieth began, an unwholesome stability was achieved by depriving nearly all Negroes, through ingenious devices, of the franchise, and by separating the race from the mainstream of community life. The latter process and the regime which it established were called *segregation*.

It is appropriate to note here a common error with respect to the supposed longevity of this system. Segregation so completely per-

* Reference Notes begin on page 292.

1

meated Southern life in sixty years that many came to look upon it as an "institution" that had existed from time immemorial. When it came under attack, not a few even among publicists and politicians of stature referred to segregation as a part of "the mores of three hundred years." The historian C. Vann Woodward brought the facts of the matter to the attention of a frequently surprised public in 1955 in his *The Strange Career of Jim Crow,* but even now it is widely true that "the national discussion over the question of how deeply rooted, how ineradicable and how amenable to change the segregation practices really are is being conducted against a background of faulty or inadequate historical information." [2]

Subservience and subjection of the Negro to the white man were indeed centuries old—but not segregation. Slavery was a very different relationship, and during an interval of more than thirty years after the Civil War neither slavery nor segregation in a general sense existed. It is true that the school facilities first provided for the newly freed Negroes of all ages who were eager for book-learning were almost always separate from the schools for whites. The Freedmen's Bureau was concerned solely with helping Negroes, and the more than four thousand schools set up by it were, of course, for Negroes only. But segregation as the mold for a dual society and as the popular and long-sought "solution" of the race problem was invented later.

It was in the 1890s that the segregation movement was born. It was near the end of the first decade of the twentieth century when its peak was reached. By then segregation had been extended, whether by law or by custom, to include hotels, restaurants, saloons, rest rooms, drinking fountains, libraries, churches, parks, hospitals, orphanages, prisons, asylums, all places of public assembly, all means of public transportation, nearly all fields of industrial employment, and ultimately funeral homes, morgues, and cemeteries. Because the resources of the Negroes themselves and the facilities and opportunities left open to them were meager, segregation generally meant in effect exclusion. The schools provided for Negroes were still few and rudimentary in their offering; employment above the level of menial or unskilled labor was almost closed to them. Thus segregation came in a large measure to replace slavery as a means of keeping the Negro "in his place"—which meant a subservient place in the life and economy of the South.

In a wave of racism at the turn of the century (which was not confined to the South), segregation proceeded with general acquiescence; it was indeed accepted by Booker T. Washington, the foremost Negro leader, in the hope of securing by this accommodation the economic and educational opportunities of which his race stood in dire need. The Negro was again submerged. In the words of Harry S. Ashmore, "the Southern Negro lapsed into the long twilight period which would continue until the New Deal years. . . ." [3] An incipient voice of Negro protest rose, scarcely audible at first, and an interracial organization founded in 1909, known as the National Association for the Advancement of Colored People, though ineffectual for a decade or more, was to become by mid-century a powerful influence in national affairs.

In the meantime a number of factors operated to increase respect for the Negro and to bring segregation into disfavor in the nation as a whole. Though still vastly inferior to the educational facilities for white youth, schools and colleges for Negroes multiplied and improved, and despite the disadvantages under which he labored, the Negro made significant progress. An increasing number of distinguished Negro intellectuals began to stand in refutation of the theory of innate Negro incompetence. In the late 1920s the production of racist literature, which had flourished since the turn of the century, almost suddenly subsided, and the theory of biological racial inferiority began to be repudiated by scholars generally.

By the middle of the twentieth century segregation, though still tenaciously defended in the South, was frowned upon in principle in most of the nation. School segregation had been abolished in all but the seventeen Southern and border states, the District of Columbia, Kansas, and a few scattered localities in three Western states. Segregation in the Armed Forces was ended in the early 1950s, following an executive order issued in 1948. The Negro vote by now was a factor in national politics. The more enlightened Negro masses were becoming acutely conscious of the incubus of segregation, and Negro leaders were urging a militant stand against it. The President's Committee on Civil Rights reported in 1947:

> The separate-but-equal doctrine has failed in three important respects. First, it is inconsistent with the fundamental equalitarianism of the American way of life in that it marks groups with the brand of inferior status. Secondly, where it has been followed, the results have been separate but unequal facilities for minority peoples.

Finally, it has kept people apart despite incontrovertible evidence that an environment favorable to civil rights is fostered whenever groups are permitted to live and work together. There is no adequate defense of segregation.

It was at this stage in history that the Supreme Court directly confronted the question: Is segregation in public schools compatible with the ideals of democracy expressed in the Constitution of the United States? The Court answered: "No." The cases before it involved only public education, but the principle which it laid down would extend in time to a variety of public services and accommodations. The decision accomplished no immediate and sweeping transformation; indeed, the edict to end segregation was not to be obeyed in all sections of the South for many years to come even in the field of public education. Nevertheless, the great decision of May 17, 1954, opened the door at last for the assimilation of Negroes as full-fledged citizens of the Republic.

The Court ruled specifically that segregation in public schools violates this commandment of the Fourteenth Amendment of the Constitution: "No state shall make or enforce any law which shall abridge the privilege or immunities of citizens of the United States; nor shall any state deprive any person of life, liberty, or property, without due process of law; nor deny to any person within its jurisdiction the equal protection of the laws."

The Court found that "separate educational facilities are inherently unequal" and hence deny to the minority race the "equal protection of the laws."

The Supreme Court had dealt with the race problem before. This 1954 pronouncement was the latest of three historic decisions, each of which was a milestone. In the advance toward enlightened interracial behavior the Dred Scott decision may be said to point to the place from which our journey began. This decision was handed down in 1857—before the Fourteenth Amendment, which was adopted in 1868, and before Emancipation. It held that slaves were property and that Congress could not set geographic limits to slavery. Looking back to the 1780s, when the Constitution was adopted, the Dred Scott opinion gave this account of the attitude toward Negroes prevailing at that time:

They had for more than a century before been regarded as beings of an inferior order and altogether unfit to associate with the white race, either in social or political relations; and so far inferior that they had no rights which the white man was bound to respect; and that the Negro might justly and lawfully be reduced to slavery for his benefit. . . .

The United States had come a long way from that concept by 1896; not slavery, but only the device of segregation, was at issue when the Supreme Court delivered its decision in the case of *Plessy v. Ferguson*. Still the Court said:

Legislation is powerless to eradicate racial instincts or to abolish distinctions based upon physical differences. . . . If one race be inferior to the other socially, the Constitution of the United States cannot put them on the same plane.

The Plessy decision sustained a Louisiana statute requiring separate accommodations for white and colored persons in railway trains, provided the accommodations were physically equal, and thus proclaimed what became known as the "separate-but-equal doctrine." Though the case involved directly only transportation facilities, the Court appeared to give incidental sanction to the separate-but-equal principle in education when it observed:

Laws permitting and even requiring [separation of the races] in places where they are liable to be brought into contact do not necessarily imply the inferiority of either race to the other, and have been generally, if not universally, recognized as within the competency of the state legislatures in the exercise of their police power. The most common instance of this is connected with the establishment of separate schools for white and colored children, which has been held a valid exercise of the legislative power even by the courts of states where the political rights of the colored race have been the longest and most earnestly enforced.

Seven justices concurred in this 1896 decision; one eloquently dissented. Justice John Marshall Harlan, a Southerner from Kentucky, whose clairvoyance was to be vindicated by a unanimous Court in 1954, declared:

In the view of the Constitution, in the eye of the law, there is in this country no superior, dominant, ruling class of citizens. There is no caste system here. Our Constitution is color-blind, and neither knows nor tolerates classes among its citizens. . . . In my opinion, the judgment this day rendered will, in time, prove to be as pernicious as the decision by this tribunal in the Dred Scott case. . . . What can more certainly arouse race hate, what more certainly create and perpetuate a feeling of distrust between these races, than state enactments which in fact proceed on the ground that colored citizens are so inferior and degraded that they cannot be allowed to sit in public coaches occupied by white citizens . . . ?

We boast of the freedom enjoyed by our people above all other peoples. But it is difficult to reconcile that boast with a state of the law which, practically, puts the brand of servitude and degradation upon a large class of our fellow-citizens, our equals before the law. The thin disguise of "equal" accommodations for passengers in railroad coaches will not mislead anyone, nor atone for the wrong this day done. . . .

The separate-but-equal doctrine was eagerly embraced as a basis for Negro-white relationship; separate but equal provision for the two races became the declared policy of every Southern state. But the emphasis was entirely on "separate." The history of the separate-but-equal doctrine is one of grotesque disregard of the "equal" end of the phrase.

The ideal of equal educational opportunity was a goal to be considered only after the needs of white children were met. The needs of Negroes were so neglected in the South during the next three decades that construction of Negro grade schools became a salient object of philanthropy. Several Northern foundations, notably the Julius Rosenwald Fund, contributed generously to this cause. The completion of a Negro school in Elizabeth City County, Virginia, in 1930, was the occasion for celebrating the five-thousandth "Rosenwald school." [4] As late as 1933 more than two hundred Southern counties with Negro populations of 12.5 per cent or more had no Negro high schools at all. After 1940 the South redoubled its efforts in the whole field of public education, and Negro children were given a considerably larger share of the total outlay than before. By 1954 school facilities for Negroes had been brought near the level of those for whites in several Southern states; but in others they were grossly inferior, and equality in this was still far short of being achieved in the South as a whole.[5]

Many have speculated that had the "equal" requirement of the separate-but-equal doctrine been adhered to in good faith the question of segregation might not have come before the Supreme Court, at least not for many more years. It is indeed possible that if the Negroes had enjoyed better school facilities they would have been prepared to accept segregation for a longer period. At the same time, however, more rapid cultural progress would doubtless have made the humiliation of segregation more poignantly felt. The question is academic now; but even before the 1954 decision was handed down, Southern leaders were seized with an impulse to hasten the expansion and improvement of Negro school facilities—in the hope, on the one hand, of presenting a stronger case to federal courts and, on the other, of dispelling the Negro urge for integration.

Lawyers of the National Association for the Advancement of Colored People had prosecuted successful suits for equalization of school plant and teacher salaries in the South within the framework of segregation. The marked improvement in public schools for Negroes which followed World War II was due in large part to NAACP prodding. In 1950 the Association resolved to launch a broad attack upon segregation itself. Its general counsel, Thurgood Marshall, convened a series of conferences of lawyers who, aided by sociologists, psychologists, and educators, both white and Negro, began to lay the groundwork for Supreme Court appeals. Langston Hughes, a noted Negro author high in NAACP councils, relates:

> It was unreasonable and unjust, they maintained, to expect Negro children to wait twenty, thirty, or forty years for the Jim Crow [segregated] school to wither away. For it was not just the physical inadequacies and curriculum deficiencies of most Negro schools in the South that were in question. Marshall argued that the very fact of segregation itself caused undeniable personality damage and serious injury to the human personality subjected to such inequalities.[6]

The walls of segregation at the university level had already begun to crumble; in the fall of 1953 only five state universities still had not opened their doors to Negroes. In a series of cases, beginning with that of a Negro applicant to the University of Maryland Law School in 1936, Supreme Court opinions had increasingly suggested that racial segregation could never afford equal opportunities in education. The Court's decision of June 5, 1950, on the suit of Hemon Sweatt to enter the University of Texas Law School was based on premises so broad as virtually to exclude separate education on the graduate and professional level. Although a separate law school had been set up for Negroes, the Court, in ordering Sweatt's admission, cited the advantages of the state university in "reputation of the faculty, experience of the administration, position and influence of the alumni, standing in the community, traditions and prestige."

To bring the issue of segregation in public schools before the Supreme Court a suit or suits were needed to be filed in lower courts, seeking the admission of individual Negro children on a non-segregated basis to schools of specific communities where segregation was practiced. These suits would ultimately reach the high tribunal on appeal as "class actions," and a decision by the Supreme Court that denial of such admission was in violation of the Constitution would make segregation unlawful everywhere. Appropriate situations were not long in presenting themselves.

One of them was already developing in Clarendon County, South Carolina, where the inadequate Negro schools were in particularly glaring contrast to the schools for white children. Parents of children attending the overcrowded Negro high school in the town of Summerton had begun to meet and discuss their grievances in 1949. When a committee waited upon the local school board and got no satisfaction, a NAACP lawyer prepared a formal petition, which a hundred and seven parents and children signed, and filed it with the school board. Nothing came of this. In 1950 NAACP lawyers filed suit in the federal district court at Charleston to end segregation in the public schools of the Summerton school district of Clarendon County.

While this case was pending in the district court, Negro dissatisfaction with inferior school facilities in a Virginia county was expressed in a more spectacular fashion. On April 23, 1951, the students of Prince Edward County's inadequate Negro high school, four hundred and fifty in number, went on strike. The Negro Parent-Teacher Association meeting two days later voted to support the students' efforts to obtain a new high school. But a NAACP attorney, addressing the meeting, pointed out that discrimination was not merely a matter of bricks and mortar and announced that the NAACP's aim now was to end segregation itself. The matter was placed in the hands of NAACP lawyers, and a petition was filed with the school board requesting that it cease making distinctions on the basis of race in the assignment of pupils. The striking students returned to their school. But the school board rejected the petition. On May 23, 1951, a petition was filed with the federal district court.

Three-judge federal district courts ruled similarly in the South Carolina and Virginia cases. (Three-judge courts are required when the constitutionality of state laws is in question.) The defendant school authorities were ordered to proceed without delay to equalize school facilities for white and Negro children, and the construction of the new schools was in fact undertaken promptly in both communities. But segregation was upheld in the lower courts, and the issue was taken on appeal to the Supreme Court. These cases, the ones that came to the Supreme Court from states of the onetime Southern Confederacy, involved two of the communities where racial segregation would be most difficult to bring to an end. The disparity between the school facilities for whites and those for Negroes was conspicuous in both counties and Negroes comprised an exceptionally large proportion of the population of each: in Prince Edward, Negroes were 45 per cent of the total; in Clarendon, over 70 per cent.

A striking contrast was presented by another community—in a non-Southern, Midwestern state—from which an appeal testing the constitutionality of segregation was on its way to the Supreme Court. In Topeka, Kansas, the Negro plaintiffs conceded that school facilities and services provided for the two races were substantially equal; they challenged only the principle of segregation, which was still practiced in the first six grades of the public schools. Segregation was not popular in Kansas. The state attorney general, in undertaking to defend an 1867 Kansas statute leaving the question to local governmental units, said: "We want it understood that we are not defending segregation"; and the Topeka Board of Education permitted its attorney to help prepare the brief only on condition that "the only issue to be argued will be the constitutionality of the Kansas law and not the moral rightness of segregation." [7] The three-judge federal court considered itself bound by Supreme Court precedent and upheld segregation, but it made the following significant observation.

Segregation of white and colored children in public schools has a detrimental effect upon the colored children. The impact is greater when it has the sanction of the law; for the policy of separating the races is usually interpreted as denoting the inferiority of the Negro group. A sense of inferiority affects the motivation of a child to learn. Segregation with the sanction of law, therefore, has a tendency to [retard] the educational and mental development of Negro children and to deprive them of some of the benefits they would receive in a racial [ly] integrated school system.

The Supreme Court considered this finding "well stated" and later embodied it by quotation in its own opinion.

In a case from Wilmington, Delaware, where unequal school facilities were complained of, appeal was taken to the United States Supreme Court from a decision of the Delaware Supreme Court in favor of the Negro plaintiffs. The Delaware tribunal, while explicitly refraining from dealing with the question of segregation as such, ordered Negro children admitted to white schools until such time as the Negro schools might be brought up to parity with those for white children. This case went to the Supreme Court by appeal on the part of the school authorities; they protested that the Delaware courts had not allowed a reasonable time for making the adjustment.

Each of the four cases described above raised the issue of public-school segregation in relation to the prohibitions applicable to the states under the Fourteenth Amendment of the Constitution. The four were heard and dealt with collectively by the Supreme Court. By long custom the name of the first in the list of plaintiffs in the first of the cases to reach the Court is given to the whole action. The name of Oliver Brown, who sought to have his 8-year-old daughter, Linda Carol Brown, admitted to a white school near her home, was by alphabetization the first in the list of plaintiffs in the Topeka suit, and this was Case No. 1 on the Supreme Court docket. The four cases were labeled *Oliver Brown et al. v. Board of Education of Topeka* and referred to informally as merely *Brown*. Thus the most momentous judicial decision of the century was to be known for all time as the Brown decision.

A fifth school segregation case before the Supreme Court, that of *Bolling v. Sharpe,* came from the District of Columbia. Since the District's school system operated directly under federal authority, it was contested under the Fifth rather than the Fourteenth Amendment. This case was to be heard at the same time, but it would receive a separate ruling.*

The five cases were argued before the Supreme Court in December 1952 and reargued one year later, the Court submitting specific questions to opposing counsel. A change of national administration occurred between the 1952 and 1953 hearings, and, because of the death of Chief Justice Fred M. Vinson, a change also in the highest judicial office: Earl Warren, governor of California, was appointed Chief Justice by President Eisenhower in time to preside over the December 1953 reargument. The Court—which was to act unanimously—was strikingly representative of the nation. Chief Justice Warren, who would write the opinion, was a Republican; the associate justices, except Justice Harold Burton, of Ohio, a Republican friend whom President Truman had appointed, were all from the Democratic party. Three were from states requiring public-school segregation: Justice Stanley Reed from Kentucky; Justice Tom Clark from Texas, and Justice Hugo Black from Alabama. The other four justices were William O. Douglas of Connecticut, Felix Frankfurter of Massachusetts, Robert H. Jackson of New York, and Sherman Minton of Indiana. The legal counsel on both sides was of the highest order. Thurgood Marshall, heading a group of able Negro attorneys for the plaintiffs, had already proved himself both a tough fighter and a brilliant lawyer. John W. Davis, a former ambassador to Great Britain, nominee of the Democratic party for President of the United States in 1924, headed the group of state and private attorneys defending segregation.

Both Democratic and Republican administrations entered the case on behalf of the plaintiffs. First, President Truman's Attorney General, James P. McGranery, and, later, President Eisenhower's Attorney General Herbert Brownell, Jr., supported the argument that public-school segregation should be declared unconstitutional. McGranery also introduced testimony of Secretary of State Dean Acheson, who wrote:

* Two more suits seeking desegregation of public schools were in litigation in federal district courts but were suspended pending Supreme Court action on the five mentioned: *McSwain v. County Board of Education of Anderson County,* Tennessee (Clinton), filed April 26, 1950, and *Bush v. Orleans Parish School Board,* filed 1952.

As might be expected, Soviet spokesmen regularly exploit [racial discrimination] in propaganda against the United States, both within the United Nations and through radio broadcasts and the press, which reaches all corners of the world. . . . The segregation of school children on a racial basis is one of the practices in the United States which has been singled out for hostile foreign comment in the United Nations and elsewhere. Other peoples cannot understand how such a practice can exist in a country which professes to be a staunch supporter of freedom, justice, and democracy. The sincerity of the United States in this respect will be judged by its deeds as well as by its words.

The NAACP lawyers now carried their well-rehearsed argument on the inequality of separateness to the highest tribunal. Psychologists and sociologists testified voluminously that available scientific evidence indicated no innate racial differences in intelligence, that segregation blocked communication and increased interracial tension, and that segregation had had detrimental personality effects upon Negro children and impaired their ability to profit from available facilities of public education.

The Court was to refer in a footnote to its decision to a number of sociological texts, adding: "And see generally Myrdal, *An American Dilemma*." Critics later would make much of the Court's apparent reliance upon sociologists, and Gunnar Myrdal, the distinguished Swedish authority, would be widely execrated in the South as a suspicious alien, probably a Communist. However, the extent to which the findings of sociologists were necessary to the disposition of the cases has been the subject of some debate among scholars. Professor Edmund Cahn has held that the decision turned on the "common sense" of the justices:

So one speaks in terms of the most familiar and universally accepted standards of right and wrong when one remarks (1) that racial segregation under government auspices inevitably inflicts humiliation and (2) that official humiliation of innocent, law-abiding citizens is psychologically injurious and morally evil. Mr. Justice Harlan and many other Americans with responsive consciences recognized these simple elementary propositions before, during, and after the rise of "separate but equal." For at least twenty years hardly any cultivated person has questioned that segregation is cruel to Negro school children. The cruelty is obvious and evident. Fortunately, it is so very obvious that the justices of the Supreme Court could see it and act on it even after reading the labored attempts by plaintiffs' experts to demonstrate it "scientifically." [8]

Fifty-eight years after the Plessy decision, counsel for the defense argued that Virginia and South Carolina at last were on the way to fulfilling both ends of the separate-but-equal doctrine. Virginia's Attorney General Almond said: "It is our policy and our determination —and our people are enthusiastically in support of it—to equalize school facilities." [9] Defense counsel warned that the elimination of segregation would destroy public-school systems. They contended that public schools, involving minors present in school under state compulsion, were a different matter from institutions of higher learning, a field in which the Supreme Court had rejected racial segregation in several recent cases. The wishes of parents had to be considered if schools were to enjoy the necessary public support.

The Court invited the views of the litigants on the question of whether or not the Congress that had submitted the Fourteenth Amendment and the state legislatures and conventions that had approved it had understood that it would abolish segregation in education. Counsel for the plaintiffs said the Fourteenth Amendment did clearly intend to abolish segregation in public schools; counsel for the defense argued eloquently that the amendment bore no such intent. The Court also raised the question of whether Congress or the Supreme Court had the power under the amendment to move against public-school segregation. The plaintiffs contended that the Court did have such power, and the briefs submitted by two United States attorneys general concurred. The defendants insisted that the state legislatures were the proper bodies to determine the racial pattern of education: they said the Court had recognized this since the Plessy decision of 1896.

The Court queried the attorneys on the question of whether, in the event desegregation should be ordered, a gradual transition ought to be permitted, and, if so, in what manner. Gradualism appealed to none of the litigants. Attorneys for the plaintiffs said they had examined "all of the plans for gradual adjustment which we could find" and concluded that "none would be effective." John W. Davis said, ". . . we find nothing here on which the Court could formulate a decree, nor do we think the court below has any power to formulate a decree, reciting in what manner these schools are to be altered at all, and what course South Carolina shall take concerning it." [10]

It was nearly a year and a half after the first arguments were heard that the opinion was finally delivered. No decision in generations had been so long pondered by the Court and so anxiously awaited by so many people. On May 17, 1954, at the stroke of noon, the nine justices of the Supreme Court filed gravely into the courtroom. Opening formalities and the disposition of minor cases consumed nearly an hour. A brief pause ensued, then the Chief Justice read the great decision. His voice was calm and deliberate. The document was not long, and not as majestically worded as befitted its place in history.

The Court reviewed briefly the history of the Fourteenth Amendment, which it found "inconclusive . . . with respect to segregated schools."

"In approaching this problem," it said, "we cannot turn the clock back to 1868 when the amendment was adopted, or even to 1896 when *Plessy v. Ferguson* was written. We must consider public education in the light of its full development and its present place in American life throughout the Nation. Only in this way can it be determined if segregation in public schools deprives these plaintiffs of the equal protection of the laws. . . .

"Does segregation of children in public schools solely on the basis of race, even though the physical facilities and other 'tangible' factors may be equal, deprive the children of the minority group of equal opportunities? We believe that it does."

The Court recalled that the Plessy decision involved "not education but transportation" and noted that its validity as a precedent in public education had already been questioned in decisions rejecting segregation in universities. Now the Court defined a new precedent—and marked the end of an era: "We conclude that in the field of public education the doctrine of 'separate but equal' has no place. Separate educational facilities are inherently unequal. Therefore, we hold that the plaintiffs and others similarly situated for whom the actions have been brought are, by reason of the segregation complained of, deprived of the equal protection of the laws guaranteed by the Fourteenth Amendment."

In a second opinion, dealing with the District of Columbia case, the Court said: "It would be unthinkable that the same Constitution would impose a lesser duty on the federal government." It found that "racial segregation in the District of Columbia is a denial of the due process of law guaranteed by the Fifth Amendment to the Constitution."

The Court did not at this time issue the decree putting its rulings into effect, but scheduled further argument on the mechanics of effecting transition to integrated schools.

Chapter 2

THE INITIAL REACTION

The event engaged the swift attention of news media throughout the world. The encyclopedic *New York Times* produced the next morning seven broad pages of information related to the great decision; research had been done earlier in the expectation that the ruling would be handed down "on a Monday morning in May. . . ." To quote from that newspaper's own account: "In all, nearly fifty *Times* staff members were involved in the operation. And by the time the decision was actually handed down, much of what they wrote was already in type.

"Monday, when the story broke, this vast news-gathering organization moved into high gear again. The Washington Bureau filed thousands of words on the ruling. Reporters and correspondents in the affected areas interviewed government and education officials for reaction. From New York, law professors, historians, sociologists, other experts were interviewed by phone. Editors tied the whole thing together."

The Voice of America began broadcasting the news to the world within one hour after the reading of the decision. It continued broadcasting it, in thirty-four languages, throughout the day and the night and the following day. A 700-word bulletin was broadcast to American diplomatic posts in sixty-five countries, where it was quickly translated and mimeographed for release to the press.

Editorial reaction in the South was cautious or aggrieved. In the rest of the United States the dominant editorial note was one of resounding applause. Applause came also from the European press. The *London News Chronicle* headlined its story: "A Black Stain Wiped Out." The *Manchester Guardian* expressed "immense relief" at America's "having put behind it what has long been its worst reproach." The *Times* of London called the ruling "among the most important decisions that the Court has ever handed down." The Laborite *Daily Herald* said it would "make every friend of humanity and every believer in democracy cheer." *Le Monde* in Paris hailed the decision as a "victory of justice over race prejudice," and the *Neue Zeitung* in Zurich called it "an impressive example of the vitality of American democracy." In India the powerful Indian Express chain of newspapers welcomed the ruling as a "healthy change in enlightened American opinion."

Southern editors, few of whom were yet aroused to frank hostility, stressed the difficulty of complying with the Supreme Court ruling in the near future. The reaction of the *New Orleans Times-Picayune* was one of unmitigated pessimism. "In the course of efforts to preserve some of the lines of separation," that paper said, "the ensuing strife will probably react unfavorably on public-school support and multiply the problems with which the schools are already faced." The *Birmingham* (Alabama) *Post-Herald* said: "Acceptance of the decision does not mean that we are stopped from taking such honorable and legal steps as may be indicated to avoid the difficulties it presents to both races."

Many Southern editors at this stage urged a calm, constructive approach to the problem. Virtually all major newspapers in North Carolina and a number in Tennessee and Florida sounded this note. In Georgia, where abandonment of the public-school system was being talked of, the pre-eminent *Atlanta Constitution* said: "Our best minds must be put to work, not to destroy, but to arrive at constructive conclusions." The Chattanooga *Times* said: "The *Times* believes that most of the Southern states will meet this situation calmly." Virginia papers discussed the problem of adjustment to the ruling with as yet no hint of rebellion. The *Richmond Times-Dispatch* felt that the Supreme Court would have been on sounder ground "if it had entered its decree yesterday in the five cases before it, and granted a specific number of years for compliance. . . . It would have been desirable if the Court had at the same time specified the abolition of segregation by stages or steps, with, say, 10 per cent eliminated the first year after the decrees became effective, 40 per cent more two years later, perhaps, and the remaining 50 per cent some years after that. In this way, all uncertainty as to the timing and method of the tremendous shift would have been eliminated at once."

Viewed in retrospect, it is interesting to note that headlines in some newspapers in former Confederate states announced in an entirely matter-of-fact tone: Change Not Immediate. Two years later the same newspapers would regard it as a foregone conclusion that there would be no extensive change in the system of segregated schools in their states for long years to come.

In the border region between North and South, where school segregation also prevailed, the editorial comment was generally constructive. The *Baltimore Sun* foresaw that "the implications will be painful to many Marylanders," but agreed with the Supreme Court "that segregation, however equal the physical facilities, does put the brand of inferiority upon Negroes." The *Washington Evening Star* said: "Concern over a dubious assumption of power by the Court . . . does not alter the fact that this decision finds much support in wisdom and fairness." The *Washington Post* rejoiced that the decision "affords all Americans an occasion for pride and gratification." The *St. Louis Post-Dispatch* acclaimed the decision as "a great and just act of judicial statesmanship," and the *Wilmington* (Delaware) *Journal* found it "based on a sound American principle."

In the remaining two-thirds of the nation, where compulsory school segregation was already a thing of the past, important newspapers applauded the decision with unwonted eloquence:

Hartford Courant: "This milestone in our history means that we still struggle successfully towards our own ideals."

Des Moines Register: "The United States Supreme Court has begun the erasure of one of democracy's blackest marks. . . ."

Denver Post: "Such an opinion had to be reached eventually in a country founded on the belief that 'all men are created free and equal.' "

Chicago Tribune: "The fact that the decision was unanimous . . . should help a good deal to discourage resistance to the findings or attempts to evade its plain meaning. . . ."

Minneapolis Morning Tribune: "The Court's momentous decision will be welcomed and embraced by all who believe that the constitutional guarantee of equal rights means just that, and nothing less."

San Francisco Chronicle: "The majesty of the democratic idea that men are created equal and are entitled to the equal protection of the laws shines through yesterday's unanimous decision. . . ."

New York Times: "The highest court in the land, the guardian of our national conscience, has reaffirmed its faith—and the undying American faith—in the equality of all men and all children before the law."

Detroit Free Press: "Those citizens of the United States who cherish the belief that the American concept of democracy is a vital, living, organic philosophy, slowly but inexorably advancing toward the ideals of the founders of this Union, will be heartened by the unanimous opinion of the Supreme Court in the historic school segregation case."

From the Negro press an exultant chorus rose, hailing "the greatest victory for the Negro people since the Emancipation Proclamation" (*Amsterdam News*) and "one of the important days in the history of this country and the fight for freedom for all the citizens of the nation" (*Atlanta Daily World*). "There ought to be dancing in the streets!" a young Negro mother in Washington exclaimed. There was no dancing in the streets. The significance was not quickly grasped by the Negro masses. But a Washington cab-driver-preacher remarked: "After they know about it a while, there will be enthusiasm." In Prince Edward County, Virginia—from which one of the cases came to the Supreme Court—a 16-year-old high-school student said to a *New York Post* reporter: "Our teacher told us it may cost her her job, but she said it may also make it possible for us to get a better job long after we have forgotten her." Among the Negro intelligentsia throughout the land and in the ranks of the NAACP there was deep and fervent rejoicing.

Ralph Bunche, director of the United Nations Trusteeship Division and a winner of the Nobel Peace Prize, read the first news in the Associated Press office in New York. When he went to a branch bank in the same building to cash a check and rushed back for the next bulletin a guard followed him with thirty-five dollars, which he had left at the cashier's window! [1] Jubilant Negro leaders crowded the NAACP offices in New York throughout the afternoon. A press conference was held. Channing Tobias, chairman of the NAACP board, said: "The National Association regards the unanimous decision . . . as a highly significant step in the forward progress of American democracy. . . ." Dr. Bunche said it would "have a very great significance in the outside world." Thurgood Marshall, who had led the Negro legal fight, noted: "The most gratifying thing, in addition to the fact that we won, is the unanimous decision and the language used. Once for all, it's decided, and completely decided." [2] Lester B. Granger, executive secretary of the National Urban League, in a statement issued later said: "Thurgood Marshall has immortalized himself." [3] In Georgia, Dr. Rufus E. Clement, president of Atlanta University and a member of the Atlanta school board, said: "It is now important for the courageous and honest people of both races in the South to approach the situation with calmness, with good will, and with intelligence." [4] Mrs. Ruby Hurley, NAACP regional secretary in the South, said the decision knocked "the props from under Russian propaganda." [5] Mary McLeod Bethune, a famous Negro crusader then in the twilight of her remarkable life, said: "Let all the people praise the Lord!" [6]

Comment was elicited from many politicians and officials in the seventeen states whose segregated public schools had been declared unlawful. In the pattern of reactions here we see a sharp line between the states which once had seceded from the Union and their immediate neighbors to the north. In the latter, the comment of important officials was generally like that of Governor Phil M. Donnelly of Missouri, who said: "The citizens of Missouri are law-abiding people and I am confident that they will endeavor to uphold the Constitution of the United States, which is the supreme law of the land"; or like that of Governor Theodore R. McKeldin of Maryland: "I am sure our citizens and officials will accept readily the Supreme Court's interpretation of the fundamental law."

In the onetime Confederate South no politician of stature expressed approval of the Supreme Court decision. All stressed the enormous difficulty, if not the impossibility, of complying with it; and some denounced it vehemently. Louisiana's two senators were then among the more conciliatory spokesmen. Senator Allen J. Ellender said: "I don't want to criticize the Supreme Court. It [the ruling] is bound to have a very great effect until we readjust to it." Senator Russell B. Long said: "Although I completely disagree with the decision, my oath of office requires me to accept it as the law." Liberal Senator Estes Kefauver of Tennessee cautioned: "While we may not agree with the decision, we must not let this disrupt our public-school system. We must not let this result in bitter strife." But Senator Richard B. Russell of Georgia called the decision "a flagrant abuse of judicial power," and Senator Burnet R. Maybank of South Carolina said it was "a shameful political, rather than a judicial decision." Senator James O. Eastland of Mississippi declared bluntly: "The South will not abide by, or obey, this legislative decision by a political court." [7]

Ironically, the most constructive comment came from officials of Virginia, the state which was destined to lead the South upon an adventure called "massive resistance." In an ephemeral phase of loyal resignation, Virginia's Attorney General J. Lindsay Almond, Jr., expressed confidence "that Virginia will approach the question realistically and endeavor to work out some rational adjustment." Governor Thomas B. Stanley, who in a matter of weeks was to turn to defiance, promised to "call together as quickly as practicable representatives of both state and local governments to consider the matter and work toward a plan which will be acceptable to our citizens and in keeping with the edict of the court." Prophetic of the attitude which was soon to dominate that state was the comment of its powerful senator, Harry F. Byrd: he called the Court's ruling the "most serious blow that has been struck against the rights of the states." [8]

The most violent reaction came from Georgia, whose governor, Herman Talmadge, had been obsessed with the possibility of such a decision from the Supreme Court for several years and had already expressed fierce opposition. Georgia and South Carolina had both taken steps to abolish public schools rather than accept racial integration. Governor Talmadge quoted a remark attributed to President Jackson after a fiercely disputed Supreme Court decision of an earlier day: "John Marshall made that decision. Now let him enforce it!" [9] Lieutenant Governor Marvin Griffin, who was soon to succeed to the Georgia governorship, smelled "meddlers, demagogues, race-baiters, and Communists." [10]

The governor of South Carolina, then seventy-five years of age, looked back upon a career of service to the Republic matched by few living Americans. During the Second World War, James Francis Byrnes, as Director of Economic Stabilization and later as Director of War Mobilization, was considered by many the most powerful individual in the nation next to President Roosevelt himself. Under President Truman he was for eighteen crucial months Secretary of State. Earlier he had served long in the Congress, as a member of the House of Representatives and as a senator. Between his service with the legislative and executive branches he had been an associate justice of the Supreme Court.

The aging statesman was profoundly saddened when the high tribunal delivered its decision. As governor of South Carolina he had launched an unprecedented program of improvement in Negro schools. In his inaugural address on January 16, 1951, he had said: "It is our duty to provide for the races substantial equality in school facilities.

We should do it because it is right. For me that is sufficient reason."

Byrnes had early exerted himself to avert the anti-segregation rul-ing. He it was who engaged Davis, whom he regarded as "the ablest constitutional lawyer in the United States," to defend the cause of segregation. When the national administrations changed between Supreme Court hearings, Byrnes has recalled in his autobiographic *All in One Lifetime,* he "expressed to President Eisenhower the hope that he would not feel bound by the position taken by the Democratic administration." Before the Supreme Court hearings began, the South Carolina governor had sounded this warning: "Should the Supreme Court decide this case against our position, we will face a serious problem. Of only one thing can we be certain. South Carolina will not now, nor for some years to come, mix white and colored children in our schools. . . . If the Court changes what is now the law of the land, we will, if it is possible, live within the law, preserve the public-school system, and at the same time maintain segregation. If that is not possible, reluctantly we will abandon the public-school system."

Now Byrnes said he was "shocked that the Court has reversed itself," but he added: "I earnestly urge all of our people, white and colored, to exercise restraint and preserve order." [11]

Public-school segregation was now unlawful by solemn pronounce-ment of the Supreme Court, and although a year was to pass before that tribunal would formulate its decree for bringing segregation to an end, a few school districts responded to the decision forthwith. We may begin therefore, to register—in what will prove to be a dismal log—the progress in effecting this vast social change.

When the Brown decision was handed down, the segregation of public schools was required in seventeen states and the District of Columbia, which is Washington, the nation's capital. In four other states school segregation was permitted by action of local govern-mental units. In these four states segregation was already on the wane. The proportion of Negroes to their total population was small, from .07 per cent in Wyoming to 3.8 per cent in Kansas. In Wyoming segregation had practically ended, and in New Mexico the last three communities with segregated schools now integrated them forthwith. Arizona entered the final phase of a desegregation program which had begun in 1953 and was to be completed in 1955. In Kansas the remnants of school segregation in ten cities were eliminated at once or scheduled for elimination the following year; in Topeka the school board in September 1953—eight months before the Supreme Court acted—had adopted a desegregation program to be completed in 1955.

In the region where segregation had been required, the cities of Washington and Baltimore proceeded to integrate their public schools when they opened the following September. The state of West Virginia moved promptly on an extensive scale: schools were integrated completely in a dozen counties and desegregation was begun in thirteen more. In Missouri the city of St. Louis took the first steps in a desegregation program to be completed in 1955, and segregation was ended in a few scattered school districts of that state. Two school districts in Arkansas, one in Oklahoma, and one in west Texas were desegregated. In Delaware the city of Wilmington, commencing a three-stage operation, integrated its elementary schools in complete tranquillity—though trouble developed in a desegregation attempt in the rural community of Milford. Outside of this small section of south Delaware, the flurries of public disorder which attended the 1954 desegregation were mild and short-lived.

In Milford semi-violent hostility succeeded temporarily in causing local officials to close public schools and to suspend their desegregation program. Incidentally, the angry rallies of white citizens in Milford, numbering up to four thousand, bore early witness to the inflammatory potential of the professional racist agitator—in this case one Bryant Bowles, who would continue to plague Delaware and carry his message farther south during coming months.

In Washington and Baltimore something like complete desegregation was promptly carried out—attended by only minor street demonstrations of protest. Approximately 60,000 of Washington's 100,000 pupils were colored—a higher percentage of Negro children than in any other American city, and, added to the difficulty of interracial mingling, two completely separate school systems had to be knit together. But by November, 74,447 Washington pupils were attending 123 integrated public schools. In Baltimore the school board followed the simple plan of removing the racial restriction from its unusual pupil-assignment system and allowing children to go to the schools of their choice; only 1376 of the city's 55,331 Negro pupils chose the first year to enter previously all-white schools.

Except for several small school districts where few Negroes lived in Texas and Arkansas, the steps of adjustment to the Brown decision were all taken in the border region.

In the eleven states of the onetime Southern Confederacy, the mild first reaction gave way to steadily rising hostility; governors and state legislatures busied themselves with plans for evasion, and organizations to stimulate popular resistance burgeoned. The Louisiana legislature censured the Supreme Court for "its usurpation of power." [12] A Texas Democratic convention declared the decision an "unwarranted invasion" of state rights,[13] and Marvin Griffin was nominated for governor of Georgia on the pledge: "Come hell or high water, races will not be mixed in Georgia schools." [14] In Virginia, Governor Stanley soon abandoned his initial appeal for rational adjustment and signaled that state's turn toward resistance with the announcement: "I shall use every legal means at my command to continue segregated schools. . . ." [15] In November the voters of Louisiana and Georgia approved amendments to their state constitutions, in the former case, to permit the state to use its police powers to maintain segregated schools, and, in the latter, to permit the operation of a "private" school system, supported by tuition grants from public funds, in the event the legislature should see fit to close public schools. In December, Mississippians voted to give the legislature authority to close public schools rather than submit to their desegregation. It was the first trickle of a flood of constitutional amendments and legislative enactments in which Southern hostility and recalcitrance would express themselves during the next five years.

When the Supreme Court declared public-school segregation unconstitutional in May 1954, as we have noted, it refrained from issuing a decree and asked for another round of briefs and arguments on the precise issue of implementation. Fully aware of the explosive nature of the problem and anxious to be reasonable and to move cautiously, the Court invited the Department of Justice, the attorneys for the Negro plaintiffs, the lawyers for the school boards in the five cases immediately before the Court, and the attorneys general of all states requiring or permitting segregation to take part in the discussion. Specifically, the lawyers were asked to address themselves to the questions of whether immediate desegregation should be ordered; or, in case gradual compliance should be allowed, whether the Supreme Court should formulate detailed decrees or remand the cases to the district judges with directions; and in the latter case, what directions should be given the district judges.

Briefs were submitted in November 1954, but oral argument originally scheduled for the following December was postponed until April 1955. Justice Robert H. Jackson had died in October and his successor's appointment was not confirmed until March 1955. The new justice was John Marshall Harlan, a grandson of the author of the famous dissent in the case of *Plessy v. Ferguson.*

Thurgood Marshall again led a battery of NAACP lawyers on behalf of the Negro plaintiffs. The five localities which were parties to the suit were represented by counsel and, additionally, Florida, North Carolina, Arkansas, Oklahoma, Maryland, and Texas sent lawyers to advise the Court. Attorney General Herbert Brownell submitted a brief, and Solicitor General Simon E. Sobeloff represented the Eisenhower Administration in the oral argument.

Marshall urged that desegregation be ordered by a fixed date, either the following September or September 1956. Brownell and Sobeloff agreed with the Southerners that the cases should be remanded to the district courts, but they urged that district judges be directed to require school authorities to submit school-integration plans within ninety days (one grade a year was indicated as an acceptable schedule); if no satisfactory plan was submitted, district judges should be instructed to order immediate desegregation. The Southern lawyers urged that maximum discretion be allowed district judges in permitting gradual adjustment—very gradual indeed.

Many observers have contended that an order requiring immediate, over-all elimination of race discrimination in the assignment of pupils to public schools would have resulted in a quicker and easier transition to the new order. It has since been abundantly demonstrated that public-school desegregation rarely proves as difficult as it is expected to be. Desegregation might have been accomplished in many localities before resistance had hardened, and it might have forestalled some organized harassment. In large Southern cities with uniformly good public schools, efficient law enforcement, and a sophisticated populace, the miracle of immediate adjustment might indeed have been

accomplished. If local authorities had grasped this fact and had proceeded simply as a constitutional duty, the transition in the South
would have been immensely accelerated.

But among persons familiar with the Southern scene, including even
the most liberally disposed, few could conceive that an order for immediate and general desegregation would have been practicable. In
many areas desegregation would have meant the enrollment of small
contingents of white pupils in predominantly Negro schools. Often in
the poorer localities it would have required the transfer of white
pupils from good or comfortable schools to the pitifully inadequate
schools which had been provided for Negroes—a step which, however
just, would have been virtually impossible to accomplish. In rural
Southern counties, too, the schools have been centers of social life to
a greater degree than elsewhere in the nation. If we add to these circumstances the intense and pervasive race prejudice in these communities—which local officials generally shared—we are bound to
conclude that a sweeping, overnight transition would have been impossible.

The painful delay in ensuing years in bringing public-school segregation in the South to an end must be traced to causes other than the
judgment of the Supreme Court on this point. The Court decided in
favor of gradualism and maximum consideration for the diversity of
local situations, but only after "a prompt and reasonable start" had
been made. It left the formulation of specific decrees to district courts,
and in remanding the cases to them on May 31, 1955, in a 900-word
opinion—again unanimous—it laid down these guide lines:

> While giving weight to these public and private considerations,
> the courts will require that the defendants make a prompt and
> reasonable start toward full compliance with our May 17, 1954,
> ruling. Once such a start has been made, the courts may find that
> additional time is necessary to carry out the ruling in an effective
> manner. The burden rests upon the defendants to establish that such
> time is necessary in the public interest and is consistent with good
> faith compliance at the earliest practicable date. To that end, the
> courts may consider problems related to administration, arising
> from the physical condition of the school plant, the school trans-
> portation system, personnel, revision of school districts and at-
> tendance areas into compact units to achieve a system of determin-
> ing admission to the public schools on a non-racial basis, and re-
> vision of local laws and regulations which may be necessary in

solving the foregoing problems. They will also consider the adequacy of any plans the defendants may propose to meet these problems and to effectuate a transition to a racially nondiscriminatory school system. During this period of transition, the courts will retain jurisdiction of these cases.

In accordance with the foregoing, district courts were required to enter the "necessary and proper" orders to end public-school segregation "with all deliberate speed." The phrase "with all deliberate speed," strange at first to the general public, became a famous and much debated designation for the tempo prescribed for school desegregation.

The South reacted to this second ruling generally with a feeling of relief. It was, as the *New Orleans Times-Picayune* observed, "pretty much what the Southern attorneys general had asked for." Some newspapers were moved to excessive optimism; the *Tampa Tribune,* for example, said: "The Court's wisdom, we think, will dissipate the thunderhead of turmoil and violence which had been gathering in Southern skies since the Court held school segregation unconstitutional a year ago. . . ." The *Norfolk Virginian-Pilot* hailed the ruling as a "superb appeal to the wisdom, intelligence, and leadership of the Southern states" and called upon Virginia to "rise to leadership in the probably long and difficult task."

Southern political leaders also expressed momentarily a degree of relief. Lieutenant Governor Ernest Vandiver of Georgia approximated the feeling of most when he said: "I think the Supreme Court in some small measure attempted to correct an obnoxious decision." [16] The text of the Court's ruling was read, as the bulletins came over teletypes, to both houses of the Florida legislature, then in session, and was greeted with cheers. The wave of hostility in the South, which had been steadily rising for a year, came to a pause. But the hiatus in that trend was to be measured in weeks.

In September schools opened with hardly any change in the rule of segregation in this region. In the western part of Texas, an area with few Negro inhabitants, sixty-five school districts did remove racial restrictions in public-school enrollment. In Arkansas one more school district, Hoxie—after an on-and-off period amid some local disorder— integrated twenty-five Negro children in formerly all-white schools. In the once highly secret "Atomic Bomb City" of Oak Ridge, Tennessee, eighty-five Negro pupils were integrated among 2526 white students in federally operated junior and senior high schools. These were the only departures from the system of segregated public schools in the former Confederate South. In eight states no Negro child was admitted in 1955 to any public school with white children.

In Prince Edward County, Virginia, an incident occurred which was grimly prophetic of events to come. Prince Edward County, it will be recalled, was one of the five localities directly under the Supreme Court order. May 31, 1955, the day of the implementing ruling, was the last day under Virginia law for the adoption of county budgets, and the Prince Edward governing board met that evening to take action on school appropriations for the coming year. Fearing that desegregation would be immediately enforced, several hundred angry white citizens appeared before the board to urge that the county give up public schools. The board acted accordingly: by unanimous vote, it cut off all funds for school operation. At a mass meeting on June 7, attended by some thirteen hundred citizens, an organization was formed and a fund-raising campaign was launched with a view to providing private schools for the county's white children. A few weeks later, however, upon the advice of state authorities and being convinced that desegregation was not imminent, the Prince Edward board reconsidered the matter and resumed public-school appropriations.

Ringing out sharply in the Southern press on the day after the May 31 ruling, was a defiant editorial in the *Richmond News Leader*. We should make the acquaintance here of the remarkable editor of that newspaper. He was James Jackson Kilpatrick, Jr., a native of Oklahoma, who, in 1951, at thirty-one years of age, had succeeded the late Douglas Southall Freeman. A writer of talent with a trenchant style, rising easily to a frenzied pitch, Kilpatrick became both a bellwether of the Southern temper and the most widely followed literary trumpeter of resistance to the Brown decision. The *News Leader*'s reaction to the May 1954 pronouncement had been to call for the formulation of "a proposal that would win the Supreme Court's approval," and to suggest: "If the court were to fix, say, a ten-year period, and permit the states to integrate 10 per cent of their schools a year . . . a solution might be found." Because the *News Leader* editorial of June 1, 1955, reflected a mood that would soon be widely prevalent in the South, it is appropriate to quote extensively from it here:

In May of 1954, that inept fraternity of politicians and professors known as the United States Supreme Court chose to throw away the established law. These nine men repudiated the Constitution, spit upon the Tenth Amendment, and rewrote the fundamental law of this land to suit their own gauzy concepts of sociology. If it be said now that the South is flouting the law, let it be said to the high court, *You taught us how.*

From the moment that abominable decision was handed down, two broad courses only were available to the South. One was to defy the Court openly and notoriously; the other was to accept the Court's decision and combat it by legal means. To defy the Court openly would be to enter upon anarchy; the logical end would be a second attempt at secession from the Union. And though the idea is not without merit, it is impossible of execution. We tried that once before.

To acknowledge the Court's authority does not mean that the South is helpless. It is not to abandon hope. Rather, it is to enter upon a long course of lawful resistance; it is to take lawful advantage of every moment of the law's delays; it is to seek at the polls and in the halls of legislative bodies every possible lawful means to overcome or circumvent the Court's requirements. Litigate? Let us pledge ourselves to litigate this thing for fifty years. If one remedial law is ruled invalid, then let us try another; and if the second is ruled invalid, then let us enact a third. . . .

When the Court proposes that its social revolution be imposed upon the South "as soon as practicable," there are those of us who would respond that "as soon as practicable" means never at all.

Chapter 3

THE BORDER STATES

The clash between local attachment to segregation and state rights and the national will was to produce for the region of the onetime Southern Confederacy an adventure and an experience peculiarly its own. Not for generations had the line that marked the outer boundary of the block of states that once seceded from the Union been so sharply drawn.

We cross that line here to observe the further response to the Supreme Court's ruling in that other extensive region where public-school segregation had been compulsory hitherto. The District of Columbia and the border states, which made more progress in school desegregation in three years than the former Confederate states have made in ten, did not accomplish it without scattered minor disorders and one briefly alarming outbreak. But save for small enclaves of persistent Southern heritage—the eastern counties of West Virginia, the "Boot Heel" of Missouri, "Little Dixie" in Oklahoma, Maryland's Eastern Shore, and sections of southwestern Kentucky and southern Delaware—these states had outlived the agrarian past which linked them with the South.

Oklahoma lay geographically the farthest south, but Oklahoma had been a state for less than half a century and it had had only faint Civil War traditions as a territory. The other five had been slave states, and they looked back to a time when their citizens were divided in their sympathies between the Confederacy and the Union. But in the middle of the twentieth century all six were firmly integrated in their economies and in their philosophy and loyalties in the mainstream of the nation.

Kentucky is the border state which we have most hesitation in separating from the "South" in this study. In terms of fried chicken, bourbon, mint juleps, Southern belles, and the strains of "My Old Kentucky Home," Kentucky is still emphatically Southern. Indeed, two years after the Brown decision, convulsions in two Kentucky localities suggested to many that that state might match the hostility of the eleven former Confederate states in the matter of school desegregation. The exemplary desegregation of schools in Louisville was the more notable for that reason. Benjamin Fine wrote in the *New York Times* of September 11, 1956, the day after Louisville schools were integrated: "When the history of this proud Southern city is written, this day will undoubtedly go down as an historic landmark. Historians will note that a social revolution took place that may advance the cause of integration by generations. Even in the South, it was shown here, integration can be made to work without violence."

Nevertheless, the manner in which integration was accepted and the firmness and calm with which the transition proceeded there after 1956 would seem to justify our plan in this study of dealing with Kentucky as a border, rather than a Southern, state.

For convenience and clarity in the remainder of this volume we shall speak of "the South" with reference only to the eleven states which formed the Confederate States of America. (It may be added that, since Kentucky's initial disturbances, this has been a common practice. Such expressions as "Southern resistance," "Southern turmoil," "Southern soul-searching," "Southern moderates," and "Southern extremists" in public discussion generally have had reference only to the eleven Secession states.)

Negroes were present in the border states in proportion to the total population as follows: Delaware, 14 per cent; Maryland, 17 per cent; West Virginia, 6 per cent; Kentucky, 7 per cent; Missouri, 8 per cent; and Oklahoma, 7 per cent. Each of the Southern states had a larger percentage of Negroes in its population than any of these, except Texas, where Negroes were only 13 per cent of the total.

When schools opened in September 1956 desegregation was far advanced in Missouri and Oklahoma, and in West Virginia public schools remained segregated in only two small counties on the Virginia border. In Delaware, Maryland, and Kentucky desegregation was proceeding more slowly, though on a scale which would have looked revolutionary in any of the states farther south. In pockets of heavy Negro population in these three states the elimination of segregation would be a further process of protracted year-by-year advance.

In Missouri the two principal cities, St. Louis and Kansas City, accounted for more than two-thirds of the state's Negro population. Both cities had completed desegregation in 1955, with the exception of some minor adjustments which were completed in 1956. Rural and small-town areas generally followed the example of these cities except in the cotton-growing "Boot Heel"; even there, ten high schools had ended segregation by 1957. This left only four high schools segregated in the entire state; some 60,000 of Missouri's 67,000 Negro pupils had been integrated with white children.

In Delaware the city of Wilmington completed its desegregation program in 1956 without incident. By 1957, fourteen other bi-racial districts out of sixty-one in the rest of the state had followed suit. A federal court put an end to a gradual grade-a-year plan being followed in some districts and ordered complete desegregation in all grades and all schools beginning with the 1961–62 term.

Apart from the prompt action in the city of Baltimore in 1954, Maryland waited for the Supreme Court order of 1955, and only eight of the state's twenty-three counties desegregated schools in the fall of that year; but within the next two years all but two of Maryland's counties having Negro residents adopted desegregation as a formal policy to be realized at varying speeds.

Oklahoma as a whole moved swiftly after the Supreme Court's 1955 ruling: of 261 school districts having Negro pupils, 136 were desegregated in 1955 and 38 more the following year; but the south-eastern corner of that state, "Little Dixie," which has the highest Negro population, settled down to a long, slow transition.

The violence which flared in Kentucky was in several respects anomalous. Sturgis and Clay are two small coal and farming communities of about three thousand and two thousand inhabitants respectively in the southwestern section, where Negroes represent about 10 per cent of the total population. The Union County Board of Education, without announcing any general desegregation plan, decided rather abruptly in the summer of 1956 to admit nine Negro children to the white school at Sturgis instead of transporting them to a Negro school at Morganfield eleven miles away. The Negroes registered without incident on August 11, but tension rose as the news circulated through the community, and when they came for the first regular day of class they were turned back by approximately five hundred whites who had surrounded the school. The school superintendent addressed the demonstrators and the crowd dispersed. The next day the crowd came back, but the Negro pupils did not appear; their parents had agreed to send them to Morganfield in return for assurance that schools would be desegregated in 1957. At this point, however, State Adjutant General J. J. B. Williams visited Sturgis and decided that troops of the National Guard were needed. Early on the morning of September 6 two hundred Guardsmen of the 240th Tank Battalion rolled into Sturgis. In this new situation the Negro parents tried again to send their children to the local white school. Guardsmen with fixed bayonets on their rifles escorted the Negro children through a mob of eight hundred heckling, shouting white people.

The unrest spread to Clay, eleven miles east of Sturgis in Webster County, where the board of education had decided to admit four Negro children to a white school. A crowd of a hundred and fifty, many of them women, stood in front of the school and turned the Negro children back, while thirty men hovered at the bottom of the hill, blocking the road to keep the press away. National Guardsmen were sent to Clay, and for a few days Negro children attended the schools in the two towns under troop protection. But the Kentucky attorney general then ruled that, since no official plan for desegregation had been formulated, the Negro pupils had been improperly enrolled in both towns, and the integration attempt was abandoned for the 1956–57 school term.

The desegregation accomplishments of Wilmington, Baltimore, Washington, Kansas City, St. Louis, and Louisville demonstrated that peaceful elimination of school segregation in large cities of substantial Negro population was possible. They were hailed as illuminating pilot operations for Southern cities. St. Louis had a total population of 875,000, of whom 175,000, or 20 per cent, were Negroes; its public schools enrolled 91,000 pupils, 35 per cent of them Negroes. On June 22, 1954, five weeks after the Brown decision was handed down, the Board of Education of St. Louis announced a desegregation program, which moved with dispatch. Teacher colleges and special schools were desegregated that September, high schools and adult education classes the following February, and elementary schools in September 1955. Technical details of the operation are set forth in a comprehensive report of the St. Louis school board, issued in September 1956, entitled *Desegregation of the St. Louis Public Schools*. The story is also told in a brochure published in 1956 by the Anti-

Defamation League of B'nai B'rith, *The St. Louis Story,* by Bonita H. Valien. Emphasizing the co-operation of community leaders in the undertaking, the school-board report related:

> Both before and after the announcement of the plan in the local newspapers, a number of key organizations of the community volunteered their assistance and support. These included the press, the League of Women Voters, the city-wide councils of parent-teacher associations, the YMCA, the YWCA, the NAACP, the Urban League, the Metropolitan Church Federation, representatives of the Catholic Church, the Lutheran Society for Better Human Relations, the Jewish Community Council, the National Conference of Christians and Jews, the Mayor's Commission on Human Relations, and others. . . .
> . . . The League of Women Voters published a booklet describing the plan in detail . . . and recommending support. The Metropolitan Church Federation set aside a Sunday for prayer of thanksgiving for public-school desegregation. . . .

In both St. Louis and Louisville the law-enforcement authorities lent systematic, but inconspicuous, co-operation. In Louisville plainclothes men mingled with possible troublemakers and as many as five hundred police were on call. But no disorder worthy of the name occurred in either city.

The preparation and execution of Louisville's school desegregation program is described in a very readable book entitled *The Louisville Story,* by Omer Carmichael and Weldon James. Carmichael was the superintendent of schools who directed the transition, and James was associate editor of the *Louisville Courier-Journal.* Louisville, once a slave-trading center of the Old South, has become a growing, progressive city, with a population at the time of school desegregation of close to four hundred thousand. Negroes composed about 16 per cent of the total, but they accounted for nearly 27 per cent of the school enrollment. A significant feature of the Louisville plan was a liberal transfer privilege in the first year of integration to serve as a "safety valve." It was anticipated that many parents of both races, particularly in the beginning, would prefer to have their children attend schools in which their own race was not in a small minority. Eleven per cent of the pupils requested transfer and they were nearly always accommodated. But after all the post-registration changes, 73.6 per cent of all pupils were in fifty-five mixed schools, leaving only eleven all-white and nine all-Negro schools.

A small Citizens' Council group offered minor harassment; wooden crosses were burned—a threat symbol adopted from the Ku Klux Klan—and a handful picketed the school-board office and City Hall for an hour or so, though none of this activity engaged many participants or gave the police authorities much concern. Press, clergy, and civic groups rallied behind the desegregation program here much as they had done in St. Louis, but in Louisville the achievement owed most to the personality and leadership of Omer Carmichael. A native of Alabama, he had dedicated himself to this undertaking with tact and skill and unwavering purpose since 1954. After the widely publicized event Superintendent Carmichael found himself in demand for national press interviews and public appearances on both lecture rostrums and television programs; he was invited to the White House for an hour's talk with President Eisenhower. This educator devoted much of his time from then on to expounding the science of peaceful school integration and witnessing to the possibility of accomplishing it—though in the South his message generally fell upon deaf ears—until he died in January 1960.

A certain science of school desegregation was indeed developing. Both in the big-city programs and in the experiences of small-town and rural school districts, valuable light was being thrown on the problems of preparing students, teachers, and the public for the change; on patterns of gradualism; and on means of providing for disparate levels of educational achievements on the part of newly integrated pupils.

Hopkins County, Kentucky, adopted a one-grade-a-year desegregation plan; under this the first grade was integrated at the start and other grades were to be integrated successively thereafter. When objections of NAACP attorneys were upheld by a federal court, the county adopted a plan for desegregation to be completed within a four-year period. But the one-grade-a-year plan remained a popular device for effecting gradualism, and it was to be approved temporarily by federal courts in more difficult situations in the South. In Kanawba County, West Virginia, grades one, two, and seven were integrated in 1956 and grades three, four, five, and six the following year. A variety of other plans were tried. Analyses of many of these plans were made under the auspices of the public education fraternity, Phi Delta Kappa, and were published in a useful book entitled *Action Patterns in School Desegregation*.

Widespread fear had been expressed that the influx of Negro pupils would lower the standards of previously all-white schools. Negro children, coming from a backward economic and cultural environment as well as from generally inferior schools—and retarded by segregation itself—were on the average considerably behind white pupils of the same age in educational progress. This problem was met in the District of Columbia, St. Louis, and Wilmington by variations of what was known as the "track system," designed to prevent backward pupils of either race from retarding the progress of others. The somewhat famous track system which the District of Columbia began to implement in 1956 distributed 13,377 senior high-school students—3026 in a basic track, 5575 in a general track, 3884 in a college preparatory track, and 892 in an honors track.

All of these findings and the growing literature on the subject were eagerly studied by sociologists and educators—but outside of the South. There public-school administrators or college professors who were known to be as much as considering the problem of school desegregation exposed themselves to popular abuse and official reprisal. The science of school desegregation became a part of the necessary homework, however, of federal district judges; and, though furtively at first, it received the attention of Southern educators as the years went by.

While the meager school desegregation in most of the South for some years to come would follow litigation and orders of federal courts, it is significant that desegregation in the border states was initiated in the main "voluntarily"—that is, without specific court orders, in spontaneous response to the constitutional mandate. A handful of lagging districts were prodded by federal court action, but during the first five years after the Brown decision over six hundred school districts were desegregated voluntarily.

By 1956 the school desegregation crisis for this region was over; the remaining transition moved quietly and uneventfully forward for most of the decade. Insofar as concerned the District of Columbia and the six border states, the Supreme Court decision posed problems of exceptional difficulty, but it met with no widespread resistance, aroused only minor threats to public order, and brought no challenge to the authority of the judicial or executive branches of the national government. In the South a far different story was unfolding.

Chapter 4

NEGROPHOBIA

For most white Southerners the essential jolt in the Brown decision was its simple recognition of the fact that Negroes are citizens of the United States. Though only a rare fanatic would admit it, there was in their instinctive attitude a remnant of the old feeling, articulated in the Dred Scott decision, that Negroes were not exactly people but "beings of an inferior order." Many of the kindest white Southerners —who "loved Negroes"—more or less unconsciously shared this feeling. The Negro minority was not quite a part of the "public" in the South. If the "public" was invited to a concert or other function under white auspices, a Negro had no assurance that he would be admitted. The normal courtesy titles of "Mr.," "Mrs.," and "Miss" were commonly denied even to cultivated Negro ladies and gentlemen. When a Southern politician referred to "my people" or to "the people" of this or that section he seldom considered the Negro element of the population in the designation. Negroes might be "Southern Negroes," but a "Southerner" in common parlance was emphatically a white person.

This concept had now been demolished by the highest tribunal in the land. The new concept had to be digested and a new structure of Negro-white relations had to be erected. But, first, the old relationship had to be destroyed. In the process a large measure of the genuine friendship which had developed under the old order had also—it seemed, inevitably—to be swept away. If interracial relations had been good before the Brown decision, as white Southerners insisted, they now deteriorated rapidly.

A racial estrangement set in that did not begin to relax for five years in some states, for six or seven in others, and that lingers still in much of the South. Choruses from Negro colleges ceased to be invited, as they had often been invited in the past, to sing for white audiences; Negro groups were excluded from holiday parades and festivities in which they had formerly taken part; and many white community leaders who had been conspicuously active in aiding and advising Negroes abandoned this activity—to lend their efforts in some cases to "anti-integration" movements. Even the Urban League, a long-respected Negro assistance organization, not involved in the school-integration controversy, was deserted by many of its white friends and supporters; the Urban Leagues of Little Rock, Richmond, New Orleans, Jacksonville, and Fort Worth were excluded from local Community Chests, in whose fund-raising campaigns they had previously shared. Some white Southerners even boycotted radio and television programs that included Negro entertainers. In an incident which was widely deplored in the South but which was indicative nevertheless of the feeling in many quarters, the celebrated Negro singer Nat "King" Cole was attacked by hoodlums in the audience when he visited Birmingham in his native state of Alabama. In situations of particular tension, hatred of Negroes expressed itself in economic sanctions and in larger outbreaks of violence.

Many white Southerners were disturbed at the seeming impertinence of Negroes in boldly claiming the rights of citizens—in going to federal courts, even the Supreme Court of the United States, with litigation aimed at a "way of life of the South." The business of "keeping the Negro in his place" has been for centuries a major concern. The spectacle now of able and sophisticated Negro lawyers matching wits with white counsel and winning case after case was both a violation of the traditional racial fitness of things and an embarrassing refutation of the myth of innate Negro incompetence. The National Association for the Advancement of Colored People became an object of consuming hatred. And the kind of hatred which this mainly Negro organization inspired in people who insisted that Negroes were hopelessly inferior creatures itself represented a breakdown of that illusion. The hatred of the NAACP partook of neither condescension nor contempt: it recognized an astute and powerful adversary.

Fear stimulated opposition to desegregation most stubbornly on two counts: fear of Communism, with which the crusade for Negro rights was believed to be somehow related; and a horror of racial amalgamation. Though seldom a part of the public discussion, fear also of economic competition from fully emancipated Negroes and the possibility of losing jobs to them was present among thousands of whites.

Miscegenation is a delicate subject from several points of view. The fact that the vast majority of Negroes in the United States are actually mulattoes, with some white ancestors, points to widespread miscegenation at an earlier period of Southern history, and illegitimate sexual relations of white males with Negro women were not uncommon at the time of the Brown decision. Yet a fear that intermingling of white and Negro children in public schools would lead to interracial marriages on a large scale has been prevalent at all levels of white Southern society and has been exploited daily by racist agitators. It is not borne out by the experience of Northern states where segregation has long since been abolished. The extent of intermarriage between whites and light-skinned mulattoes in the North is impossible to determine, but known cases of intermarriage between whites and individuals obviously Negro are still rare. No significant increase in miscegenation could be observed anywhere following public-school integration. Nevertheless, the fear of interracial marriages has been perhaps the most insistent single ingredient in Southern hostility to the desegregation ruling. When the question, "Would you like for your daughter to marry a Negro?"—is asked, it is supposed to put an end to any argument on the subject.

The idea that the movement to end racial segregation was part of a Communist conspiracy took hold among a vast number of white Southerners. Many were ready to believe that Communists dominated not only the NAACP, but the federal government and the Supreme Court of the United States. The merchants of hate, whom we shall presently describe, stocked this canard heavily among their wares. These people wasted little time in rational criticism of the Brown decision but referred to that action matter-of-factly as a Communist plot and plastered many a tree and signboard with the slogan, "Impeach Earl Warren."

Learned and thoughtful criticism of the Supreme Court decision was not lacking; there were rational considerations which caused many Southerners to regret the Brown decision. In due course we shall discuss the Southern protest as it manifested itself on a higher level. We examine here the Negrophobia which spread over the South, its background, and the men and organizations which promoted it.

Without reaching farther back into the long history of race prejudice, account should be taken of the residual poison left by the racist literature which was popular in both North and South during the first quarter of the twentieth century. This was the period when the segregation craze was moving to its most absurd extremes. It was also the period when the present older generation of Southerners was in the formative years of adolescence and early manhood. The books of Madison Grant and his racist contemporaries were still available in the 1950s to reinforce the more literate segregationists. In the field of bestselling fiction, Southerners above middle-age were likely to have read some of the novels of Thomas Dixon—of which five million copies had been sold.

Dixon is best remembered as the author of *The Clansman,* upon which the early motion-picture extravaganza *The Birth of a Nation* was based. This cinematographic apotheosis of the Ku Klux Klan, even after repeated expurgation, is still tinged with anti-Negro venom. In the 1930s, having been seen by an estimated one hundred million people, *The Birth of a Nation* virtually disappeared.[1] After the Brown decision it was revived and shown in a number of Southern cities. It was running in Little Rock on the eve of the 1957 riots there, and it was also shown in New Orleans during periods of interracial strife. During a convention of the NAACP in Atlanta, Georgia, the film was exhibited in a suburban theater under the auspices of the Ku Klux Klan itself; a handbill, issued by the "United Klans," read in part:

> The NAACP dares you—white man—to see: THE BIRTH OF A NATION. . . . Thousands of NAACP members are here—to take over your city—and do your thinking—UNLESS—you dare to stand your ground and join the thousands of white people who have decided that the white man shall retreat no further. . . .

In the 1950s the old silent movie was not a resounding box-office success, nor was its current showing a major factor in the rising tide of anti-Negro feeling. But there were few among the older generation of Southerners—or, indeed, of Americans—who had not sat through *The Birth of a Nation* at least once at some time in their lives.

As for Dixon's novels, such as *The Clansman* and *The Leopard's Spots,* it would be difficult to imagine reading matter better calculated to put salt on lingering sores of the Reconstruction era and instill hatred and fear of the Negro. Dixon described the Negro (using a Clansman character as his mouthpiece) as a "creature, half-child,

half-animal, . . . a being who, left to his will, roams at night and
sleeps in the day, whose speech knows no word of love, whose pas-
sions, once aroused, are the fury of the tiger. . . ."

The amateur racist anthropologist was given this kind of basic
material:

> . . . Since the dawn of history the Negro has owned the Con-
> tinent of Africa—rich beyond the dream of poet's fancy, crunching
> acres of diamonds under his bare black feet. Yet he never picked
> one up from the dust until a white man showed him its glittering
> light. His land swarmed with powerful and docile animals, yet he
> never dreamed of a harness, cart or sled. . . . He lived as his
> fathers lived—stole his food, worked his wife, sold his children, ate
> his brother, content to drink, sing, dance and sport as the ape! [2]

In *The Leopard's Spots*—which the *Atlanta Journal* of that day
called "an epoch-making book, packed with truth stranger than fiction" [3]—a Dixon character declares:

> One drop of Negro blood makes a Negro. It kinks the hair,
> flattens the nose, thickens the lips, puts out the light of intellect and
> lights the fires of brutal passion. . . . [4]

Probably the first book-length diatribe to appear in the wake of the
Brown decision, and one of the most widely circulated, was written
by Thomas P. Brady, judge of the circuit court of the fourteenth
district and later an associate justice of the Supreme Court of Mississippi. This was entitled *Black Monday* (with reference to Monday,
May 17, 1954, when the decision was handed down.) [5] One might
suspect that Judge Brady had just put down an old copy of *The
Leopard's Spots* when he wrote:

> The Negro proposes to breed up his inferior intellect and whiten
> his skin and "blow out the light" in the white man's brain and
> muddy his skin.

One senses an echo of Dixon also in this comment:

> You can dress a chimpanzee, housebreak him, and teach him to
> use a knife and fork, but it will take countless generations of evolu-
> tionary development, if ever, before you can convince him that a
> caterpillar or a cockroach is not a delicacy. Likewise the social,
> political, economic and religious preferences of the Negro remain
> close to the caterpillar and the cockroach. . . .

Such was the tenor of literature which thousands of white Southerners found in their mailboxes or on their doorsteps after the Brown decision. The stuff was sometimes sponsored by a Citizens' Council or a unit of the Ku Klux Klan; more often the source was anonymous. The indigenous output was supplemented by several hate publications in the North which, long given to vilification of Negroes, Catholics, and Jews, now focused their attention upon Negroes.

Black Monday itself became a sort of handbook for the burgeoning Citizens' Councils, in which Judge Brady was a leading spirit, and which were to become the largest segregationist organization in the South. The book was an embodiment of virtually the whole militant segregationist syndrome. Many charged that the Supreme Court and the federal government were deliberately fomenting the interracial turmoil that they themselves were strenuously engaged in promoting, but few could match the purple prose of Judge Brady, who expressed it thus:

> Oh, High Priests of Washington, blow again and stronger upon the dying embers of racial hate, distrust and envy. Pour a little coal oil of political expediency and hope of race amalgamation upon the flickering blaze which you have created, you will start a conflagration in the South which all of Neptune's mighty ocean cannot quench. . . . A law is never paramount to mores. . . . Sacred mores are invulnerable to the dagger of any Brutus. When a law transgresses the moral and ethical standards of the mores, invariably strife, bloodshed and revolution follow in the wake of its attempted enforcement.

A maudlin revival of the cult of Southern womanhood was reflected in Judge Brady's apostrophe: "The loveliest and purest of God's creatures, the nearest thing to an angelic being that treads this terrestial ball, is a well-bred, cultured Southern white woman or her blue-eyed, golden-haired little girl." The cult was related, of course, to a horror of contact between white women and Negro men. It had fired lynching mobs in the past. It was to have a part again in a few months in Judge Brady's own state in the savage murder of a Negro boy.

Among the most conspicuous characteristics of race prejudice are its swift contagion at times of public excitement and the ease with which it can be turned by even a moderately skillful agitator into

hysteria and frenzy. In the unrest following the Supreme Court's desegregation decision, it provided a means by which a previously unimportant and little-known person could quickly attract a large following, get into the limelight, and enjoy a sense of power. Bryant Bowles,
whom we left in the midst of the commotion in the Milford area of
Delaware, was one of the first to discover this possibility. The harvest
of publicity which he reaped in those early disturbances may have
carried a suggestion of similar opportunities elsewhere. Many also
went into action out of unfeigned hostility to the Supreme Court ruling. At any rate, anti-integration agitators were not long in coming
forward in every Southern state. Most of them confined their activities
to their own communities, but some kept a sharp eye on the broad
spectrum of the crisis and moved in wherever local unrest seemed to
offer the best promise of drama, turmoil, and publicity.

The most notorious of these interstate rovers was not a Southerner
at all but a native of New Jersey, named Frederick John Kasper.
Twenty-five years of age, Kasper had attended Columbia University
and had run a bookstore which had sold anti-Semitic literature in
Greenwich Village. More recently he had worked in a bookshop in
Washington, D.C. (He cultivated a friendship with the poet Ezra
Pound, then in a mental hospital in that city.) In a tireless campaign
to stimulate resistance to the Supreme Court's order and to "race-
mixing," Kasper harangued Citizens' Councils, Ku Klux Klan meetings, and—at times of crisis—angry mobs. He had a large hand in
the violence that plagued Tennessee in 1956 and 1957, and he became
a hero to thousands of Southerners. Admiral John Crommelin, a retired naval officer from Montgomery, Alabama—himself a racist agitator—told a rally in Clinton, Tennessee: "You may not see it, but
someday a statue will be erected on this courthouse lawn to John
Kasper." [6]

Kasper spent most of 1958 and 1959 in a federal prison, but his
popularity by then was already fading. This strange young man, who
incessantly preached hatred of the Negro, had earlier—during the
Greenwich Village phase of his career—fraternized conspicuously
with Negroes. The revelation in 1957 of this scandalous detail from
his past resulted in widespread disenchantment among his following. [7]

Bryant Bowles promoted a so-called "Association for the Advancement of White People," and Kasper headed a short-lived "Seaboard
White Citizens' Council"; but these men actually operated as inde-

pendent prima donnas. The great majority of the racist agitators crusaded within the framework of the more stable anti-integration organizations that were being formed in all sections of the South and of the ancient Ku Klux Klan, which was stirring again.

The Ku Klux Klan that galloped mysteriously across the pages of Reconstruction history had an aura of idealism and chivalry which in a troubled time invited the participation or elicited the sympathy of many of the most respectable Southerners. In its lofty declaration of principles this secret order sought to succor the weak and unfortunate and to protect members of the white race in "life, honor and property" from molestation by the newly freed and enfranchised Negroes. In fact, its actual *raison d'être* was to keep the Negro in his place, and to accomplish this it played upon the superstitions of ignorant ex-slaves by parades and night forays of silent horsemen covered with white sheets and wearing masks, by lighting up "fiery crosses," and by other eerie signs and warnings. Also, to an extent which the public never knew, it engaged in acts of murderous violence. This "Invisible Empire," as it was called, reached the peak of its activity and power in 1869; thereafter it gradually fell into disrepute and disbanded.

An unmounted Ku Klux Klan appeared in 1915 and, flourishing during the "roaring twenties," spread across the nation until it attained an estimated membership of four million. The Klan in this reincarnation stood not only for "womanhood" and white supremacy, but for Protestant Christianity and "pure Americanism"—which made it hostile to Catholic, Jewish, and foreign-born citizens. In some areas it added organized labor to its list of foes. This aberration gradually subsided after 1928, and, as Arnold S. Rice has observed in *The Ku Klux Klan in American Politics,* "During the early 1950s there were indications that the Klan might disappear permanently from the American scene." [8]

The Supreme Court's 1954 decision brought the Ku Klux Klan to life again. Klaverns, as local units were called, were organized and fiery crosses lighted up the sky in many sections of the South. Like the Invisible Empire of Reconstruction days, the revived Klan was limited to the South, and its attention and its terroristic exhibitions were focused upon Negroes and "Negro-lovers." White sheets and regalia were brought forth and much of the old mumbo-jumbo was reinstated. The burning of crosses near the homes or meeting places of suspected "integrationists," whether colored or white, became a standard symbol of local tension. Hundreds of cross-burnings were reported, for this ritual was often practiced by other than authentic Klansmen. Klansmen were identified with some of the most ferocious anti-Negro outbreaks, especially in Alabama, and shocking atrocities were laid at their door.

However, the Ku Klux Klan had a bad name now even in the South. In spite of much sympathy with its aim of "keeping the Negro in his place," it was frowned upon by most of the public. It was also torn with schism and rivalry among its leaders—who incidentally profited from the collection of fees and the sale of regalia. There was really no single over-all Ku Klux Klan but a number of rival Klan organizations. They established several hundred Klaverns and enrolled at one time or another probably fifty thousand members,* but these were drawn almost entirely from fanatic, hoodlum, and lawless elements, and the movement was able to gain a foothold in only a part of the South.

Alabama was the chief stronghold of the revived Ku Klux Klan. It had substantial strength at times also in the Atlanta area of Georgia, Northern Florida, and the northeastern corner of South Carolina. In the Upper South, Klan emissaries were coldly received. Virginians would have no truck with the organization, and only small Klan nuclei developed in Arkansas, Tennessee, Louisiana, and Texas. In Mississippi an omnipresent Citizens' Council organization pre-empted the racist field.

North Carolina was afflicted with considerable Klan activity; but the sinister order was to receive a rebuff in that state which resounded across the nation as one of the few genuinely humorous incidents which the desegregation crisis afforded. In March 1958 a Klan expeditionary force, led by Wizard James Cole, of Marion, South Carolina, staged a full-dress demonstration in Robeson County, North Carolina, to warn the thirty thousand Lumbee Indians there against association with their white neighbors. The Lumbees, who are a sophisticated and thoroughly modernized tribe, responded in a spirit of indignation mingled with hilarious amusement. Gathering around their white-robed visitors, they fired hunting rifles into the air until the

* The Anti-Defamation League of B'nai B'rith, which followed Klan activities closely, estimates that the membership never exceeded this figure.

Klansmen fled in terror, whereupon Lumbee jokers wrapped discarded Klan sheets and regalia around themselves and danced merrily.

By far the most influential molders of the movement of resistance to desegregation were the organizations which sprang up in every Southern state and either coagulated in what became the "Citizens' Councils of America, Incorporated" or allied themselves with that body. At first there were many "White Citizens' Councils" and an "Association of Citizens' Councils"; local groups also used such names initially as "National Association for the Preservation of the White Race," "States' Rights League," "Hermitage Crusade," "Southern Gentlemen"—or "Pond Hollow Segregation Club." Strong state organizations which, with varying degrees of integration in the Citizens' Councils of America, preserved their separate identity were: the States' Rights Council of Georgia, the North Carolina Defenders of States' Rights, the Tennessee Federation for Constitutional Government, and the (Virginia) Defenders of State Sovereignty and Individual Liberties. The Ku Klux Klan was emphatically not an affiliate. Although their memberships sometimes overlapped and the two groups joined forces in some demonstrations, the Klan with its notorious propensity to violence was officially shunned by the status-seeking Citizens' Councils.

The first Citizens' Council came into being in July 1954, when fourteen citizens met in the town of Indianola on the Mississippi Delta. It soon had about a hundred members. Its organizer was Robert B. Patterson, a plantation manager who continued as executive secretary of the Citizens' Councils of Mississippi and became a leading figure in the expanding movement. Within six weeks councils had been set up in seventeen counties. By the end of 1954 councils were operating in more than one hundred Mississippi towns and were forming in several other states.

In March 1955 W. J. Simmons, a wealthy planter's son, organized the Jackson Council and joined Patterson in making a career of Citizens' Council promotion. More and more, the former's office in Jackson rather than Patterson's in Greenwood became the headquarters. The polished, sophisticated Simmons became in time—as editor of the Citizens' Council monthly publication and president of the Citizens' Council Forum—the movement's most influential leader. The sale of *Black Monday* was pushed throughout the South, and a

flood of pamphlets began to pour forth. Judge Brady was not only the
intellectual leader of the burgeoning movement, but he also went into
action as a vigorous organizer; according to his own account, he made
six hundred speeches during the first couple of years. The movement
slowed down during the period of waiting for the Supreme Court's 1955
decree and then spread rapidly until it claimed to have over three
hundred thousand members. Informed observers agree that at its peak
the membership of the Citizens' Councils of America, with its affiliates,
probably reached several hundred thousand.

Among the best-known leaders of the expanded Citizens' Council
movement were State Senator Sam Engelhardt, the dynamic organizer
of the Alabama Councils; Hugh G. Grant, a former United States
Minister to Thailand and president of the States' Rights Council of
Georgia; Emory Rogers of South Carolina; State Senator William
Rainach of Louisiana; and Roy V. Harris, a prominent Georgia
politician, who became president of the Citizens' Councils of America.
Segregationists of all types—including many of the Ku Klux Klan
mentality—found a place in the movement. But the Citizens' Councils
placed great emphasis on respectability, and in some sections mayors,
state legislators, sheriffs, clergymen, and business and professional
men of the first rank were to be found on Citizens' Councils rolls.
Mississippi, the birthplace and headquarters of the movement, was
enveloped in it virtually to the saturation point.

With these influences at work to stimulate hostility to the school
desegregation order and to Negroes, one may well ask what influences
were operating in the opposite direction. Did any voice ring out to
halt this trend? Did anyone to whom the masses of Southerners would
listen say: Stop; this is immoral, this is unpatriotic, or this is unwise?
or this is making the inevitable change more difficult and dangerous
for us? The answer is No. The counteracting influences, during the
first post-Brown decision years at least, were feeble indeed. Clergymen
who spoke out against the trend were rare. Some newspaper editors
sought cautiously to combat it, but most either avoided the subject or
urged the extremists on in inflammatory editorials. Those politicians
who called for calm and respect for the law of the land spoke so
softly that their voices were hardly heard in the anti-integration din.

There were, of course, thoughtful white Southerners who either believed that the Supreme Court had correctly interpreted the Constitu-

tion or realized that its decision was binding and would not be revoked, and who foresaw that public-school segregation would somehow have to be brought to an end. But we are unable to form any reliable estimate of how many held such views because public expression of them was so rare. Whether from fear of criticism and abuse, or from a sincere belief that an outspoken approach would impair their ability to exert a quiet influence in some phase of the crisis, such sentiments for the most part were carefully concealed. Public acknowledgment that the Supreme Court decision was the law of the land—though this concession generally was coupled with insistence upon a personal preference for segregation—invited bitter criticism and required courage in the highest degree. Emphasis on moderation and interracial friendship, even law and order, aroused suspicion and had to be voiced with caution.

There had long been an organization in which respected white Southerners joined with Negro leaders in working for interracial friendship and understanding. Formed in 1919 as the Commission on Interracial Co-operation, it was reorganized in 1944 as the Southern Regional Council. This organization, with a regular staff and an office in Atlanta, engaged in continuous and much-needed research on race relations, while in statements, publications, and speeches by its members it sought both to inform the public and to advance the cause of interracial justice. In 1952 the Southern Regional Council took a position against race segregation. It welcomed the Brown decision when it came in 1954, and its activities thenceforth were intensified and expanded. Affiliated with the Council, or working independently, were half-a-dozen small interracial state groups of dedicated people working for the same cause. White people were also working for better interracial relations in the South through national organizations, notably the Anti-Defamation League, the American Jewish Committee, and the American Friends Service Committee. The number of such organizations in the field and the volume of their activities would later assume substantial proportions. But in the first post-Brown decision years, relatively few even knew of their existence. In 1956 the white Southerners working actively for friendship between the races could be counted, not in tens of thousands, but in hundreds.

It was inevitable that the mounting hostility to the desegregation order and the mounting anti-Negro feeling, encouraged by dynamic

organizations—in which sheriffs and police were often members—
would express themselves in acts of violence.

The Southeastern Office of the American Friends Service Committee, the Department of Racial and Cultural Relations of the National
Council of the Churches of Christ in the U.S.A., and the Southern
Regional Council collaborated in compiling and publishing a report
on the eleven Southern states during the period from January 1, 1955,
to January 1, 1959, entitled *Intimidation, Reprisal and Violence.* The
information was culled from reports of the Associated Press, the
United Press, the International News, the *Southern School News,* and
a score of newspapers, the source being given in each case. Among the
two hundred and twenty-five acts against private liberties and public
peace listed were the following:

  6 Negroes killed

  29 individuals, 11 of them white, shot and wounded in racial
incidents

  44 persons beaten

  5 stabbed

  30 homes bombed; in one instance (at Clinton, Tennessee) an
additional 30 houses were damaged by a single blast; attempted
blasting of five other homes

  8 homes burned

  15 homes struck by gunfire, and 7 homes stoned

  4 schools bombed, in Jacksonville, Nashville, Chattanooga,
and Clinton

  2 bombing attempts on schools, in Charlotte and Clinton

  7 churches bombed, one of which was for whites; an attempt
made to bomb another Negro church

  1 church in Memphis burned; another church stoned

  4 Jewish temples or centers bombed, in Miami, Nashville,
Jacksonville, and Atlanta

  3 bombing attempts on Jewish buildings, in Gastonia, N.C.,
Birmingham, and Charlotte

  1 YWCA building in Chattanooga and an auditorium in Knoxville dynamited

  2 schools burned

The victims or the targets of these outrages were nearly all Negro.
Among exceptions were a few white people who conspicuously be-
friended Negroes, were accused of "race-mixing," or urged "moderation," and a wave of bombings of Jewish temples occurred in 1958.

Under the headings of "Intimidation" and "Reprisals" the report listed numerous other instances of cross-burnings and threats, of less violent demonstrations, and scattered instances of persecutions of white persons who associated with Negroes or otherwise dissented from extreme segregationist orthodoxy.

These incidents were reported more comprehensively in Northern than in Southern newspapers. They were deplored by Southern editors, but many Southern publicists held that they were the inevitable result of a provocative and improper Supreme Court decision. John Temple Graves, a distinguished Southern newspaper columnist, said that "the Court made us necessarily more race conscious than we have been since Reconstruction," and added: "It has taught us to disregard the law." [9] Criticism was often countered with the charge that crime and violence were equally prevalent in the great cities of the North.

It is possible that this blunt tabulation of outrages could give an impression of a kind of anarchy which did not exist. The incidents listed occurred in a region of forty million people over a period of four years, and most Southerners knew of them only through news media. Nevertheless they reflected a degree of malignancy and lawlessness more serious and more pregnant with crisis than many realized.

In the first incidents to arouse nationwide concern, public-school desegregation was not directly at issue. These included the revolting murder of a Negro boy in Mississippi, the series of disturbances in the struggle of Negroes for equal treatment on the city buses of Montgomery, Alabama, and the rioting precipitated by the admission of a Negro woman to that state's university. They signaled—especially the first and last of these—extraordinary mobilizations of newspaper and camera men, magazine writers, and the television and radio services; they were the subject of interminable examination, analysis, speculation, and debate, as well as colorful and sensational narrative.

The slaying of Emmett Till in Sumner, Mississippi, and its aftermath were naked manifestations of Negrophobia, a reversal to the worst days of anti-Negro brutality in the South. This 14-year-old Negro boy was kidnaped and murdered in August 1955 when a white woman said that he had tried to "date" her, uttered an obscenity, and "wolf-whistled"! The case was widely known as the "wolf-whistle" murder. The trial of the two men charged with the deed, the woman's husband and a companion, drew large crowds and was followed with

THIS BOOK IS THE PROPERTY OF
THE NATIONAL CITY PUBLIC LIBRARY

avid interest throughout the nation. In the ugly tradition of cases in which white men are accused of killing Negroes, nobody was punished.

The protracted Negro boycott of city buses in Montgomery, Alabama, made history in two respects: it marked the beginning of a new era of aggressive nonviolent action on the part of Southern Negroes and it thrust into national prominence a remarkable new Negro leader. It was a significant forerunner of the Negro upheaval which was to spread across the nation in 1963.

On Thursday, December 1, 1955, when a bus carrying white and Negro passengers made a downtown stop, the driver asked four Negroes to give up their seats to white passengers. One of the Negroes, Mrs. Rosa Parks, refused. She was taken to the police station and charged with violating city segregation laws. Saturday, printed leaflets were circulated asking Negroes to stay off the buses Monday, the day of Mrs. Parks' trial. Almost 90 per cent of them did; they went to work in private automobiles, Negro taxis, in wagons, on foot or bicycle. Mrs. Parks was found guilty and fined fourteen dollars. That night five thousand Negroes crowded into the Holt Street Baptist Church and by the end of the evening the Montgomery Improvement Association was formed. Its president was the Reverend Martin Luther King, Jr.

This was the beginning of a year-long bus boycott, during which King's home was bombed, a dynamite cap exploded in the home of another leader, and one hundred Negroes were indicted on charges of violating Alabama's anti-boycott laws. Meanwhile, a suit was filed in federal court. On November 13, 1956, the United States Supreme Court unanimously ruled that Montgomery's bus segregation laws were unconstitutional. The Negroes called off the boycott and resumed riding on the newly desegregated buses. But acts of violence continued. During the months following, four Negro churches, the homes of two ministers, and a taxi stand were bombed; snipers fired at buses, in one instance wounding a Negro woman; and a 15-year-old Negro girl was beaten by several young white men near a city bus stop.[10]

(A Negro boycott of city buses in Tallahassee, Florida, which developed in a similar manner in the summer of 1956 and was accompanied by tension and some violence, was also terminated as a result of the Supreme Court decision in the Montgomery case.)

The leader of the Montgomery Negro movement, Dr. Martin Luther King—he had won a doctorate at Boston University—was a talented preacher and writer, even a philosopher, as well as a calm, indomitable crusader. King became the apostle of a new doctrine of nonviolent resistance and protest, drawing its inspiration in part from Mahatma Gandhi, and rose quickly to the top rank of national Negro leadership, revered by Negroes and execrated by Southern segregationists.

In February 1956 public interest turned from the bus boycott in Montgomery to focus excitedly on the city of Tuscaloosa in the same state, where a Negro woman, Autherine Lucy, was admitted briefly to the University of Alabama. The lifting of racial barriers in Southern colleges and universities had begun before the Brown decision and had proceeded peaceably in half-a-dozen Southern states. Approximately a hundred and twenty-five public and private universities and colleges in Southern and border states—including one Alabama institution, the Catholic college of Spring Hill in Mobile—had admitted Negro students. By the beginning of the 1955–56 school year, Negroes had been admitted to state universities in all but five Southern states: Alabama, Florida, Georgia, Mississippi, and South Carolina. In these states university integration was now linked in the minds of segregationists with public-school integration, which they were prepared to resist to the end.

Miss Lucy, now twenty-six years of age, had first sought admission to the University of Alabama in 1952 and been refused. Her case had been in litigation, in the hands of NAACP lawyers, for three years when the definitive federal court order came. She attended her first class on Friday, February 3, 1956. That night a crowd of twelve hundred students, attracted by a burning cross, assembled on University Avenue and exploded firecrackers, sang "Dixie," and marched through the women's dormitory area. After a basketball game the next night students massed before the Student Union Building for further demonstrations. Many outsiders were noted among the university students—high-school pupils, workers from a nearby plant, and members of the Ku Klux Klan. Monday, a crowd of about three thousand roamed the campus, jeering, cursing, and throwing eggs and stones at officials accompanying Miss Lucy to her classes—the latter lying in the bottom of the car. Some peered in classroom windows, shouting: "Where is the nigger? Lynch her! Kill her!" Finally Miss Lucy was removed from the campus under heavy police escort and university officials suspended her indefinitely, expressing fear for her life.[11]

Not all of the students, or the townspeople were stampeded into folly. Indeed, Dr. O. C. Carmichael, president of the university, said: "The lawlessness . . . represents a small percentage of the student body." [12] The legislature of the student government association called for action to protect students' safety; the International Relations Club criticized the "ineffectiveness of the forces of law and order"; law-school students adopted a resolution supporting Dr. Carmichael in his determination not to tolerate further disorder; and seven hundred and fifty students signed a petition requesting that those leading the rioting "be apprehended and subjected to severe disciplinary action up to and including permanent expulsion." [13] A group of civic leaders in Tuscaloosa also called for law and order, and the calls for decency and decorum in the *Tuscaloosa News* won for its editor, Buford Boone, a Pulitzer Prize.

At the end of the month United States District Judge H. Hobart Grooms ordered that Miss Lucy be readmitted. But within hours she was expelled permanently. Something had happened which angered the university officials and furnished a not unwelcome excuse for ending the Lucy incident on disciplinary grounds. In her suit for reinstatement Miss Lucy had charged that the university had conspired with the mob. In court Thurgood Marshall dropped all charges of conspiracy, saying: "After careful investigation we are unable to produce any evidence to support these allegations." The board of trustees announced that it "felt impelled because of the nature of the charges made against its members and the officials of the university to take action expelling Autherine Lucy." [14] On petition by Miss Lucy to re-enter the university, Judge Grooms ruled that her expulsion was justified. Later the board of trustees announced that Leonard Wilson —the 19-year-old leader of the rioting mob—had been expelled, four other students had been suspended, and twenty-five had been disciplined.

On February 17 a Citizens' Council had been formed in Tuscaloosa for the first time. Over a thousand flocked to the organization meeting —of which sophomore Leonard Wilson was temporary chairman. Wayne Phillips wrote in the *New York Times Magazine* of February 26, 1956:

Saturday, the day after the white council meeting, there was something in Tuscaloosa the outsider had not felt before. There was hate, and there was fear.

Hate literature was circulated through the regular Saturday shopping crowds on the main street. Negroes were publicly ridiculed by men with whom they had lived in peace for years. Strangers were shunned or, if recognized as Northerners, taunted. Violence was something to be laughed at, boasted of, and gloried in. . . .

Chapter 5

THE PEOPLE'S
CHOSEN REPRESENTATIVES

On January 29, 1960—by which time North Carolina had achieved only token integration in nine out of a hundred and seventy-three school districts but had been spared radical resistance contortions or serious public disorder—the governor of that state addressed the Harvard Law School Forum. Looking back over the past few years, Governor Luther H. Hodges (later Secretary of Commerce), described in a temperate and elevated tone the difficulties which confronted a Southern state executive and the course which North Carolina had followed. He said that he did not wish "to dwell on the differences of opinion among competent lawyers and scholars concerning the 1954 decision, nor to take a great deal of time stating certain facts having to do with tradition, community mores, and strongly held convictions with respect to maintaining separate public schools for different races," but he wanted "to make the point that the governor of North Carolina did indeed face a very difficult, overwhelming problem brought about by the 1954 change in the interpretation of the Federal Constitution," and he continued:

It is accepted history that the Fourteenth Amendment to the Federal Constitution was adopted in the aftermath of the War Between the States. And the Congress which debated and approved the language of the Fourteenth Amendment for submission to the vote of the states also enacted federal statutes providing for operation of separate schools within the District of Columbia. It is also a matter of history that through the decades immediately following the adoption of the Fourteenth Amendment no less than twenty-five states, at one time or the other, had statutes either authorizing or requiring separate schools for the races. The states either permitting or requiring such practices were not by any means limited to those which we now group together and refer to as "Southern states." For example, at various times there were California, Delaware, Illinois,

56

Indiana, Kansas, Missouri, Nevada, New Jersey, New York, Ohio, and Pennsylvania, all outside the Southern or border-state category. It is also a matter of historic fact that in various cases decided before 1900, as well as after 1900, the United States Supreme Court gave express approval to what is called the "separate-but-equal" rule.

Whatever the niceties of constitutional interpretation involved in the decision of those cases which came before our highest court before 1900, many states and local governments did proceed to establish and operate racially separate schools and the Supreme Court did not, until very recent times, indicate that the rule of "separate but equal" might be in jeopardy so far as judicial interpretation was concerned.

It is thus clear that the 1954 decision amounted to a drastic change of the judicial mind, or a complete reversal of long-established interpretation by the Supreme Court.

This fact in and of itself did, in my opinion, make the problem vastly more difficult for the governor of a state which had chosen to maintain separate public schools for the races.

The governor traced the development of public education in North Carolina since the Reconstruction era and recalled the "background of extreme travail and difficulty through which Negro citizens had to come to citizenship responsibilities," resulting in the development of segregated school systems "in many states of the Union." From the time that he "was suddenly called upon to assume the responsibilities of governor in November 1954, and without knowing how North Carolina would meet the ever-darkening crisis," he had set for himself two objectives: "(1) To maintain, if possible, a system of public education for all the children of North Carolina; and (2) to maintain law and order.

"I frankly confess to you today," Governor Hodges said, "that there were many times during that period when it seemed that not only were the pillars of education about to fall, but also the pillars of stable and responsible government. . . . There were times when it seemed almost that our state, our region, and indeed the whole nation must suffer an orgy of great internal discord, and that we must pass through a period of neighbor against neighbor, citizen against citizen, state against state, and in truth a nation divided against itself. . . .

"By early 1955 our state legislature was in regular session, and the

Advisory Committee on Education under the chairmanship of Mr. [Thomas] Pearsall . . . in due time recommended to me, and I . . . in turn recommended to the General Assembly, the repeal of all our statutes which then required that white and Negro children be assigned to separate schools. At the same time we recommended, and the General Assembly enacted, a pupil-assignment law which placed in the local boards of education throughout the state full authority and responsibility for assignment of the pupils to the public schools in each local unit in accordance with valid and reasonable standards. . . ."

The governor recalled further that he had suggested "that it would be in the interest of our public schools and in the interest of maintaining peace . . . for all of our citizens to observe voluntary separation of the races in the public schools." (It may be noted that this suggestion aroused no enthusiasm among North Carolina Negroes.)

"As the people of our state were increasingly concerned," he called the legislature in special session in July 1956 and recommended as "safety valves" an amendment to the state constitution "which would (1) authorize tuition grants to be paid to the parents of any child assigned against the wishes of his parents to a school in which the races were mixed, such grants to be available for education in a private school chosen by the parents . . . ; (2) authorize the people in any locality, by majority vote, to discontinue the operation of the public schools in that community. . . ."

However, speaking in January 1960, the North Carolina governor was able to say of his state with pride: "In no instance that I recall has an election been called by citizens at the local level for the purpose of voting to close schools. Also, I understand that up to the present time there has been no case in which the parent has withdrawn his child from a public school and applied for a tuition grant on the grounds that he objected to his child attending school with a person of another race."

Governor Hodges closed on this lofty note: "We must always keep before us the great promise of America, which is the promise of freedom under responsible and democratic government—and I mean freedom for all citizens irrespective of race, religion, or creed. While our day-to-day progress toward more perfect realization of these ideals may seem to falter, and while all of us at one time or the other despair of doing good works, the spirit of America must always remain alive in our hearts."

There was on the whole a more constructive spirit among the state governors in the South than among the representatives of the people in the state legislatures and in the halls of Congress. All elected officeholders were conscious of the political advantages of catering to the racist fever. But the chief executive bears a unique responsibility for the maintenance of public order and the general equilibrium of his state. The legislator, who can cast but one vote in a numerous assembly, feels freer to voice extravagant opinions and to join in impulsive gestures. Some governors were equally uninhibited, and the picture changed somewhat with the rising tide of fanaticism at the grassroots of political power. Moderate incumbents in Alabama and Mississippi were to be replaced by irresponsible extremists; the governor of Arkansas, who was then pursuing a decorous course, was—surprisingly—to become a symbol of Southern rebellion against federal authority. But in the summer of 1956 more Southern governors were looking in the direction of adjustment to the Supreme Court's desegregation ruling than were facing the other way.

Marvin Griffin, who had succeeded Herman Talmadge as governor of Georgia, and George Timmerman, Jr., who had succeeded Governor Byrnes in South Carolina, were men of smaller stature than their predecessors. Griffin was an even more reckless advocate of resistance, both in Georgia and as a roving ambassador of turmoil in other Southern states; and Timmerman, who held that "the mixing of children of two biologically different races" was "contrary to the divine order of things," pledged that "not in a thousand years will the schools of South Carolina be integrated." [1] In Texas, Governor Allan Shivers frowned upon school-closing proposals but placed himself emphatically on the side of resistance to desegregation. Governor Thomas B. Stanley, after initial hesitation, yielded to the pressure of a political machine and proclaimed resistance in Virginia.

On the other hand, half-a-dozen Southern governors, in addition to Hodges of North Carolina, were in varying situations resisting segregationist hysteria. In Tennessee the moderate policy of Governor Frank Clement was put to a dramatic test on the morning of January 23, 1956, when approximately three hundred vociferous segregationists drove from Memphis and Chattanooga and converged on the state capitol in Nashville. Cars in the two motorcades were decorated with Confederate and American flags and banners bearing pro-segregation slogans, including one demanding "Segregation or War." The governor listened for an hour to twenty of their spokesmen, then lectured them firmly and made no concession to their demands. State Attorney General George McCanless, who accompanied the governor, said: "I am a Southerner, and I believe in segregation. But we in this country are a government of laws and not men, and the decisions of the Supreme Court are applicable to the whole country and not just somewhere else." [2]

Tennessee was unique among Southern states in that not only the governor, but the two representatives of that state in the United States Senate, Estes Kefauver and Albert Gore, expressed moderate views on the desegregation issue, though they took little part in the controversy. Jim McCord, a former governer, state conservation commissioner under Clement, also said, following the January demonstration: "If calmness and patriotism alone had activated the members of the United States in the 'Fifties, war might have been averted. And, if the people of today will lend themselves to calm purposes and Christian-like ideals, these questions can be settled adroitly and to the best interests of Tennessee." The fact that Tennessee was blessed with such leadership at the highest level increases the blame to be placed at the door of the roving racist agitators who converged upon that state when it became the scene of the most violent explosions yet registered over the desegregation of public schools.

Governor LeRoy Collins of Florida, a handsome and attractive public figure, won the title of "the moderate Southern governor" from many national observers by his repeated appeals for Christian tolerance and respect for law. A polished gentleman and a devout Episcopalian, he spoke the language of idealism. Collins was cautious, if not negative, in his approach to the actual implementation of the Supreme Court decision. He averted much segregationist criticism by a vague insistence that "we can preserve segregation," and he put through the Florida Assembly a series of enactments which, though relatively moderate, were expressly designed to accomplish that purpose. No Negro child was admitted to any white public school in Florida until 1959. But it was due to the courage and skill of LeRoy Collins that Florida was spared some of the legislative excesses which afflicted other Southern states, and his lofty utterances helped a certain candle of liberalism to burn more brightly in the South.

Governor Orval Faubus of Arkansas—in 1956—was wavering in

his "moderate" stand, yet he campaigned successfully for re-election against two extremist opponents whom he called "hate preachers." He favored action to prevent "sudden and complete integration," but he pointed with a kind of pride to the fact that in Arkansas three public-school districts and all the state institutions of higher learning, one of which his son attended, had been desegregated.

Governor Earl Long had neither the moral nor the physical stamina to stem the rising tide of hostility and intolerance in Louisiana. However, he was sympathetic with the Negroes; their votes had been a factor in his election and he would seek to keep their friendship to the end. He was to battle segregationist extremists fiercely—though he would embrace many of their proposals. "Extremists on both sides are injuring the cause," he said, and added with great truth: "There are a lot of fakers trying to advance themselves politically by using the race issue to befuddle the people." [3] Being "soft on integration" was one of the many charges to be leveled at his confused and unhappy administration.

In judging the actions and public utterances of the governor of a state which is seething with anti-Negro and anti-integration feeling, the political exigencies and limitations which surrounded him must be taken into account. A degree of compromise with extremism was the price of election to office in the first place, and only by marching some distance down the road of defiance with the majority was it possible to exercise an influence against going all the way to disaster. Without a leaven of politicians who reasoned thus, the most reckless element would have held unchallenged sway. Alabama and Mississippi were the two Southern states where hostility to desegregation would express itself in the most violent form. The governors of those states at this time insisted upon their attachment to segregation and their determination to preserve it, but from a study of their behavior in its peculiar context—aided by the writer's talks with them—it can be said with assurance that these two governors deplored the resistance furor and desired to move toward some orderly adjustment.

Alabama's colorful Governor James ("Big Jim") Folsom was habitually kind to Negroes and was regarded by most of them as a friend of their cause. He discouraged legislative excesses, sometimes withholding his signature from segregationist measures, and his early groping toward orderly adjustment to the desegregation ruling led some national observers—wrongly—to remove Alabama from the classification of "resisting" states. Speaking before the Alabama Education Association in 1955, Folsom said: "I would like to remind you that we always hear more noise from those who are guided by blind prejudice and bigotry than is ever the case with those who try to think through and be fair in their approach." [4] His "soft" attitude aroused bitter opposition during his term of office and appeared to close the door to any return to political power on his part in the future.

Mississippi, of all the Southern states, has had the highest percentage of Negroes in its population and the strongest attachment to white supremacy among its white citizens. Any public expression bordering on liberalism, or even moderation, on the segregation issue was politically perilous there. Governor James P. Coleman, who had been a congressman of liberal leanings, resisted extremist pressure in a number of critical situations and was criticized for his "softness on integration"; he refused to join the Citizens' Council. Coleman's words and actions often shocked liberals who viewed them from afar, but among the too silent moderate minority in Mississippi he was regarded as the state's best hope. When most of the Southern members of Congress joined in a sensational manifesto of protest against the Supreme Court's decision, Governor Coleman recalled the situation in the South on the eve of the Civil War and cut through the loud applause in Mississippi with the comment: "Those in positions of responsibility must think things through before they take positions of no return. . . . The greatest need of the time is for cool thinking on racial problems. This is no time to let hotheads make us lose our perspective and go beyond the point of no return." [5]

Southern members of Congress were much heard from. Senator Eastland of Mississippi attacked the Brown decision day in and day out and seized upon every semblance of argument in sight to support his contentions. Many others—conspicuously Senator Strom Thurmond of South Carolina, Senator Herman E. Talmadge of Georgia (elected to the Senate in 1956), Representative John Bell Williams of Mississippi, and Representative James C. Davis of Georgia —criticized the desegregation ruling unceasingly and without restraint. The demur of a handful of liberal Southern members was scarcely audible. A disproportionate number of Southern senators were high in national councils. The seniority rule and the usually long tenure in office in the one-party South had made Southerners the ranking Democratic members of the most powerful Senate committees. Eastland was the ranking Democrat on the Judiciary Committee; Russell of Georgia, Walter George of Georgia, and Byrd of Virginia were ranking Democratic members of the Armed Forces, Foreign Relations, and Finance Committees respectively. Russell inveighed against the desegregation ruling with a degree of restraint; George registered his disapproval, but his unwillingness to take the warpath of defiance was largely responsible for his retirement from the Senate in 1956. Byrd was bitter, though not voluble, on the subject; in his direction of a famous political machine in his own state and in his skillful maneuvering among his colleagues in Congress this Virginia senator gave a powerful stimulus to the movement of resistance in the South.

Byrd was generally regarded as the chief architect of the "Southern Manifesto," which boomed across the nation in March 1956. It was part of his plan to "organize the Southern states for massive resistance," as he had already organized his own state of Virginia. The manifesto, which was signed by an overwhelming majority of the Southern members of Congress and introduced in the House and Senate on March 12, 1956, attacked the Supreme Court decision sharply and commended "those states which have declared the intention to resist enforced integration by any lawful means."

The manifesto began to take shape at a meeting of twenty Southern senators in the office of Senator George, who consented to serve as chairman of a drafting committee. The first draft was stronger than the final document written by Senator Russell. Many Southerners hesitated to sign it; Senator George himself was clearly lacking in enthusiasm. But under pressure from manifesto promoters—who reminded them of the feeling back home and the possibility of being labeled "betrayers" of the South—nineteen out of twenty-two Southern senators went along. The only ones who refused were the two from Tennessee. Lyndon Johnson of Texas, being the Senate majority leader, was not asked to sign.

In the House of Representatives, twenty-four Southern members refused to lend their names to the manifesto. Three North Carolina members withheld their signatures—Representatives Thurman Chatham, C. B. Deane, and Harold D. Cooley. Chatham said: "I personally will not sign anything that will tear down the power and prestige of the Court as the final arbiter of justice." [6] (Chatham and

Deane were defeated in their bids for re-election two months later; Cooley survived.) But eighty-two Southern representatives signed the document. The delegations of Alabama, Arkansas, Georgia, Louisiana, Mississippi, South Carolina, and Virginia gave the manifesto their unanimous support.

The Southern Manifesto was received without comment in the House of Representatives. In the Senate the reaction of most non-Southerners, after the initial shock, was one of sorrow more than anger: some were relieved that the Southerners had not been more violent in their protest. Outside of Congress, both President Eisenhower and Adlai E. Stevenson, who would face each other again in the forthcoming presidential election, emphasized the fact that the Southerners had committed themselves to support their views only by lawful means. No personage at a high official level answered the broadside against the Supreme Court. The high tribunal itself, as it must, remained silent.

As the Southern Manifesto, officially entitled the "Declaration of Constitutional Principles," brought the highest segregationist prestige and talent to bear in presenting the case against the Brown decision, it is appropriate to quote salient passages here:

> We regard the decision of the Supreme Court in the school cases as a clear abuse of judicial power. It climaxes a trend in the federal judiciary undertaking to legislate, in derogation of the authority of Congress, and to encroach upon the reserved rights of the states and the people.
>
> The original Constitution does not mention education. Neither does the Fourteenth Amendment nor any other amendment. The debates preceding the submission of the Fourteenth Amendment clearly show that there was no intent that it should affect the systems of education maintained by the states.
>
> The very Congress which proposed the amendment subsequently provided for segregated schools in the District of Columbia. . . .
>
> In the case of Plessy v. Ferguson in 1896, the Supreme Court expressly declared that under the Fourteenth Amendment no person was denied any of his rights if the states provided separate but equal public facilities. This decision has been followed in many other cases. It is notable that the Supreme Court, speaking through Chief Justice Taft, a former president of the United States, unanimously declared in 1927 in Lum v. Rice that the "separate-but-equal" principle is ". . . within the discretion of the state in

regulating its public schools and does not conflict with the Fourteenth Amendment." . . .

Though there has been no constitutional amendment or act of Congress changing this established legal principle almost a century old, the Supreme Court of the United States, with no legal basis for such action, undertook to exercise their naked judicial power and substituted their personal political and social ideas for the established law of the land. . . .

With the gravest concern for the explosive and dangerous condition created by this decision and inflamed by outside meddlers:

We reaffirm our reliance on the Constitution as the fundamental law of the land.

We decry the Supreme Court's encroachments on rights reserved to the states and to the people, contrary to established law and to the Constitution.

We commend the motives of those states which have declared the intention to resist forced integration by any lawful means.

We pledge ourselves to use all lawful means to bring about a reversal of this decision which is contrary to the Constitution and to prevent the use of force in its implementation. . . .

With the legislatures of the eleven Southern states the Brown decision and matters related to it became a continuing obsession. Extraordinary sessions were called again and again—in March 1956 the Alabama legislature was in special session for the fourth time in fourteen months—and regular sessions were often so taken up with the segregation problem that little time was left for the public business which normally crowded their agenda.

Public-school appropriations received much attention. Appropriation bills offered opportunities to strengthen the dikes of segregation, but a certain beneficial effect of the re-examination of the "separate-but-equal" policy also appeared. The Mississippi legislature struggled with the problem of financing an ambitious "school equalization" program; Governor Timmerman boasted that in South Carolina "schools for Negroes are now superior to any in the nation" as a result of a $127,000,000 construction program in which Negro schools had received 60 per cent of all funds allocated. Discounting such exaggerations, Southern states were moving with considerable new impetus to close the gap between white and Negro school facilities.

The volume of pro-segregation legislation grew steadily. In 1956 state assemblies launched upon a veritable legislative binge. Politicians lay awake nights concocting schemes to baffle the NAACP and outwit the federal judiciary, and, except where one proposal duplicated or interfered with another, they all stood a good chance of being enacted into law. The legislatures of Alabama, Georgia, Mississippi, South Carolina, and Virginia—each in session during the first three months of 1956—adopted no less than forty-two pro-segregation measures. By the end of the year the number of such enactments in the eleven Southern states had reached a total of a hundred and six, and the flood showed no signs of subsiding.

In examining the mood of Southern legislatures during this period it is important to note the disproportionate representation of the rural areas, and particularly of those counties with the heaviest Negro population. It was among the white people of these sections that race prejudice was most deeply rooted. The excessive influence in the legislatures of the Black Belt, the fiercest stronghold of resistance to desegregation, was striking. Patrick E. McCauley, assistant to the director of the Southern Education Reporting Service, in a study for *With All Deliberate Speed,* pointed out that "in Alabama 16 Black Belt counties with 13.5 per cent of the state's total population have 27.3 per cent of the House representation and 28.5 per cent of the Senate seats. Georgia's 37 Black Belt counties with 11.5 per cent of the population have 19 per cent of the House seats and 22.7 per cent of the Senate seats. Fourteen Louisiana Black Belt parishes (counties) have 13.8 per cent of the House representation and 18.4 per cent in the Senate, with only 8.4 per cent of the population. . . ." The Black Belt was limited for this purpose to contiguous counties having populations over or near 50 per cent Negro. McCauley noted further that the Black Belt counties re-elect the same representatives over greater numbers of years than do other sections, giving them "added influence in terms of prestige, committee, and leadership appointments and greater parliamentary experience." [7]

An element of stampede and a certain fetish of unanimity contributed greatly to the fever which seized the state legislatures. The same phenomenon was discernible at the congressional level in the recruitment of supporters for the Southern Manifesto. The dissenter faced the dreadful political consequences of being labeled an "integrationist," "a friend of the NAACP," etc.; he was often denied support in unrelated objectives and excluded from important committees, which impaired his usefulness as a legislator. The resentment of extremist colleagues was not unlike that visited upon a conspirator who shrinks from a desperate enterprise upon which his comrades have embarked.

At the outset there was in every state assembly a minority, generally a substantial minority, who objected to extravagant measures of resistance to the Supreme Court ruling. A number of the earlier bills found division in debate and were passed by only moderate majorities. But as the futility of opposition became more and more apparent, potentially far-reaching enactments were adopted swiftly by a vote which, if not unanimous, was less than half-a-dozen votes short of that goal. The stampede sometimes began before a bill was introduced. Some of the most drastic bills adopted by the Virginia legislature were signed by more than a majority of the members of one chamber before they were thrown into the hopper. Resolutions of protest, or "interposition," against the Supreme Court ruling were adopted by the unanimous vote of the Alabama and North Carolina Senates and the unanimous vote of both houses in Louisiana and South Carolina; in the lower chambers of Alabama and North Carolina the opposing votes were four and two respectively; in Virginia opposition was registered by only five votes in the House and two in the Senate. In Georgia half-a-dozen bills to aid and encourage private schools cleared the Senate unanimously. In Louisiana a dozen pro-segregation bills were passed without a single dissenting vote in either chamber. When the Florida legislature approved a five-bill program the Senate acted unanimously; in the House of Representatives only one opposing vote was cast—that of Representative John B. Orr, Jr.

Orr's gesture was so rare as to be sensational in the Southern scene; this young legislator actually declared his belief that segregation was "morally wrong." It is interesting to note that his courage brought praise from several colleagues and a barrage of commendatory messages, and that his constituents in the relatively liberal city of Miami returned him to office for one further term before his segregationist opposition laid him low.

The strange pile of legislation beginning to clutter the statute books of Southern states included provisions for the following: the use of police powers to prevent the admission of Negroes to white public schools; the placing of schools under the control of the governor or the state legislature (where it was hopefully calculated they could not be reached by federal courts); the financing of litigation opposing

desegregation; investigation of pro-integration and pro-segregation activities (with emphasis entirely on the former); commissions to pub-
licize the "Southern point of view"; the closing of public schools to
prevent desegregation and the sale or leasing of public-school property; and aid and encouragement for private schools. Compulsory
school-attendance laws were modified or repealed in half-a-dozen
states. In order that Negroes should be penalized equally with whites
in any school-closing, several legislatures provided for the closing
of all public schools in any district in which Negroes should be enrolled in one or more schools. Among the more subtle safeguards
against racial integration was the Georgia legislature's decree that a
schoolteacher could instruct only pupils of his or her own race. A
number of enactments sought to hamper or frustrate the NAACP.
Several legislatures memorialized their delegations in Congress, urging them to seek legislation to curb the powers of the Supreme Court,
and the Georgia Assembly called for the impeachment of six Supreme
Court justices whom it accused of "attempting to subvert the Constitution of the United States and of high crimes and misdemeanors in
office."

Mississippi provided for a fine or a jail sentence for any white person attending a school also attended by Negroes. The Mississippi legislature sought to provide fines, imprisonment, and civil liability for
federal officers who tried to enforce desegregation, but this bill was
vetoed by Governor Coleman. Coleman gave his approval, however, to
an act setting up a State Sovereignty Commission to "do and perform
any and all acts and things deemed necessary and proper to protect
the sovereignty of the State of Mississippi and her sister states from
encroachment thereon by the federal government or any branch, department, or agency thereof." This commission was voted $250,000
for its work. For the first three years it engaged mainly in propaganda,
but it was equipped with an investigating division empowered to em-
ploy secret investigators and paid informers.

Two types of action taken by nearly all Southern legislatures invite
special attention. One was the "pupil-assignment" or "pupil-placement" laws, setting up elaborate requirements and criteria "other than
race" to regulate the assignment of children to schools. Hopeful liberal
observers saw in some of these a means of effecting selective gradualism in adjusting to the Supreme Court ruling; but the object of most

of their proponents was to make it possible to deny Negroes admission to white schools or to hold desegregation to a minimum when it could no longer be prevented.

In the Virginia legislature liberal Senator Stuart B. Carter, who rivaled the lonely stand of Florida's State Senator Orr in averring publicly a "conscientious belief in integration," supported the pupil-assignment plan at one stage. "The best method of making the change," Carter said, "is to have gradual orderly integration, where necessary, controlled and regulated by the people in the school district." We have already quoted Governor Hodges' reference to the Pearsall Plan of pupil assignment in North Carolina. William T. Joyner, vice chairman of the committee which drafted the North Carolina bill, expressed the philosophy of many supporters of pupil-assignment plans when he said: "I do not hesitate to advance my personal opinion, and it is that the admission of less than 1 per cent— for example, one-tenth of 1 per cent—of Negro children to the schools heretofore attended only by white children is a small price to pay for the ability to keep the mixing within bounds of reasonable control." [8]

The principle of establishing criteria to regulate the assignment of pupils was given qualified approval by federal courts. But in their operation the plans adopted gave rise to interminable litigation; it was difficult, for instance, to establish an intent to comply with the Supreme Court ruling when the same legislature that set up the assignment plan enacted laws requiring the closing of schools to prevent the admission of Negroes. Nevertheless, a trickle of integration began in North Carolina in 1957, and in Virginia—after revision of its law and a radical change of policy in 1959—integration was to proceed somewhat more extensively under a pupil-placement plan.

Most pupil-assignment laws were transparently designed to exclude Negroes from white schools. While the words "segregation" and "Negro" were avoided, school authorities in determining the schools in which pupils should be placed were given such factors to consider as ". . . the possibility or threat of friction or disorder among pupils or others; the possibility of breaches of the peace or ill will or economic retaliation within the community; the home environment of the pupil; the maintenance or severance of established social and psychological relationships with other pupils and with teachers; etc. etc." [9] Abundant excuses were thus provided for rejecting the applications of Negroes to enter white schools. Cumbersome systems of appeal—

promising long delay and possible expense—were calculated further to deter Negro applicants.

The climax of hostility on the part of Southern state legislatures was reached in a gesture called "interposition." This was the doctrine, once held by many Southern leaders, that a state had a right to "interpose its sovereignty" between the federal government and its people. In blunter language, this meant that a state could nullify the effects of an edict of the federal government within its boundaries, that the state in the last analysis was in fact independent. In the middle of the twentieth century the word "interposition" had been forgotten by all but historians, and the doctrine had been long since buried by the Civil War. Both were now exhumed. The word became familiar to the general public and the doctrine was embraced by the legislatures of most Southern states.

Interposition was succinctly invoked in a statement issued in August 1955 by a group of white citizens in South Carolina, known as the "Committee of 52," which attracted little attention. These South Carolinians urged their legislature "to take such steps as may be necessary or desirable to interpose the sovereignty of the State of South Carolina between federal courts and local school officials with respect to any effort of such courts to usurp state authority in the matter of public education." [10]

Credit for the disinterment of the doctrine has also been given to an elderly Virginia lawyer named William Old—who was later honored for this accomplishment by the legislature of his state by being named a circuit court judge. But it was the *Richmond News Leader* which broadcast the idea in Virginia and the South, and its editor Jack Kilpatrick, has been rightly regarded as the "father" of modern interposition.

Old put the results of his research into a pamphlet which came to Kilpatrick's attention in October 1955, and to the latter—now a zealous resister and groping for a formula—Old's findings were pure gold. Most of the *News Leader*'s editorial page was given over to interposition. The Virginia and Kentucky interposition resolutions of 1798 and 1799 were reprinted in full. Voluminous editorials, written with the solemnity of great state papers, appeared daily alongside three-column portraits of Jefferson, Madison, Calhoun, and other pre-Civil War Southern immortals. "After six weeks, and fifty thousand words in the *News Leader,* the strange new word 'interposition' had entered the vocabulary of most adult Virginians and of politicians all across the South. Reprints of the interposition editorials had been distributed beyond the *News Leader*'s circulation range. A group of extreme segregationists, meeting in Memphis, Tennessee, urged Virginia to 'interpose its sovereignty' when the legislature met in January and called on all Southern states to fall in line. . . ." [11]

The five Southern states whose legislatures were in session in January 1956 raced to adopt resolutions of interposition in one form or another. Alabama had the honor of being the first across the interposition line. The Virginia legislature haggled longer over the wording, but in the debate and in earlier drafts it had led the way. The Virginia General Assembly resolved in part as follows:

> That by its decision of May 17, 1954, in the school cases, the Supreme Court of the United States placed upon the Constitution an interpretation, having the effect of an amendment thereto, which interpretation Virginia emphatically disapproves;
>
> That with the Supreme Court's decision aforesaid and this resolution by the General Assembly of Virginia, a question of contested power has arisen: The Court asserts, for its part, that the states did, in fact, in 1868, prohibit unto themselves, by means of the Fourteenth Amendment, the power to maintain racially separate public schools, which power certain of the states have exercised daily for more than eighty years; the State of Virginia, for her part, asserts that she has never surrendered such power. . . .
>
> [That Virginia] anxiously concerned at this massive expansion of central authority . . . is in duty bound to interpose against these most serious consequences, and earnestly to challenge the usurped authority that would inflict them upon her citizens. . . .
>
> And be it finally resolved that until the question here asserted by the State of Virginia be settled by clear constitutional amendment, we pledge our firm intention to take all appropriate measures, legally and constitutionally available to us, to resist this illegal encroachment upon our sovereign powers and to urge upon our sister states, whose authorities over their own most cherished powers may next be imperiled, their prompt and deliberate efforts to check this and further encroachment by the Supreme Court, through judicial legislation, upon the reserved powers of the states.

Resolutions adopted by five other states in 1956 also contain significant passages:

Alabama: [The Supreme Court decisions] are, as a matter of right, null, void, and of no effect; and the legislature of Alabama declares to all men as a matter of right, this state is not bound to abide thereby . . .

Georgia: It is the duty of the State in flagrant cases such as this to interpose its powers between its people and the efforts of said Court to assert an unlawful dominion over them.

South Carolina: The State of South Carolina as a loyal and sovereign State of the Union will exercise the powers reserved to it under the Constitution to judge for itself of the infraction and to take such other legal measures as it may deem appropriate to protect its sovereignty and the rights of its people.

Mississippi: Said decisions are in violation of the Constitutions of the United States and the State of Mississippi, and therefore, are considered unconstitutional, invalid and of no lawful effect within the confines of the State of Mississippi.

Louisiana: Until the usurpation herein complained of . . . be settled by legal constitutional amendment . . . the legislature of Louisiana does hereby solemnly declare the decision of the Supreme Court . . . and any similar decisions that might be rendered in connection with the public-school system and public parks and recreational facilities, insofar as such decisions may affect or apply to the sovereign State of Louisiana, to be in violation of the Constitution of the United States and of the State of Louisiana. . . .

Chapter 6

THE PROBLEM
OF ENFORCEMENT

"The decision in *Brown v. Board of Education* created the greatest problem of compliance since the Marshall period," observes the Encyclopædia Britannica.

The Supreme Court said pointedly in its 1955 pronouncement: ". . . It should go without saying that the vitality of these constitutional principles cannot be allowed to yield simply because of disagreement with them." But how in a region in hostile disagreement was that ruling to be enforced? The question touched the foundations of the system of government under which we live.

The Russian dictator Joseph Stalin, speaking of the Roman Catholic Pope, once asked scornfully: "How many divisions has he?" The Supreme Court has no divisions of soldiers at its command, and no police and no enforcement agency. It has no direct means of invoking the power of the Government of the United States to enforce its decrees. In the normal course its place in the constitutional division of power, its Olympian prestige, and the long tradition of matter-of-fact obedience to its fiats are sufficient. But in most of the South after the Brown decision these values appeared to have lost their force. In the constitutional crisis which arose and which involved far more than public schools, the power of the President—even military force —would ultimately be used to insure compliance with limited local and specific orders of federal courts. But the broad ruling that public-school segregation violated the Constitution brought no steps on the part of the executive or the legislative branches of the government looking to its general abolition.

President Eisenhower strove to follow a course of disinvolvement in the controversy; Congress took no action which even suggested approval of the Brown decision. On one occasion when the President was chided by congressional critics for his apparent indifference to resistance to the ruling, he replied, via special counsel: "The President

would not make any assumption that the judicial branch of the Government is incapable of implementing the Supreme Court's decision." [1]
To newspapermen and others, President Eisenhower spoke frequently of "progress"—"progress" which had been made or "progress" which should be made—but his personal opinion of the Brown decision and of school desegregation was left in doubt. "There are very strong emotions on the other side," he once remarked—"people that see a picture of mongrelization of the race, they call it." Calling for "education," "patience," and "moderation," he criticized "extremists" and seemed to place those working for compliance and those working for defiance together. His comments on massive gestures of resistance were in the nature more of extenuation than of rebuke.

Commenting on the Southern Manifesto, the President said with singular complacency: "Now, the first thing about the manifesto is this: that they say they are going to use every legal means. No one in any reasonable position anywhere has talked nullification, because— and there would be a place where we get to a very bad spot for the simple reason that I am sworn to defend and uphold the Constitution of the United States and, of course, I can never abandon or refuse to carry out my own duty.

"But let us remember that the Supreme Court itself talked about emotionalism in this question, and it was for that reason that it said 'progress must be gradual.' " [2]

Nullification was expressly present in some of the interposition resolutions adopted by Southern state legislatures. Asked for his comment on these, the President said: "Now this is what I say: there are adequate means of determining all of these factors. The Supreme Court has issued its own operational directives and delegated power to the district courts.

"I expect that we are going to make progress, and the Supreme Court itself said it does not expect revolutionary action suddenly executed.

"We will make progress, and I am not going to attempt to tell you how it is going to be done." [3]

Suggestions were made in many quarters that the President should invite Southern leaders to discuss the problem with him at the White House. In February 1956 Adlai E. Stevenson proposed that the President call a meeting of Southern white and Negro leaders "to explore ways and means of allaying rising tensions over racial integration in the South." [4] Governor Collins of Florida asked the President to call a conference of Southern governors and attorneys general. The Textile Workers Union of America asked him to summon the Southern governors. No such conferences were held. President Eisenhower told a news conference on May 23, 1956, that he believed any such conference would tend to inflame rather than alleviate racial tension and that the participants probably would feel compelled to stand by long-established positions.

The inaction of Congress did not signify disapproval of the Supreme Court decision. On the contrary, if members of Congress reflected the sentiments of their constituents, a large majority must have approved—and they probably did approve—of the desegregation ruling. A Gallup poll in July 1954 found that, in spite of overwhelming disapproval in the South, 57 per cent of those with opinions in the nation approved of it. Those approving were: in the Far West, 68 per cent; in the Middle West, 61 per cent; and in the East, 76 per cent. However, not only was the powerful and determined Southern bloc to be reckoned with, but there was difference of opinion even among liberals as to what action, if any, Congress should take. Theodore R. McKeldin, who as governor of Maryland was leading his state to compliance in good faith, said in 1959: "We don't need a special act . . . to tell us what the Supreme Court has stated rather clearly. . . . We have the powers now, in the Presidency and in the Department of Justice, to act as a nation against any state's act of rebellion against the Constitution. There is a practical question, too, as to the kind of federal integration law which would suit the condition and popular temperament of, say, Maryland and Kentucky, and at the same time those of Georgia and South Carolina." [5]

On the other hand, many felt that, in view of the far-reaching implications of the desegregation ruling and the extraordinary hostility in the South, the executive and legislative branches of the federal government should share the responsibility for its implementation. A number of plans were suggested. Governor Collins advanced a proposal in 1957 for the creation of a federal commission in each state with primary responsibility for the direction of desegregation in public schools. Under this plan the commissions would offer counsel to individuals and school authorities, investigate allegations that persons were being denied admission to public schools on account of race, consider any plan for desegregation upon the request of school authorities, and approve or disapprove of them or direct modifications. Southern governors, to whom the plan was first submitted, were cool to any plan looking to school integration; others found the Collins plan impracticable or an encroachment upon the scope of the federal judiciary. The proposal is of interest, nevertheless, as indicative of a needed service for which no governmental machinery existed.

Senator Lyndon B. Johnson introduced a bill in the Senate in 1958 for the creation of a federal community relations service to conciliate "disagreements in communities in the various states disruptive to peaceful relations among citizens of such communities." In the same session of Congress, Senator Paul H. Douglas of Illinois, with the co-sponsorship of seventeen colleagues, introduced a bill with comprehensive provision for legislative implementation of the desegregation ruling. This bill endorsed the Brown decision unequivocally as expressing "the moral ideals of the nation" and "the supreme law of the land." It provided for technical and financial assistance to state and local communities confronted with the problem of adjustment, including available information, surveys, national and local conferences, trained specialists, and local advisory councils. An appropriation of forty million dollars annually was contemplated to assist local governments to meet the costs of additional educational measures which might be taken to facilitate the transition. The Douglas bill also provided for positive action on the part of the Department of Health, Education and Welfare to promote, and on the part of the Department of Justice to force, desegregation.

The bill, which became the Civil Rights Act of 1957, included under a famous Title III provision for the initiation of desegregation suits by the Department of Justice, but Title III was deleted before the bill's passage. The Commission on Civil Rights in its 1959 report requested authorization to "establish an advisory and conciliation service to assist local school officials in developing plans designed to meet constitutional requirements and local conditions. . . ." The Commission's 1961 report recommended: "That Congress enact legislation making it the duty of every local school board which maintains any public school from which pupils are excluded on a basis of race, to file a plan for desegregation with a designated federal agency within six months after the adoption of such legislation, said plan to call for at least a first step toward full compliance with the Supreme Court's decision in the *School Segregation Cases* at the beginning of the following school year, and complete desegregation as soon as practicable thereafter. . . ."

In the period here under review none of the above proposals was adopted. But they are nonetheless illuminating as representing steps which the magnitude of the problems suggested.

The Supreme Court administers only the lower courts in the national judicial system, and it had given responsibility for the implementation of its ruling to them. The task of accomplishing the vast social change thus fell upon district courts and circuit courts of appeal. It fell upon "58 Lonely Men," the federal judges in the South—of whom J. W. Peltason said in his book by that title: "Perhaps not since pre-revolutionary years, when royal governors imposed imperial orders on colonials, have any American officials been placed in the center of such a cross fire, a cross fire of such intensity that even the dignity of high office offers little protection." [6]

All but five of the Southern federal judges were born in the region and, privately, a majority of them probably favored race segregation. They understood better than most the difficulties which stood in the way of adapting public-school systems to the new order, and they had strong ties of friendship and sympathy with local officials and community leaders. But except for the rebellion of half-a-dozen aging jurists, they strove to carry out the instructions of the Supreme Court and to adhere to the principles laid down in its decisions. Many of these judges displayed high qualities of serenity, firmness, and courage—in some cases a degree of heroism—in the midst of turmoil and hostile pressures. When suits were filed in federal courts, orders could be confidently expected—though not without possibly lengthy litigation—to admit Negroes to white schools. In the few instances where district courts failed, the federal courts of appeal were sure to bring them into line.

A number of school districts in western and southern Texas, like most border-state districts, proceeded to remove racial barriers in response to the broad ruling that public-school segregation was unconstitutional. A few scattered school districts elsewhere accepted token integration "voluntarily"—though largely to forestall court action, with expensive litigation, which they realized must come. It was hoped that the example of court-ordered integration would set off a general movement of voluntary adjustment. But, outside of southern

and western Texas, no such movement developed in the South. For
the most part departure from the system of segregated public schools
in a region of forty million people had to wait upon the district-by-
district action of forty-eight district judges plus ten circuit judges of
the federal judiciary. It was a frail mechanism to propel a social
revolution.

Moreover, it was not self-starting. A federal judge could not order
a school board to cease segregating pupils until someone with proper
standing invoked the jurisdiction of his court. The courts could act
only when cases were brought to them; complaint of denial of constitutional rights had to be filed and adjudicated. Litigation took a variety
of forms, but the standard procedure was this: a group of Negro
children would apply for admission to white schools, the application
would be rejected or ignored by the white school authorities, and the
children and their parents, with legal counsel, would then go to the
federal district court for relief. Negroes who were bold enough to
launch upon this onerous and often dangerous operation needed
advice, moral support, and, above all, legal counsel. By and large there
was just one source from which these could be obtained—the National
Association for the Advancement of Colored People and the NAACP
Legal Defense and Educational Fund. By a caprice of history and
circumstance, the NAACP organizations thus became an accessory of
the enforcement mechanism. No instrumentality of government, but
the NAACP, became in effect the activating agent.

We may pause here to take another look at the organizations upon
which this immense responsibility fell. The NAACP's forty-four-year
struggle for Negro rights had reached a climactic triumph in the
Brown decision. Now, in its efforts to secure the implementation of
that ruling, it enjoyed a larger membership and more financial support and enlisted more legal talent than ever before. Its growing roll
of dues-paying members—about three hundred thousand in 1956—
did not give the full picture of its representative capacity: it spoke for
eighteen million Negroes in the United States.

It had a headquarters office in New York, staffed by about one hundred employees, and its members met regularly in eleven hundred
branches scattered widely over the nation, more than half of them in
the Southern and border states. Dues collections and special donations to the NAACP and its Legal Defense and Educational Fund in

1955 totaled $1,179,605. The NAACP Legal Defense and Educational Fund is a separate corporate entity, established in October 1939, to obtain new sources of income to meet the rising cost of the association's legal activities. The Fund confines itself to "those portions of the NAACP program which have been judged by the United States Treasury to be clearly eligible for tax-deductible contributions."

Although the great majority of the members of the NAACP were Negroes, there were also white members, and white individuals had been prominent among its leadership from its beginning. Its president was Arthur B. Spingarn, a white man; another white man, Lloyd Garrison, was chairman of its legal committee. Mrs. Eleanor Roosevelt, widow of the late President Roosevelt, was among a distinguished group, white and Negro, on its board of directors. In 1958 its members included Herbert H. Lehman (former senator and former governor of New York); W. Averell Harriman and Nelson A. Rockefeller (successively governors of New York), Governor G. Mennen Williams of Michigan, Chester Bowles (former governor of Connecticut), Walter Reuther, Harry Golden, and Richard Cardinal Cushing. United Nations Undersecretary Ralph Bunche and Robert C. Weaver (administrator of the Housing and Home Finance Agency) were among nationally famous Negroes high in NAACP councils.

The chief spokesmen for the NAACP were its Negro executive secretaries—Walter White, the veteran crusader, who died in 1955, and Roy Wilkins, the dynamic and personable leader who succeeded him. Thurgood Marshall, who led the successful fight for the historic Supreme Court decision, was a hero to many. Marshall and his associates in that fight—Robert L. Carter, Jack Greenberg, Louis T. Redding, James Nabrit, George E. C. Hayes, and Spotswood W. Robinson—continued to be the dominant influence in the important legal phase of NAACP activities. The legal committees of local branches, which had primary responsibility for lawsuits, were aided and guided by Marshall and his staff.

The wide gulf between the thinking of white people and that of Negroes in the South—at all cultural levels—was nowhere better illustrated than in their attitudes toward the NAACP. The flood of vilification and the incessantly repeated smears had led many, even among white people who were otherwise moderately disposed, to regard the NAACP as an evil influence. To most white Southerners it was a mysteriously diabolical thing. In contrast, Southern Negroes looked up to the NAACP with admiration and respect; to most of them it was above criticism, an institution which all men of good will should support. The attitudes of political leaders North and South toward the NAACP offered another striking contrast: in the North politicians cultivated its friendship, were happy to appear publicly with NAACP leaders; in the South any friendly contact with an NAACP official might be enough to end a politician's career.

The basic complaint of Southern segregationists, underneath the synthetic charges of Communism and miscellaneous villainies, was that the NAACP was "stirring up" the Negroes and thus inciting racial turmoil. The NAACP did emphatically encourage Negroes to seek what the Supreme Court had declared to be their constitutional rights, but it insisted at all times upon orderly recourse to courts of law. It may have been a blessing even from the point of view of those Southerners who believed most strongly in segregation that the inevitable rebellion against segregation on the part of the Negroes should have been guided by an organization so devoted to peaceful procedure.

Addressing a NAACP convention a few weeks after the Supreme Court decree of May 31, 1955, Marshall said: "In all school districts we will insist that the first and minimum evidence of 'good faith' shall be the recognition by the school board that students cannot be assigned on the basis of race. . . . Next we will insist that a plan for desegregation be worked out as soon as possible but not later than September 1955. . . . We will insist that the plan include step-by-step desegregation during the next school year. Finally, we will insist that desegregation be completed not later than the school term beginning September 1956." [7]

This ambitious program was not inconsonant with the momentum of desegregation in the border states. But with respect to the former Confederate states of the South, as we look back upon it, it seems a fantasy without relevance to the actual situation which was developing.

First to receive district court attention in the South were the two cases—that of Clarendon County, South Carolina, and that of Prince Edward County, Virginia—which had been remanded specifically by the Supreme Court. In July three-judge courts heard each of these cases and in each ordered that discrimination in the admission of children to public schools should be terminated "with all deliberate speed." But no date was fixed for compliance. These two Black Belt counties were among the most difficult communities in the entire South from the standpoint of both practical obstacles and intransigent hostility among white citizens. Years would go by and desegregation would be accomplished in many other Southern localities before the first Negro would attend school with white people in either of them.

In the Clarendon County case an opinion rendered July 15, 1955, by a three-judge district court, with Circuit Judge John J. Parker presiding, proved one of the most important glosses of the Brown decision; it would figure prominently in segregationist planning and argument thereafter. The court ordered desegregation of the county's schools without fixing a date and said:

> It [the Supreme Court] has not decided that the states must mix persons of different races in the schools or must require them to attend schools or must deprive them of the right of choosing the schools they attend. What it has decided, is that a state may not deny any person on account of race the right to attend any school that it maintains. . . . Nothing in the Constitution or in the decision of the Supreme Court takes away from the people freedom to choose the schools they attend. The Constitution, in other words, does not require integration. It does not forbid such segregation as occurs as the result of voluntary action. It merely forbids the use of governmental machinery to enforce segregation." [8]

Thus compliance with the ruling would not necessitate the arbitrary and sweeping reshuffling of pupils that some had believed to be demanded. The statement was widely interpreted to mean that desegregation could be postponed until Negroes took positive steps in each locality to secure admission to white schools, and segregationist efforts were intensified to prevent Negroes from doing that.

Formal application was already being made by hundreds of Negro children in widely scattered districts. By September desegregation petitions had been filed with local school authorities—thirteen in Alabama, four in Florida, five in Georgia, two in Louisiana, five in Mississippi, fourteen in North Carolina, ten in South Carolina, two in Tennessee, and six in Virginia. A majority of the signers of these petitions yielded to segregationist pressure and withdrew their names; many of the petitions were withdrawn; most would be ignored by school authorities.

Intimidation in Mississippi and Alabama effectually put a stop to Negro applications for enrollment in white schools for years to come.

In Yazoo County, Mississippi, the Citizens' Council published a full-page advertisement in a local paper giving "an authentic list of the purported signers to an NAACP communication to our school board." Many of the signers promptly lost their jobs; a plumbing contractor was taken off the two construction jobs which he had under way and was refused plumbing supplies by a wholesale house. Economic reprisals against the signers of school desegregation petitions were reported in three Alabama counties, Dallas, Bullock, and Butler. In Selma, the county seat of Dallas, White Citizens' Council Chairman Alston Keith estimated that of the twenty-nine Negro petition signers "about sixteen—probably all of them who had jobs—were fired," and explained that some were self-employed.

In the South Carolina city of Orangeburg economic reprisals were carried to sweeping extremes. This episode was even more significant in that it represented the first important instance of Negro retaliation. For several years after the Brown decision economic pressure was widely hailed among segregationists of the Ku Klux Klan-Citizens' Council school as a sure means of extinguishing Negro initiative. It was used also to intimidate white businessmen who refused to join Citizens' Councils or who betrayed some measure of sympathy with the Negro cause. But economic reprisals could not be carried out on a large scale without loss or hardship to some of their perpetrators. Judge Brady had said in *Black Monday:* "It will be inconvenient upon the white women of the South to discharge their maids and cooks, but this can be done." He little understood the Southern housewife, who would regard doing her own floor-scrubbing and dishwashing a high price to pay even for state rights and white supremacy. Few economic relationships between whites and Negroes could be terminated without some harm to both parties. And in Orangeburg the Negroes struck back.

In this city of seventeen thousand the economic struggle began when fifty-seven Negroes petitioned the school board in July 1955, asking that immediate steps be taken to "reorganize the public schools on a non-discriminatory basis." The *Orangeburg Times Democrat* said: "The petition stunned citizens who had taken pride in the equalization of schools and of teachers' salaries, and who were sincerely convinced that they had dealt fairly and intelligently with racial problems. . . ."

Indignant whites promptly organized a Citizens' Council, and three thousand gathered in a mass meeting, at which a campaign of reprisals was launched against the petitioners, their families, and members of the local NAACP. In the January 24, 1957, issue of *The Reporter* magazine, Edward Gamarekian gave this picture of the economic sanctions which were applied:

"Those who worked for white employers were fired. Those who rented from white landlords were evicted. Those who bought from white merchants and suppliers were denied further credit and asked to settle outstanding accounts at once. Some were no longer able to buy in some places, even for cash.

"Mayor Jennings, who was the president of the Orangeburg Coca-Cola Bottling Company, the Palmetto Baking Company, and the Orangeburg Ice & Fuel Company, cut off the supply of Cokes, bread, and ice cream to three Negro grocers and a gas-station owner who signed the petition. The Coble Dairy stopped the delivery of milk to these grocers and to all the petitioners on its home delivery routes. . . . A Shell service-station operator was forced out of business by the owner-distributor.

"Petitioners were refused new insurance policies. Immediate payment was demanded on loans and mortgages where agreements were oral or loosely drawn. Banks, loan companies, and individual lenders refused to give any further financial assistance. Teachers related to petitioners were threatened with the loss of their jobs when their contracts expired at the end of the school year. A few of the petitioners receiving welfare aid were told it would be cut off."

The Negroes, who constituted 63 per cent of the population of Orangeburg county and who united generally behind the petitioners, replied with the only weapon available to them—the boycott. They ceased to patronize the white merchants who were leading the reprisal movement.

The fall of 1955 and the winter of 1955–56 was a period of business stagnation in Orangeburg, and one of privation for many Negroes. Food, clothing, money, and messages of sympathy were sent to the Orangeburg Negro community by the NAACP and various churches, organizations, and individuals in the North. On the white side, one grocer went out of business, the laundry closed its pick-up station in the Negro section, and many merchants saw their sales dwindle. By the spring of 1956 the white business community was ready in effect to cry enough; normal business intercourse was resumed and economic peace returned to Orangeburg.

On the basic issue—the desegregation of Orangeburg public schools —the Negroes lost: there would be no public-school desegregation in South Carolina for some years to come. The case was not taken to federal court. But twenty-five Negroes stood fast to the end in refusing to withdraw their names from the petition, and it was impressively demonstrated that the economic weapon was not the exclusive property of the white man.

NAACP lawyers were kept busy. A variety of problems claimed their attention in the South, including the unfinished business of removing racial barriers in institutions of higher learning. Litigation was under way for the desegregation of universities in Georgia, Florida, Alabama, Louisiana, and Tennessee. In several states NAACP lawyers found themselves engaged in a struggle to defend the very existence of the NAACP and its right to operate locally. They were also prodding lagging public-school districts in the border states, and in the South a few hardy petitioners were laboring through the application procedure to the filing of school-desegregation suits. A few suits seeking the admission of Negroes to white public schools had been filed during the period when the cases leading to the Brown decision were in litigation and had been held in abeyance pending the outcome of that supreme effort. These cases were now reactivated. In Southern and border states by mid-1956 federal courts had handled sixty-five suits requesting desegregation of public schools and thirty other related cases.

Desegregation litigation was under way before the end of 1955 in Anderson County (Clinton) and Nashville, Tennessee; Big Spring, Wichita Falls, Mansfield, and Dallas, Texas; Atlanta, Georgia; Pulaski County, Virginia; Bearden, Arkansas; two North Carolina counties; and two Louisiana parishes; suits were filed early in 1956 in Miami, Florida; Charlottesville and Newport News, Virginia; and Little Rock, Arkansas. In Atlanta, New Orleans, and Bearden, and in Anderson and Pulaski Counties, pre-1954 suits were revived. In McDowell County, North Carolina, an old equalization suit was changed to one requesting desegregation. In Little Rock, NAACP lawyers sought to force quicker action by a school board that had announced a gradual desegregation program.

Two litigations proceeded without NAACP involvement: in Bearden, where local Negroes moved independently, and in Hoxie, Arkansas, where a school board sought an injunction to prevent segregationist interference with a desegregation program which it had voluntarily adopted. The Hoxie case produced one of the first clashes with organized segregationist agitators and was significant in several other respects. After integrating schools peacefully for a brief summer term in 1955—and receiving some national publicity as a result—the Hoxie school board was besieged by Citizens' Councils and other itinerant segregationists from around the South who converged on the town. Under harassment and pressure to return to segregation, the school board went to the federal district court for relief. The district court granted a permanent injunction restraining the agitators from "acts of trespass, boycott or picketing" and any other form of interference,[9] and the Hoxie schools continued to operate on an integrated basis. The district court held that federal courts have jurisdiction in equity to deal with attempted denial of constitutional rights and that the right of free speech does not include a right to incite disobedience to the law. Nearly a year later the district court action was affirmed by the federal court of appeals. The argument of the case on appeal brought a rare instance of intervention on the part of the Eisenhower Administration; the Justice Department, under Attorney General Herbert Brownell, filed a brief as a "friend of the court" on behalf of the Hoxie school board. (The FBI had investigated the harassment earlier at the request of Brownell.) The state of Georgia filed a brief as a "friend of the court" on behalf of the segregationist defendants.

Initial rulings in the desegregation cases were generally inconclusive: in most cases school boards were allowed more time without a fixed deadline or the door was left open for further litigation; when ground could no longer be found for delay in district courts, appeal was nearly always had to higher federal courts. Nevertheless, as the beginning of the 1956–57 school term approached, two cases were headed for a stormy climax. In Mansfield, Texas, the federal circuit court of appeals had overruled a district court that refused to order immediate desegregation and had rejected a request of the school board for more time. In Clinton, Tennessee, the Anderson

County school board was preparing to comply with an order issued by Federal District Judge Robert L. Taylor in January that the county high schools should be desegregated "by a definite date . . . fixed not later than the beginning of the fall term of the present year of 1956."

Chapter 7

MANSFIELD AND CLINTON

For all concerned with the public-school desegregation problem the month of September each year was a time of anxiety and suspense. That was when summer vacations ended and pupils enrolled for a new term. Sometimes the term started in the last days of August, and in several instances desegregation difficulties caused the start to be postponed until October or even early November; but September was generally the month of school-opening, of desegregation attempts, and of crisis. September 1956 saw disturbances in Kentucky at Sturgis and Clay and reassuring progress in Louisville, as we have already related; it also saw convulsions in Texas and Tennessee. National magazines and news media were hard put to deploy reporters and photographers to scenes of turmoil sputtering simultaneously in three states.

Texas furnished the first clear-cut example of failure of enforcement of a federal court order for desegregation of a public school. It furnished an example also of failure in the case of an institution of higher learning, which—unless the anomalous outcome of the attempt of Miss Lucy to enter the University of Alabama be taken as a failure of enforcement of a court order—was the first in this category. The performance of Texas was in some respects paradoxical. Among the eleven Southern states, Texas had the best record of compliance with the Brown decision. While eight states made no move toward public-school desegregation in 1955 and 1956, racial barriers in school enrollment were dropping fairly briskly in this state. The Supreme Court of Texas, in October 1955, had accepted the decision of the United States Supreme Court and declared the provisions of the constitution and statutes of Texas requiring public-school segregation void. Segregation had come quietly to an end in the three high schools of Austin, the state capital. By the fall of 1956 desegregation had taken place in 104 of the state's 1857 public-school districts. Negroes had been admitted to nineteen state-supported and ten church-supported colleges and universities that previously had been restricted to white students.

But peaceful adjustment to the new order had been almost entirely confined to the wide expanse of western Texas where Negroes were few. In the populous northeastern part of the state, in which approximately 90 per cent of the Negro population resided, a radically different spirit prevailed. This section resembled Louisiana and Mississippi in its deeply rooted race prejudice. The Ku Klux Klan had been active here in the 1940s; lynchings were still remembered. A report (later proven false) that a white woman had been raped had precipitated a sensational race riot in Beaumont in 1943, resulting in two deaths, one white and one Negro. The hostility of this region to desegregation was reflected in the state administration and in the state political hierarchy.

East Texas produced in one week the two incidents in which federal court desegregation orders were allowed to yield to local hostility. Texarkana Junior College, a segregated white institution, had been ordered by a federal district court to cease discriminating on account of race and specifically to admit two named Negro students. Local opposition was encouraged and in effect endorsed by Dr. W. H. Stillwell, president of the college, who told an audience of protesting citizens: "If integration results in lowering educational standards, it is not only your right but your duty to resist it." [1] An effigy of a Negro was hanged on the campus, a cross was burned, and a shotgun blast was fired at a filling station owned by a Negro leader. Four Texas Rangers, who came to preserve order, arrested four Negro teenagers for throwing stones at an automobile containing white youths but refused to escort the Negro students through the white mob surrounding the college. The Negroes were driven back and the integration attempt was given up—though order was restored in Texarkana.

The village of Mansfield on the outskirts of Fort Worth presented the first test of court-ordered public-school desegregation in hostile East Texas, and one of the first in the South. Mansfield had a population of approximately fifteen hundred, of whom some three hundred fifty were colored. A one-room schoolhouse without indoor plumbing had been replaced in 1954 by a four-room grade school for Negroes, but Negro high-school students still had to ride approximately forty miles daily by public bus to attend high school in Fort Worth, and the schedule involved a two-hour wait in that city. In April 1955 the Negroes complained to the school board of a variety of school deficiencies, including this hardship, which they hoped to have relieved by the assignment of a regular school bus. When they were unable to secure satisfaction, some of the bolder Negroes decided to apply for the admission of their children to Mansfield High School, a segregated school for whites only.

After unsuccessful efforts in July and August and at school-opening in September, a suit was brought in federal court in October on behalf of twelve Negro students. In November, Federal District Judge Joe E. Estes dismissed their petition as "premature and precipitate"— on the ground that the school authorities had not had sufficient time for the transition to an integrated system. In June 1956 the Fifth Circuit Court of Appeals reviewed the case and ruled that, the obstacle being only "a difficulty arising out of the local climate of opinion," the defendants should have been ordered to abolish segregation in Mansfield High School—"acting promptly, and completely uninfluenced by private and public opinion as to the desirability of desegregation. . . ." On remand, the district court issued the necessary orders and a plea for a year's postponement was denied.

During the summer the little community was subjected to a steadily increasing barrage of anti-Negro and anti-integration propaganda, in which the local newspaper joined. A cross was burned on August 22, and another on August 23, in the Negro section of the town. On August 28 a dummy representing a Negro was hung over Mansfield's main street, with signs reading: THIS NEGRO TRIED TO GO TO A WHITE SCHOOL and WOULDN'T THIS BE A HORRIBLE WAY TO DIE? Other Negro effigies were hanged on the flagpole (in lieu of the national flag) and over the entrance to Mansfield High School. A White Citizens' Council was formed.

Registration at the school took place on Thursday and Friday, August 30 and 31, and after the Labor Day week-end on Tuesday, September 4. A turbulent crowd of whites, sometimes estimated at as high as five hundred, surrounded the school each registration day, prepared to turn back any Negroes who appeared. On September 4, the Reverend C. W. Clark, an Episcopal clergyman from Fort Worth, who urged a "Christian attitude," was harassed and had to be rescued by a Texas Ranger. Two Rangers had been sent to Mansfield by Governor Allan Shivers to restore order.

Governor Shivers was faced squarely with the question which in time would confront three other Southern governors: whether to

preserve order in compliance with federal court desegregation rulings
or to preserve order by causing, or allowing, those rulings to be
flouted. In a crisis which occurred almost simultaneously in Tennessee,
the governor of that state chose the former course. The governor of
Texas chose the latter. Governor Shivers announced on August 30
that he had urged "that the Mansfield school board go ahead and
transfer out of the district any scholastics, white or colored, whose
attendance or attempts to attend Mansfield High School would be
reasonably calculated to incite violence," and that he had "asked
Colonel Garrison [of the Texas Rangers] to instruct his men to arrest
anyone, white or colored, whose actions are such as to represent a
threat to the peace at Mansfield."

The governor added: "I am taking this action not in a spirit of defiance of federal authority but as the only course I can conscientiously
pursue in upholding my constitutional responsibility for maintaining
law and order in Texas. Should the resulting actions on the part of
the Mansfield school authorities be construed as contempt of the
federal courts, I respectfully suggest that the charge should be laid
against the governor and not the local people." [2]

Calm was restored in Mansfield. But the mob accomplished its purpose. Mansfield High School has remained segregated to this writing,
seven years later. The procedure followed by the governor of Texas
had in it an element of rebellion which, when manifested later elsewhere—on a larger scale, in a more spectacular fashion, and more
sharply under the eyes of the nation and the world—would invite
the intervention of federal military forces. But in tiny Mansfield the
incident was quickly closed.

The Mansfield incident drew from President Eisenhower an interesting revelation of his attitude toward the Brown decision and the
problem that it posed in the South. In his press conference of September 5, 1956, the following colloquy took place:

> ROBERT E. CLARK, *International News Service:* Do you think
> there is anything that can be said or done on the national level to
> help local communities meet this problem without violence?
>
> THE PRESIDENT: Well, in each case I think the local governments
> have moved promptly to stop the violence. And let us remember
> this: under the law the federal government cannot, on the ordinary

normal case of keeping order and preventing rioting, cannot move into a state until the state is not able to handle the matter.

Now, in the Texas case there was—the attorney for the students did report this violence and asked help, which apparently was the result of unreadiness to obey a federal court order.

But before anyone could move, the Texas authorities had moved in and order was restored, so the question became unimportant.

SARAH MCCLENDON, *El Paso Times:* Mr. President, in doing so, Governor Allan Shivers sent Rangers to defy the court order, reassign out the Negro pupils, and said in a public statement which was carried in the newspapers:

"I defy the federal government," he said. "Tell the federal courts if they went to come after anyone to come after me and cite me in this matter."

I have wonder if you have discussed this with anyone in the Department of Justice?

THE PRESIDENT: I have not discussed it because you are quoting both an order that I have not read and a statement that I have not seen.

Now, I have—we have—actually sent for the district court order to know what it says. I don't know what it says. And remember that the Supreme Court placed in the hands of the district judges the primary responsibility for insuring that progress in every sector was made.

Now, just exactly what Governor Shivers said I don't know. This is the first I have heard of it.

JOHN L. STEELE, *Time:* With the schools opening up this week and next in places of serious tension I wonder if there is anything you would like to say, through us, to the younger people who are going to school regarding this problem?

THE PRESIDENT: Well, I can say what I have said so often: It is difficult through law and through force to change a man's heart. It seems to me that all of us who are so interested in this question of equality of rights regardless of religion and of race and color should do more about it. I try to miss no opportunity to urge people—I have done it; I have asked the clergy in and I have asked them to help. I have asked educators in; I have asked them to help.

Whenever I see a governor I ask him to help.

But I do believe that we must all, regardless of our calling in this world, help to bring about a change in spirit so that extremists on both sides do not defeat what we know is a reasonable, logical conclusion to this whole affair, which is recognition of equality of men.

Now, there—the South is full of people that are adamant and are so filled with prejudice that they can't keep—they even resort to violence; and the same way on the other side of the thing; the people who want to have the whole matter settled today.

This is a question of leading and training and teaching people, and it takes some time, unfortunately.

ARTHUR SYLVESTER, *Newark* (N.J.) *News:* Mr. President, in view of your statement just now, do you endorse the finding of the Supreme Court on segregation or merely accept it as the Republican platform does?

THE PRESIDENT: I think it makes no difference whether or not I endorse it. What I say is they—the Constitution is as the Supreme Court interprets it; and I must conform to that end and do my very best to see that it is carried out in this country.

ROBERT G. SPIVAK, *New York Post:* Governor Shivers, when he made his announcement last week, ordered the removal of Negro students from the Mansfield school after mob action had been in effect in that area. I wonder if you think that that is a surrender to mob rule?

THE PRESIDENT: Well, you don't know for how long he has ordered this. I don't know whether he has ordered the permanent transfer of these people or until the situation is under control.

The—I want to re-emphasize this— Certainly, every liberal will be very jealous of protecting the locality's right to execute the police power in this country.

When police power is executed habitually by the—and exercised habitually by the federal government we are in a bad way. So, until states show their inability or their refusal to grapple with this question properly, which they haven't yet, at least as any proof has been admitted, we'd better be very careful about moving in and exercising police power.

Clinton, Tennessee, received the biggest headlines of September 1956. The agony of Clinton was a demonstration above all of the incendiary capabilities of visiting agitators in a peace-loving community. It was a reminder also of a related phenomenon that would continue to aggravate and expand disorders in the South, and one which needs to be borne in mind by law-enforcement authorities everywhere: that is, the universal availability today of automobile transportation. Hoodlums and lovers of excitement, of whom every community has its share—not to mention Negrophobes and pro-segregation extremists—are able, from as far as a hundred miles, to converge upon any point of seething unrest within a few hours and return to their homes the same night. Riots, therefore, are not necessarily spontaneous or of local instigation. Those in Clinton were neither. The Clinton story was exciting fare for newspaper and magazine readers; it was one of villains and heroes, of hysteria and courageous common sense, of irresponsible fanaticism and steadfast dedication to the public good, of drama, tragedy, and pathos—ending at long last in the triumph of embattled decency. It illuminated many aspects of the problem of the transition to the new order in the South and merits examination in some detail.

Clinton was a pleasant town in Anderson County, in the Cumberland Mountains of East Tennessee, about fifteen miles northwest of the metropolis of Knoxville—where Clinton Negroes had been sent heretofore to a segregated high school. It had a population of 3712, including 220 non-whites, by the 1950 census. In the federally run "Atomic City" of Oak Ridge, nine miles north of Clinton, high schools had been peacefully integrated a year earlier. It is to be noted, too, that the desegregation controversy here was devoid of any suggestion of nostalgic Confederate loyalty: this section of Tennessee had stood with the Union in the Civil War.

The Anderson County school board, which had charge of the Clinton high school, had been involved in federal court litigation since 1950. Once the Brown decision appeared, thoughtful citizens of the area had sensed that it would be implemented before long in the local case. When in January 1956 the district court issued a definitive order for the desegregation of Clinton High School, the town authorities resolved to do everything possible to insure a smooth and peaceful transition. D. J. Brittain, Jr., the high-school principal, instituted a program of theme assignments and debates to make students aware of their coming responsibilities. The correspondent of the scrupulously objective *Southern School News* wrote in August for its September issue: "Based on interviews with parents and other citizens in the community, it is fair to describe their attitude as one of resignation."

Both before and during the turmoil that came, the performance of local officials was on the whole exemplary; and they were supported by the town's leading business and professional men. Horace Wells, editor of the local weekly newspaper, received the 1957 University of Southern Illinois Elijah P. Lovejoy Award for "realistic devotion to law and order." The faculty and a large majority of the students of Clinton High School behaved admirably. The police power of the state was exerted on the side of order within the law.

School was scheduled to open Monday, August 27, 1956. On August 23, the Anderson County school board reaffirmed its intention, announced the previous autumn, "to comply with any and all court mandates. . . ."

But on Saturday afternoon, August 25, John Kasper arrived in town. This roving missionary of white supremacy immediately started buttonholing people on the street and, as he later testified in court, "went from door to door and talked with each neighbor about the pending integration." Sunday he told a little crowd gathered in front of the courthouse that "people are superior to courts"; he urged the students present to picket the high school and stay away from classes. His inflammatory crusade began to arouse apprehension. Town and county officials, editor Wells, and others met Sunday afternoon to plan for the protection of the school on Monday—and to decide what to do about Kasper. When efforts to persuade him to leave town failed, Kasper was arrested on charges of inciting to riot and vagrancy.

Monday, with Kasper in jail, twelve Negro and 715 white students began attending classes together at Clinton High School. Some disorder occurred outside the school, where a crowd of about fifty had gathered, but inside the Negro students were received peacefully, even with some cordiality. One of their number, Jo Ann Allen, an attractive 14-year-old junior—drawn out in friendly questioning by her teacher —was elected vice-president of her home-room class.

Tuesday, attendance at the school reached a full 806. But John Kasper was free again. Tried at nine A.M. and his case dismissed for want of evidence, the racist betook himself to the high school and told the principal to "run the Negroes off or resign." "I told him," Brittain said later, "I would resign if 51 per cent of the parents with students in school wanted it." [3] Kasper went to work distributing anti-Brittain signs demanding that the principal resign. Tuesday evening he delivered a fiery speech to several hundred on the courthouse square.

The next day Brittain, who had been bombarded with anonymous phone calls—some of them threatening his life—called an assembly of the students and turned it over to Jerry Shattuck, president of the student council; he told Shattuck to conduct a poll while teachers and principal were outside of the auditorium. The vote of confidence in the principal was unanimous. It was followed by a singing of the school song. Hearing this, Brittain returned and received an ovation. He asked the students to poll their parents when they got home. The returns from his poll were 447 to 6 in favor of Brittain.

A crowd of over one hundred gathered outside the school Wednesday. Negro students now were attacked or chased; some were slipped out of the back door of the school to protect them from the mob. In the evening about one thousand gathered in the square to hear Kasper. His speech was interrupted by a federal marshal, who served a court order temporarily restraining him from interfering with school desegregation and notification of a hearing the next day on a permanent injunction. But Kasper resumed his harangue.

Thursday, August 30, his federal court hearings began, and Kasper was jailed again. He would remain in jail for the next eight days— the period of greatest turbulence in Clinton.

Many who have analyzed the crisis have concluded that this community would have adjusted itself to the school change without serious difficulty if John Kasper had stayed away. Certainly this tall, brooding fanatic, with his tone of literate sophistication and his ability to cast a strange spell over the ignorant, was the foremost kindler of the blaze that ignited there. He aroused hundreds, even thousands, and a few score became his slavish disciples. But there were other factors. The Clinton area was not without its criminal element, and practically all its white citizens objected to the mixing of races in public schools. Kaspar also had many extremist allies from afar, who were all too ready to carry on the work he had started while he languished behind prison bars.

Clinton had had no segregationist organization; now several imported ones got into the picture. Emissaries of the Tennessee Federation for Constitutional Government had arrived in Clinton shortly before Kasper. Incidentally, TFCG had filed suit in the state court demanding that state funds be cut off from Clinton High School and that county officials be restrained from admitting Negroes to it. (Five of the fifteen local residents listed as complainants said they did not understand that their names would be used in the suit and four took legal action to have their names removed.) Judge Taylor on August 28 rejected the petition.

Without Kasper, a crowd of about three hundred persons milled around the school Thursday, hurling stones, tomatoes, and epithets at the Negroes when they left for home. Three youths were arrested. A score of miscellaneous segregationists harangued the crowd on the square in the evening. Friday, attendance at the school dropped to 446, including ten Negroes. Meanwhile, in the federal court, Kasper was found guilty of contempt and sentenced to one year in prison.

Friday night saw a kind of pandemonium. One Asa, or "Ace," Carter had arrived in town from Alabama. Among the roving segregationist agitators of 1955 and 1956, Carter, a busy organizer of both Ku Klux Klan and White Citizens' Councils, was less famous only than Kasper himself. He came to substitute for Kasper at the Friday night mass meeting. If Carter lacked the latter's mystical magnetism, he was no less capable of setting a large crowd on fire. He attacked Negroes, the NAACP, the Supreme Court, and the "carpetbagging judge that put Kasper in jail"—and he left immediately after his speech.

The crowd quickly became a rioting mob which spread over the town, shouting, "We want Kasper!" Some marched to the mayor's home and threatened to dynamite it. The cars of Negro tourists were attacked. Frenzied teenagers began blocking traffic on Highway No. 25, which is a major north-south road and Clinton's main street. Cars carrying Negroes were stopped and tilted, windows and windshields were smashed, and air was let out of tires. The rioting continued until about one A.M. The harried police made no arrests: to have sent two officers to escort a prisoner to jail would have immobilized one-third of Clinton's six-man force!

Saturday the Clinton board of aldermen declared the town in a state of emergency and issued formal requests to the governor of Tennessee on the one hand and to citizens of Clinton on the other to assist in restoring order. Sheriff Glad Woodward joined the town board in the appeal to the governor, which was put in writing and flown to Nashville by chartered plane. Governor Clement also received approximately fifty telegrams from Anderson County asking for help. Meantime a volunteer force of auxiliary police was quickly formed in Clinton. Leo Grant, Jr., a 28-year-old lawyer who took the lead, related afterwards: "Forty-seven were rounded up in all—preachers, doctors, clerks—and most of us mighty scared, but also mighty provoked." [4]

The rally Saturday night was sponsored by five organizations previously foreign to little Clinton—the Tennessee Federation for Constitutional Government, the Pro-Southerners, the White Citizens' Councils, the Tennessee Society to Maintain Segregation, and the States' Rights Council of Tennessee. The crowd began to gather soon after six P.M., and by eight it had reached an estimated two thousand.

The story from then on suggests a moving-picture melodrama, though its climax might be considered too neat for plausible fiction. We let a reporter for the *Chattanooga Times* tell it, noting that the facts are amply borne out by other witnesses. This happened in an American town in the middle of the twentieth century:

> Gradually at one corner of the courthouse square, a crowd gathered. At its center was the hard nucleus of teen-age hoodlums and segregation extremists who had been the leaders of the last riot. They milled about, shouting about "nigger-lovers," "coon-hunting," and "let's run the niggers out."
>
> The situation was rapidly getting out of hand. Leo Grant, burly 220-pound commander of the "home guards," wearing a .45 pistol and carrying a sub-machine gun, mustered the regulars and volunteers in a skirmish line across the courthouse lawn.
>
> They moved, shoulder to shoulder, toward the crowd. In civilian clothes and carrying shotguns, rifles, an assortment of pistols and clubs, they resembled a colonial Minute Man platoon setting off against the British.
>
> They reached the mob and halted. The police and the mob stood face to face. A foot apart. Neither gave an inch. The air was so charged with electric tension you almost could have lighted a cigarette on it.
>
> Grant ran back into the courthouse and returned with tear-gas grenades. The police line drew back.
>
> "Psst! Psst!" Three grenades exploded in the crowd and gas billowed over the lawn. The crowd began scattering. Three more grenades followed.
>
> But the tough element which was giving this town such a difficult time began assembling again. The police, regulars and volunteers, drew into a knot near the courthouse.
>
> "Let's take their guns and kill the 'nigger-loving ———,' " some-

one in the mob shouted. More shouts went up. The mob was on the rampage again, madder than ever. Another minute and the war would be on.

At that precise moment, over the hill southeast of town, came 39 highway patrol cars. They moved down on the town, 39 sirens wailing, all 39 red dome lights flashing. They sped down the hill, turned with tires screaming, and circled the courthouse square. They screeched to a halt.

Out of the first car stepped Gregg O'Rear, 6 feet, 7 inches tall, 290 pounds, two stars of a highway patrol inspector glistening on his shoulder, his hand on his pistol, his campaign hat cocked over his right eye, a grim expression on his face.

He walked down the middle of Main Street, followed by 109 state troopers carrying riot guns and sub-machine guns at the ready, and night sticks.

Deadly silence fell. . . .[5]

Sunday at about noon a National Guard detachment moved in to relieve the state troopers—633 battle-equipped Guardsmen behind seven M-41 tanks and three armored personnel carriers, under the command of State Adjutant General Joe W. Henry. Further disorders occurred Sunday night and Monday (Labor Day)—the nightly rally in the square was attempted again, until a crowd of a thousand was dispersed by two platoons of guardsmen with bayonets fixed—but as the military made their presence felt the community gradually quieted down. On Monday, General Henry issued stern orders for the town: outdoor public-speaking, parking cars or assembling in the courthouse square after six P.M., and the use of public-address systems out of doors were prohibited.

The unrest having spread to the nearby town of Oliver Springs, two tanks and seventy-one Guardsmen were dispatched to quell rioting there.

Tuesday, September 4, attendance at the high school dropped to 266, including nine brave Negroes; but it increased daily thereafter until it reached a total of 652, including all twelve Negro pupils, by September 15. The last contingent of the National Guard withdrew on September 11. The town police force had been doubled and the sheriff's deputies had been multiplied until nearly two hundred local law-enforcement officers were ready for any further emergency.

On Thursday, September 6, Federal District Judge Taylor granted

Kasper right to bail and issued a permanent injunction against further interference with desegregation. Friday two Clinton admirers put up the required $10,000, and Kasper was released. On September 25 Kasper went to jail again, briefly, until released on another bond, of $2000—this time under a different jurisdiction. The reader will be taxed, as the public was, to keep up with Kasper's legal vicissitudes. He was arraigned now in the Anderson County Criminal Court, after grand-jury indictment, under Tennessee law, on charges of sedition and inciting a riot. His next appearance in court would be for his trial on these charges, set for November 5.

Violence flared in late September with the blasting at night of a Negro home. In mid-October, a hundred and twenty-five carloads of hooded Ku Klux Klan members paraded through Clinton; four crosses were burned; newsmen were chased from the vacant lot near the town where hooded speakers denounced integration. Otherwise, quiet settled over the area until November.

The August attempt of the Tennessee Federation for Constitutional Government to halt Clinton high-school desegregation by state court injunction backfired. An application to the Supreme Court of Tennessee for *certiorari* produced a ruling from that body on September 3: "We are of the unanimous opinion that the question is fully foreclosed by the United States Supreme Court. The application is denied." After a rehearing, in a comprehensive opinion on October 3, the state court said: "The plain fallacy of this insistence is that the Segregation Statutes referred to are not now in full force and effect, the same having been declared unconstitutional in *Brown v. Board of Education. . . .*"

The Tennessee court cited the following opinion, which had been rendered earlier by the Supreme Court of North Carolina: "In the interpretation of the Constitution of the United States, the Supreme Court of the United States is the final arbiter. Its decision in the Brown case is the law of the land and will remain so unless reversed or altered by constitutional means. Recognizing fully that its decision is authoritative in this jurisdiction, any provisions of the Constitution or statutes of North Carolina in conflict therewith must be deemed invalid."

It noted that the Supreme Courts of Florida and Oklahoma had reached similar conclusions. The Texas Supreme Court also, as we

said earlier in this chapter, had invalidated that state's school segregation laws.

The Kasper trial dragged through two weeks of November. Crowds,
mainly of Kasper sympathizers, packed the courtroom as a stream of
witnesses and the irrepressible defendant recalled events of early
September and revived bitter controversy in the town. Acquitted
November 20, amid loud cheers, Kasper immediately announced plans
to continue his fight against school integration in Tennessee.

A political contest now began to rage around the school-segregation
issue, with the White Citizens' Council backing extremist candidates
for mayor and alderman. White Youth Councils, organized by juvenile
Kasper devotees, introduced a new rancor and unrest within Clinton
High School. A handful of these young white supremacists, who had
been out of school since early September, now returned—mainly, it
seemed, for the purpose of making life unbearable for the Negro
students.

As tension increased, inside now as well as outside the high school,
a nervousness which was not present in the earlier anarchy was apparent among the Negro community and the Anderson County school
board. Wednesday, November 29, the Negroes, after their long brave
attendance record, stayed out of school. But they were not ready to
give up. The school board was. In a fatuous hope of calling off the
desegregation attempt, the board suggested to the Negroes that they
be transferred back to the segregated Negro high school in Knoxville.
The Negro parents would have nothing to do with this "voluntary
withdrawal plan." Friday five Negro students started to the school
again, but now the youngsters, seeing a truck and adults standing
ominously in front of the building, were frightened away. Negro
parents appealed to the school board for protection of their children.
Chairman R. G. Crossno said he knew of nothing it could do. On
December 3 the board sent a letter to United States Attorney General
Herbert Brownell in which it declared:

> Considerable confusion has arisen as a result of the Board's
> conscientious attempt to comply with the Court's order abolishing
> segregation while at the same time the federal authorities fail to
> enforce the same Court's injunction forbidding anyone, including
> students, from interfering with the integration.
> . . . The Board feels that under no circumstances should the

school authorities be expected to police the carrying out of such an order—but rather it is a matter for the appropriate federal authorities. Local FBI agents and United States district attorney's officers . . . for some unexplained reason are oblivious to the internationally known Clinton integration problem.

The Anderson County School Board must know whether the Department of Justice intends to continue lack of enforcement of the federal Court injunction. If so, it might become necessary to close the Clinton High School so long as we are under Court order to abolish segregation.

Tuesday, December 4—election day—saw another of those Clinton incidents which flashed across the nation. The Reverend Paul W. Turner, a 33-year-old white clergyman who had preached for eight years at the First Baptist Church, Clinton's largest church, had sent word to the Negro children that if they wanted to return to school he would come and walk with them. That morning the Reverend Turner, accompanied by two fellow townsmen, Sidney Davis and Leo Burnett, met six Negro boys and girls on a hillside nearby and carried them past about fifty jeering whites safely into the school. After the three adults had walked away and separated, half-a-dozen plug-uglies fell upon Turner and beat him. Blood stained the sidewalk and spattered on the car against which he was leaning when police came to his rescue. Fortunately, the minister's injuries, several cuts on the face, proved slight.

News of this barbarity spread rapidly through the community. It had an undoubted effect upon the town election: apathy at the polls in the morning was changed to waiting lines of voters in the afternoon. But the election results reflected more than sympathy with a beloved clergyman; they proved that in spite of all the poison that had been spewed in its midst, Clinton remained basically healthy. All the extremist candidates were badly defeated. James B. Meredith, its candidate for mayor, received only 343 votes to 1241 for T. Lawrence Seeber, a respected and moderate former county judge.

Added to the events of that crowded election day was the announcement by principal Brittain at noon that Clinton High School would be closed until further notice. A delegation headed by Mayor Lewallen conferred with the federal district attorney in Knoxville, and, at the latter's instance, Judge Taylor ordered the arrest of sixteen persons on charges of violating his injunction against interference with school desegregation. While the writs were being drafted Attorney General Brownell in Washington was responding to the school board's call for help. He announced that the FBI had been ordered to investigate the Clinton case and promised that the federal government would prosecute "all persons" who attempted to block public-school desegregation as ordered by a federal court. During the next two days federal marshals rounded up the sixteen named by Judge Taylor.

Brownell also said, however, that responsibility for the protection of students rested with state and local authorities, and that "this is fully understood and recognized by the governor of Tennessee." Governor Clement confirmed this, saying: "I have had no official request from officials of Anderson County or Clinton. I am still of the opinion that the State of Tennessee and its local authorities should handle their own problems and that the federal government should not unnecessarily intervene."

On December 10 the school opened again, with the Negroes in attendance. In what *Time* magazine described as "one of the most forthright Southern law-enforcement performances thus far in the desegregation struggle," [6] County Attorney Eugene Joyce lectured the students sternly in Clinton High School auditorium, warning them that misconduct in the school would be "dealt with severely and swiftly." None of a serious nature was reported thereafter.

We move ahead of our larger Southern story now to carry the reader to the end of Clinton's travail and its terminal tragedy. Except for minor incidents during the winter and spring of 1957, the little Tennessee community disappeared from the headlines of out-of-town newspapers for nearly two years. Occasional racist visitors made unsuccessful attempts to blow the embers of dissension into flame again. Retired Admiral Crommelin came from Alabama to address a White Citizens' Council meeting; Kasper and Carter returned for a joint appearance. But segregationist rallies were mild now and drew several hundred people at the most. Violence was underground, when it occurred, and the authors were rarely apprehended. One of several dynamitings destroyed a Negro restaurant and damaged thirty Negro homes; Clinton white citizens raised funds to repair the damage. A Negro student, a 21-year-old senior with a "poor scholastic record," charged with striking a white boy and drawing a knife, was expelled from Clinton High School. Another Negro boy stood, with no unpleasantness, among the graduating class of May 1957. The sixteen Clinton defendants on federal contempt charges were acquitted or released on probation.

Kasper was in and out of jails in Clinton, Knoxville, Nashville, and Washington, D.C., and his trials, retrials, and appeal hearings consumed much of the time of state and federal courts. He settled down to a long imprisonment only in November 1957. When he was taken by United States marshals from Knoxville to the federal prison in Tallahassee, Florida, he was observed to be carrying a copy of *Mein Kampf!*

Eight Negroes entered Clinton High School in September 1957 "without a taunt or a jeer." A year of quiet descended upon the little town. School-opening in September 1958 was similarly tranquil, with eleven Negroes in school. Clinton appeared to have been forgotten by the sowers of discord.

But this was not quite the case. Early in the morning of October 5, 1958, Clinton High School was shattered by three dynamite blasts and its classrooms were reduced to rubble. Officials at Oak Ridge promptly offered the use of an empty school building, and on October 9 the Clinton students, driven in fifteen buses—Negroes included—resumed classes in their improvised place of education. The perpetrators of the outrage were never discovered.

Efforts to secure federal funds for rebuilding the school met with complications and little success. Columnist Drew Pearson called for nationwide contributions and in mid-December he presented the Anderson County school board with a check for $27,000. Private contributions eventually reached nearly $50,000, from 3617 individuals. Insurance yielded $73,000. The federal government finally found it possible to contribute $45,000 from funds for areas under the impact of federal installations. The apparent niggardliness of the federal contribution was resented by Anderson County citizens, who felt, not without reason, that their high school had been destroyed in a war between Southern fanatics and the federal judiciary. The school rejected a proffered contribution of $14,200 from the Tennessee state treasury "on principle." "We feel," Chairman Crossno said, "that this is a federal responsibility." [7] In the spring of 1959 the county sold $500,000 worth of bonds and went forward with plans for rebuilding and enlarging the school.

Clinton High School opened in September 1960 in its new building.

Fourteen Negro students now attracted little notice. It was a festive occasion. Four hundred local citizens and visiting celebrities gathered at a dinner in the high-school cafeteria. Drew Pearson, introduced by editor Wells, was the principal speaker. All America, Pearson said, "stands in need of the sort of courage and determination shown by the people of Clinton." [8]

Chapter 8

TRIBULATIONS OF THE
DISTRICT OF COLUMBIA

While Clinton was still simmering, three determined Southerners were conducting an investigation in Washington, D.C., designed—no one doubted—to prove that the desegregation of that city's public schools had been a mistake. Probably no other municipal school system was ever the subject of such intense scrutiny, analysis, and far-ranging controversy as that of the District of Columbia during the period of this study. There was good reason for attention to be focused on the Washington experience: the District had over three hundred thousand Negroes (284,031 by the 1950 census) in its population, more than any Southern city; and it had undertaken to end public-school segregation almost at one stroke, immediately after the Brown decision of 1954. Many thousands of laudatory words were written about its accomplishment, on the one hand; and, on the other hand, in the eleven Southern states it was denounced with passionate insistency as an inept and iniquitous performance.

In June 1956, with thirteen of the twenty-five members of the House of Representatives Committee on the District of Columbia meeting in closed session, eleven of the thirteen voted to create a subcommittee "to investigate public-school standards and conditions and juvenile delinquency" in the District. Representative James C. Davis of Georgia, who became chairman, and Representative John Bell Williams of Mississippi—two of the Southern spokesmen most vociferously hostile to desegregation—together with William Gerber of Memphis, Tennessee, who was selected for chief counsel, conducted most of the investigation. Representatives Joel T. Broyhill of Virginia and Woodrow W. Jones of North Carolina took little part in the hearings but concurred in the findings of the other Southerners. Three of these four members were Democrats; Broyhill was a Republican.

The two other Republican members, Representatives A. L. Miller of Nebraska and DeWitt S. Hyde of Maryland, stayed away from the subcommittee's sessions and afterward in a dissenting minority report said: "In a close reading of the hearings we must come to the conclusion that the technical staff presented leading questions to a selected group. . . . Persons with views not in accord with those of the counsel were not given full and fair opportunity to testify."

Earlier in the proceedings a Republican member of the House Committee, Representative Roy W. Wier of Minnesota, demanded that Counsel Gerber be replaced, declaring that "his sole object seems to be to prove that integration has not worked . . . and to prevent it from working in the future." [1]

After the first week of hearings twenty-six civic and religious leaders formed a Washington Committee for the Public Schools "to make available dispassionate, unprejudiced, and accurate information. . . ." They said that the hearings "demonstrated that the members of the congressional subcommittee have little or no interest in determining the full facts" and that "they appear to be unconcerned about the solution of the serious problems confronting our school system, such as overcrowding, inadequate teaching staffs, and lack of facilities." [2] The *Washington Evening Star* said on September 21: "The Davis investigation of integration in Washington is of course designed to delay its acceptance elsewhere"; and the *Washington Post and Times-Herald* observed on September 23: "Counsel Gerber has already compiled just the record he wants. . . ."

The subcommittee's findings appeared at the year's end in a 48-page report. This document dwelt at some length with the "abuse and name-calling directed at members of the committee and its chief counsel" and harassment by "protestants apparently fearful of the impending revelation of the truth. . . ." Then it gave its own version of the truth in a panorama of disorder, sexual immorality, juvenile delinquency, and lagging educational accomplishment in the schools, resulting in an "exodus of white residents from the District of Columbia." Excerpts were quoted from the remarks of teachers and principals who had appeared before the committee. Some witnesses were quoted twice in separate places and four were evidently identified with the same school. The testimony reflected with singular uniformity a deterioration of Washington schools as a result of racial integration. The majority report—which referred at the outset to "a public admonition by the President of the United States that they [the District schools] should serve as a model of integrated schools to be copied by the rest of the country"—concluded that "the integrated school system of the District of Columbia is not a model to be copied by other communities. . . ." It offered ten relatively mild remedial proposals and, by way of "Additional Views," recommended—apparently oblivious of the Brown decision—"that racially separate public schools be re-established for the education of white and Negro pupils in the District of Columbia."

From the press and public of the District came a flurry of comment —predominantly dissenting from the House Committee's report—and the school situation was scrutinized and debated in Washington from time to time during the next seven years. Educators and sociologists elsewhere gave more than ordinary attention to the Washington performance. North of the Potomac the District's school administration was believed to be grappling effectively with a monumental problem.

But in the South the Davis Committee Report became a major item of Citizens' Council and other segregationist propaganda; it was given wide circulation by Southerners in Congress at government expense. The image of confusion and mischief in the bi-racial schools of the nation's capital was luridly embellished and firmly established in the minds of thousands. Few Southerners bothered to read any favorable or extenuating reports on the Washington schools. Years later, segregationist Southern orators were still pointing to interracial strife and "the livid stench of sadism, sex immorality, and juvenile pregnancy infesting the mixed schools of the District of Columbia." [3]

Carl F. Hansen, associate superintendent during the initial desegregation operation, and later superintendent, of the District's public schools, discussed the situation in many reports and public speeches. He prepared a brochure in 1957, entitled *Miracle of Social Adjustment,* and brought the subject up to date in 1960, in *Addendum.*[4] It was clear from his data that the educational accomplishment of the schools had improved under integrated, or "unified," operation. The improvement among Negro pupils was remarkable; some improvement in the accomplishment of white pupils was also apparent.

A movement of whites away from the vicinity of Negroes was increasingly visible in the District's residential pattern—a tendency which, accelerated by real-estate speculation and the continuing urbanization of the Negro population, was becoming an acute national problem. Some white families undoubtedly decided to move because of the change in the schools. But as Dr. Hansen indicated, emigration of whites to suburbs—a striking trend of the 1950s—was observable in nearly all large cities, including some, like Charleston and Atlanta in the South, where schools were still segregated.

When the District's public schools opened for the 1962–63 school year, the Negro proportion of the total enrollment had reached the startling figure of 83.4 per cent. In the prevailing tendency to sensationalize the Washington situation it was seldom noted that 18,750 Washington children were attending non-public schools, in which the Negro proportion was only 32 per cent. Catholic parochial and private schools served 13,345, of whom 34 per cent were Negro. The total school population was approximately 75 per cent Negro. Incidentally, there had been no rush to non-public schools by whites from the predominantly Negro public schools. Non-public school enrollment had actually declined from a total of 20,330 in 1953.

Yet prejudice and disorder were present in the District public schools to a greater extent than the superintendent's office appeared to realize. Dr. Hansen, and many others, underestimated what the *Washington Evening Star*—in a survey of the Negro community in June 1961—termed the "wells of bitterness." [5] Particularly embarrassing was Dr. Hansen's failure to foresee the possibility of repressed racial animosity exploding in the excited atmosphere of athletic contests. His reports referred repeatedly to "unexcelled good sportsmanship on the playing field." In March 1962 he said to a subcommittee of the House Committee on Education and Labor: "The proudest achievement and the greatest measure of good intergroup relations is found in interscholastic athletics."

Eight months later—and eight years after desegregation—at the close of the annual high-school Thanksgiving Day football game, before fifty thousand spectators, in the District of Columbia Stadium, rioting broke out. The all-Negro team of Eastern High School, the public-school champions, had been defeated by the boys of predominantly white St. John's College High School, the champions of the Catholic parochial schools. A hundred police officers had difficulty in restoring order; after about one hour, fourteen arrests were made.

Washington's public-school exhibit as a model for the South suffered a disastrous blow. Representative Williams of Mississippi called for an investigation by Congress of this "unprovoked mass attack by thousands of Negroes—many armed with clubs, knives, iron pipes, pop bottles, and the like—against white spectators. . . ." He said:

"The incident, coupled with the skyrocketing rate of Negro crimes of violence against white people, is making Washington's show of integration ugly indeed." [6]

The outbreak was in startling contrast to disorders over the race issue in the South, which had been a long, monotonous story of white aggression against nonviolent Negroes. Dr. John J. O'Connor, of Georgetown University—a well-known champion of racial integration —in his column "Washington Reporter" in the *Interracial Review,* gave a no less shocking account of the after-game melee: "What followed was a demonstration of savage, vindictive, and criminal lawlessness perpetrated by Negro youth on white spectators. Forty or fifty people required hospital treatment. Many more were assaulted, insulted, thrown to the ground, and spattered with mud. The same barbarous treatment was meted out impartially to white people, old and young, boys and girls. Additional fights and rock-throwing occurred outside the stadium and on the parking lot."

But Dr. O'Connor found the answer to the question of why "a young Negro hoodlum element . . . simply went berserk" in "rampant discrimination in employment" and "a woeful lack of suitable housing for minority groups." [7]

Washington Negro leaders issued a signed expression of concern and joined many whites in calling for some kind of investigation. "A few persons led a crowd to animal-like behavior," they said; but they added that the incident reflected "ominous overtones" of resentment of many aspects of race discrimination in Washington.[8] Both public- and Catholic-school authorities noted that the instigators of the convulsion were non-students in their twenties; they agreed, however, that the championship games between the two school systems should be discontinued.

Dr. Hansen asked a group of distinguished residents of the District to conduct an investigation. The committee was headed by Shane MacCarthy, former director of President Eisenhower's Council on Youth Fitness. The MacCarthy Committee's report, made public on January 9, 1963, was highly critical of the District public-school system, though it noted that "school officials are caught in a vise— they have no money to do the things they know need doing." In submitting the report Chairman MacCarthy said: "Not a single teacher to whom I have spoken in the past few weeks was surprised that the outbreak took place. Uniformly came the response, 'Why should we be? We live with this brand of conduct every day in the schools.' "

The committee recommended greater firmness on the part of teachers, school administrators, and police in maintaining discipline in the schools, the formation of a race-relations detail in the Police Department, and the appointment of a full-time "human relations coordinator" for the public-school system. But the committee recognized in the incident "a serious symptom of a larger problem." [9]

Plans were announced for tightening school discipline and for closer co-operation between schools and police. The continuing comment, however, placed heavy emphasis on the "larger problem." A fresh *Washington Post* survey concluded that "Washington's chief school difficulties of a disciplinary nature are caused by idle, frustrated, rebellious youth"—in the case of Eastern High School, "by out-of-school thugs, bums, and perverts who roam the halls, shoot dice in the washrooms, and invade classrooms." [10] Editorially, the *Post* observed that "segregation, discrimination, and exclusion from full citizenship and opportunity remain the rule of life in the District of Columbia. . . . And Negroes suffer disproportionately from cultural deprivation, from denial of equal opportunity, and from the poverty, ignorance, and moral laxity growing out of these disadvantages. . . ." [11]

The magnitude of the problem within the District of Columbia is indicated by the fact that by the 1960 census Negroes represented 53.9 per cent of its total population. But statements that Washington had become a predominantly Negro city were misleading: in the Washington metropolitan area—which includes large suburbs in Maryland and Virginia—the Negro proportion of the total population was only 24.3 per cent and had remained fairly stable for half a century. In the rapid population increase of the previous twenty years the Negro element had been crowded into the core of the greater city, which is the District of Columbia. Many white families were fleeing from the proximity of Negroes to suburban residential neighborhoods where Negroes found it difficult, if not impossible, to obtain housing. But the matter-of-fact assumption of segregationists that Washington whites were "fleeing from integration" was more misleading, for public schools had been integrated in the suburban areas of Maryland and Virginia to which whites were moving. In the District the swollen Negro population and the segregated residential pattern were resulting in some return to school segregation: twenty-six public schools had an all-Negro enrollment of 23,010; three schools served 1066 students, all of them white.

Another widespread distortion of the Washington situation was the exaggerated picture which was painted of it in racist quarters as a lawless and crime-ridden city—due, it was argued, to its failure to maintain school segregation and to the congenital perversity of Negroes. A number of sensational crimes had been committed in Washington. A Uniform Crime Report of the FBI revealed a shocking increase in crime throughout the nation in 1962. But in the FBI report Washington stood seventh among the nation's twelve largest cities in the number of crimes committed per hundred thousand population.

Chapter 9

THREE NORTH CAROLINA
CITIES AND NASHVILLE

In 1957 Negroes were admitted for the first time to previously all-white public schools in five Southern cities: Charlotte, Winston-Salem, and Greensboro in North Carolina; Nashville, Tennessee; and Little Rock, Arkansas.

These cities were comparable in many ways, including size. Their population within corporate city limits ranged, by the 1960 census, from 107,813 in Little Rock to 201,564 in Charlotte. When its populous environs are taken into account, Nashville was the largest, with a total of 399,743 inhabitants. The metropolitan area population of the other four was: Charlotte, 272,111; Greensboro, 246,520; Little Rock, 242,980; and Winston-Salem, 189,428. The proportion of Negroes to the total population in each—widely regarded as a useful measure of the magnitude of the local race-relations problem—was as follows: Nashville, 37.9 per cent; Winston-Salem, 37.1 per cent; Charlotte, 28 per cent; Greensboro, 26 per cent; and Little Rock, 23.5 per cent.

One disturbance in North Carolina, small but ugly and much publicized, and the bombing of a school in Nashville by unknown fanatics, together with the staggering events in Little Rock—in the wake of the disorders at Sturgis, Mansfield, and Clinton the previous autumn—gave a widespread impression of rebellious violence, approaching anarchy, in the South, and aroused the deepest pessimism. It was indeed during the thirteen months from August 1956, through September 1957 that disorder in connection with public-school desegregation reached its apex. Nevertheless, the desegregation operation itself in Nashville was not conspicuously disorderly; and no serious violence occurred in the North Carolina cities.

Hostility to school desegregation had been expressed in North Carolina in much the same manner as elsewhere in the South, but the volume of resistance agitation was somewhat less in comparison with the sobering influences at work in that state. Dr. Frank P. Graham, who had been president of the University of North Carolina, governor, and United States senator, and who was then a mediator for the United Nations, supported the Brown decision vigorously. Irving Carlyle of Winston-Salem, a former state senator, was a rare example of a Southern politician who not only accepted the desegregation ruling but became a crusader for compliance with it. Two literary celebrities, Harry Golden of Charlotte and playwright Paul Green of Chapel Hill, were distinguished foes of every kind of race discrimination. The constructive attitude of the state administration was more than matched by that of the press. No important daily newspaper in North Carolina descended to inflammatory opposition and most of them counseled orderly adjustment to the Brown ruling. In the three cities where public-school desegregation was first essayed, the local newspapers rendered invaluable service in preparing the public for the change. Three of their editors—C. A. McKnight of the *Charlotte Observer,* Reed Sarratt of the *Winston-Salem Journal,* and Henry Kendall of the *Greensboro Daily News*—were noted students of the Southern race problem; McKnight was the first editor, and Sarratt is the latest editor, of the indispensable *Southern School News.*

Fifty-eight Negro children filed applications for admission to white schools in June: forty-one in Charlotte, nine in Greensboro, seven in Winston-Salem, and one in Raleigh. All but twelve of these applicants were eliminated; the Raleigh application was rejected. The Charlotte, Greensboro, and Winston-Salem school boards, which decided to take the perilous desegregation plunge, followed identical schedules and took frequent counsel together. Negro pupils were assigned to white schools—five in Charlotte, six in Greensboro, and one in Winston-Salem.

The school boards moved toward the showdown with no little trepidation. They announced the assignments at simultaneous meetings Tuesday night, July 23. In opening the Charlotte meeting, a board member, Richard Brown, called upon the Almighty: "We pray for those who disagree. Enter into their minds and hearts, grant them enlarged understanding, patience, and forbearance. . . . Place Thy protecting arm around our children." Afterward a spokesman for the North Carolina Patriots, Inc., presented a spectacular petition said to bear sixteen thousand signatures and, pointing a threatening finger at Charlotte board members, denounced this "ungodly thing"; a majority of some forty visitors present applauded. In Greensboro about seventy-five heard a North Carolina Patriot deliver a vehement oration—"You shall be condemned, vilified, damned and cursed!"[1] In Winston-Salem only four visitors attended the school-board meeting, where a Patriot protested with relative restraint.

The North Carolina Patriots, Inc., was a somewhat dignified relative of the Citizens' Councils, headed by Dr. Wesley George, a University of North Carolina professor; it was cool toward the likes of John Kasper—who, by the way, appeared on the scene. Out of jail for the time being, Kasper visited each of the three cities a few days before school opening. His coming was hailed by officials and the press in the spirit of a *Winston-Salem Journal* editorial, headed: "Unwelcome." An audience of about two hundred gave him a jeering reception in Winston-Salem, about three hundred heard him in Greensboro, and about four hundred listened impassively to his harangue in Charlotte. Ku Klux Klansmen also appeared in Charlotte, but they folded up their robes and dispersed when police broke up their picket line. On September 3 Governor Hodges warned against "any lawlessness or violence" and, in answer to a reporter's question, did not rule out the use of the National Guard if it should be needed to preserve order.

The opening of schools and the integration of the Negro pupils on September 4 was anti-climactic. Press dispatches agreed that the North Carolina breakthrough "proceeded with relative calm." Disturbances did occur at Harding High School in Charlotte in connection with the arrival and departure of its one Negro student, Dorothy Counts. When Miss Counts walked home she was pursued by a rowdy crowd of juveniles—evidently indoctrinated by adult racists—jeering, spitting, and throwing pebbles, sticks, and paper balls. A white girl, who spat in Dorothy's face, and a white boy, who threw a stick, were arrested. However, Negroes entered three other white high schools in Charlotte without incident. There was some heckling but no suggestion of violence in Winston-Salem and Greensboro. Disorder in all three cities was almost entirely limited to the first day, although Miss Counts continued to be made uncomfortable in Harding High School.

Photographic excellence and an exceptional view through the camera lens of the distressing little scene in Charlotte gave the world an exaggerated impression of turmoil in North Carolina. It was a striking example of the manner in which the dramatic, the colorful, and the photogenic in school-desegregation crises often received a degree of publicity inconsistent with a balanced appraisal of events. The essential news from North Carolina was that white schools in three cities had admitted Negro pupils without serious public disorder.

The Dorothy Counts incident spoke eloquently nonetheless, while it offered one of the finest opportunities for expressive photography that the commotion in the South had produced. Dorothy was the 15-year-old daughter of the Reverend Herman L. Counts, an instructor at Johnson C. Smith University. A comely young lady of unmistakable gentleness and breeding, in a neat plaid dress, she walked in front of the bawling mob with a quiet dignity that made theories of Negro inferiority seem grotesque. A *Charlotte Observer* columnist, Kays Gary, was inspired to comment in verse, under the heading: "Her Skin Was Dark and Her Head High." His poem read in part:

> They spat and she was covered with it;
> Spittle dripped from the hem of her dress;
> It clung to her neck and arms and she wore
> it.
> They spat and they jeered and screamed:
> Debris fell on her shoulders and around her
> feet;
> And the posture of the head was unchanged.
> That was the remarkable thing.
> And, if her skin was brown, you had to
> admit her courage was royal purple.[2]

Photographers met the challenge with distinction. Dorothy's walk home from school carried her all over the United States, to London and Paris, and around the world. One of the photos won the World Press award.

To the dismay of many, after one week Dorothy Counts—seeing no hope of enjoying tolerable relations with her white schoolmates—withdrew from Harding High School and enrolled in a bi-racial private school in suburban Philadelphia.

Nashville received more attention from John Kasper and the Ku Klux Klan, as well as from more respectable segregationist organizations, than the North Carolina cities; and at the same time longer and more thorough efforts were made in the Tennessee capital to condition the public for the change. The issue was fervently contested there on both sides and from every angle. Nashville, with such noted universities and colleges as Vanderbilt, Fisk, Scarritt, and Peabody—all bi-racial to some extent—was a renowned study center for Southern problems; it was the home of both the *Southern School News* and the *Race Relations Law Reporter.* The city's large Negro community was progressive and politically alert; Negro participation in public affairs in Nashville was unique among Southern cities: two Negroes sat in the city council and one on the board of education. The city had already witnessed successful desegregation in Catholic parochial schools, the public library, the municipal golf courses, and the railroad station.

One of the city's two daily newspapers, the afternoon *Banner,* attacked the desegregation rulings bitterly. The press of Tennessee was predominantly critical of the Brown decision. But two Tennessee newspapers were outstanding in their call for orderly adjustment to it. One of these was Nashville's morning paper, the *Tennesseean.* The other was the *Chattanooga Times,* a relative by family ties of the *New York Times,* which labored diligently to combat resistance sentiment in Chattanooga and the South.

Though Governor Clement had vetoed several earlier pro-segregation bills, when the legislature met in January 1957 he endorsed a school-bill package which included a pupil-assignment plan and a measure called in Tennessee the "School Preference Law." The latter, resembling a "Freedom of Choice Plan" adopted in Alabama the year before, was a specious device which theoretically would set up three school systems and allow parents to choose for their children between white or Negro schools, according to their race, and integrated schools. It required little imagination to see that in the South such a scheme would result in little—or, more probably, no—change in the existing segregated pattern, and the law was invalidated the following September by a federal district court. At the same time Clement was more forthright than any other Southern governor in upholding the Supreme Court decision and in urging a sympathetic approach to the problem of the Negro. In his address to the legislature he said this was not only America's greatest crisis, but "our greatest opportunity"; and: ". . . We must not overlook the fact that the Negro is equal to the white in the eyes of the law and in the sight of God. . . ." In a letter to the chairman of the Anderson County school board a few weeks later the governor said: "I am sure you are aware of the fact that no gubernatorial or legislative action can overturn a decision of the United States Supreme Court." [3]

The admission of some Negro pupils to white schools in Nashville became a definite prospect in January 1957, when Federal District Judge William E. Miller gave tentative approval to a school-board proposal to begin compliance with the Brown decision with the desegregation of all first-grade pupils the following September. This plan—the impact of which was greatly reduced by a liberal transfer privilege—was the germ of what would become the "Nashville Plan" of one-grade-a-year desegregation.

William A. Bass, the superintendent of schools, began meeting in April with principals, supervisors, and both white and colored Parent-Teacher Associations in pursuance of a school-board resolution to "inform, elucidate, and help solve problems which may grow out of the effort . . . to comply with the ruling. . . ." Many Nashville clergymen asked their congregations to accept school desegregation in a "Christian spirit." Not all of them were willing to meet the issue squarely in their churches, but, as was often the case in this controversy, ministers' courage rose when they assembled in clerical meetings. Moreover, a divinity school and several church-related colleges and some denominational headquarters had brought to Nashville an exceptional number of ministers who did not have to answer to local congregations for their liberal views. The Nashville Ministers' Association and the Association of Churches addressed letters to all Protestant clergymen, suggesting that they help prepare the public in statements, sermons, or at least prayers for the children, parents, and teachers involved. The association arranged helpful television programs. Catholics and Jews were also active. The Nashville Community Relations Conference, a bi-racial organization formed the previous year, labored effectively to mobilize public sentiment behind the desegregation move. It secured six hundred signatures to a memorial in support of it, which was published in the press along with the names of the signers, many of whom were well-known religious, educational, business, and civic leaders. Sixteen other organizations supported the memorial and added three hundred and fifty more names before it was presented to the school board. Literature both pro and con circulated in abundance.

On the segregationist side, a Parents' School Preference Committee

and the Tennessee Federation for Constitutional Government urged
that the school board abandon its desegregation plan and fall back on
the recently enacted Tennessee legislation; the petition they presented
to the school board bore six thousand names. The Ku Klux Klan and
John Kasper confronted the embattled school board with harsher demands. These two were not congenial collaborators. Kasper's extremist
friends had been steadily deserting him, and now the KKK told him
to "go back to New Jersey"; he was ordered away from a Klan meeting and Klansmen chased him out of a neighboring restaurant. The
rallies of the KKK generally drew a handful instead of the thousands
anticipated in Klan advertising, but Klansmen were blusteringly persistent—and Kasper no less.

He addressed himself especially to the poorer white quarters of
Nashville, where he found abundant scope. During the first half of
1957 Kasper's battered convertible had traveled much on the roads
connecting Clinton, Knoxville, and Nashville, while he attended to the
exigencies of police, courts, and jails and filled the intervening time
with agitation to keep the white race pure and the Negroes segregated.
"I'll never desert the white race in Tennessee," Kasper said, "until
the outcome of our struggle is crystal clear and spells victory over the
race mongrelizers." [4] Sometimes in Nashville he stayed at the home
of the Reverend Fred Stroud, pastor of a "Bible Presbyterian Church"
(not affiliated with other Presbyterian bodies), who gave Kasper his
blessing. Stroud was himself a busy segregationist agitator, who proclaimed: "The Lord is on our side." Asa Carter from Alabama also
found time to pay Nashville a visit. Representative Davis of Georgia
—he of the District of Columbia school investigation—came to address the TFCG and urged that Nashville parents boycott the public
schools and send their children to private schools.

The desegregation plan provided for first-grade pupils to be assigned
first to schools indicated by the residential pattern without regard to
race, but Negro pupils assigned to schools in which they found themselves in a racial minority were permitted to transfer back to predominantly Negro schools, and a similar privilege was extended to
white pupils. As was to be expected, all the white pupils elected to stay
in predominantly white schools, and most of the Negro pupils chose
the easier and safer course—not without an element of intimidation—
of continuing to attend what remained in effect segregated Negro
schools. However, nineteen Negro pupils held to their assignments to

white elementary schools. That was the extent to which the pattern of segregation was broken. When the schools opened on September 9 the nineteen Negroes entered five schools along with whites, without incident other than some minor scuffling of pickets with police and the arrest of several white women for throwing rocks. Crowds which gathered at several places that night were more obstreperous—one group was addressed by Kasper—but police had the situation well under control.

Shortly after midnight of school-opening day, early on September 10, a dynamite blast was heard in East Nashville. One wing of the Hattie Cotton School, a previously all-white elementary school which had admitted one 6-year-old Negro girl, had been demolished. (The damaged rooms were replaced four months later at a cost of $71,000.) When daylight came and the news spread, Nashville was seized with a degree of panic. Police deployed before the desegregated schools and barricades were erected on the streets a block away from each. Hattie Cotton was closed; attendance at the other six desegregated schools was down to less than 40 per cent of normal. During a day of tension, twenty-nine arrests were made. But within a week street barricades had been removed, attendance at the desegregated schools had risen to approximately 90 per cent—with eleven Negro children still in schools with whites—and the situation had returned to normal.

From the first news of the Hattie Cotton School bombing, fingers of suspicion pointed at Kasper, who had talked of "the shotgun, dynamite, and the rope." [5] He was arrested along with half-a-dozen other suspects; but evidence linking him, or anyone else, with the crime was never found. Kasper, however, faced many charges. His adventures with police and courts reached a crescendo at this point. Arrested in a general crackdown on troublemakers, he was charged with vagrancy, loitering, and two counts of disorderly conduct. He had just posted a $2000 bond and was walking toward his car when he was arrested again and charged with illegal parking; this called for an additional bond of $500. Twelve hours later he was pulled from his bed and arrested by a constable and taken to the jail of Davidson County (which shared jurisdiction with Nashville), on the charge of inciting to riot. Before he could settle down in this jail, city police "borrowed" him to be tried and convicted in the city court on the first charges; temporarily short of cash now, Kasper paid a visit to the city workhouse. When he raised the $200 city court fine, he was hustled back to the county jail once more; in the county court he was indicted by a grand jury for inciting to riot, scheduled for trial in November, and placed under a $2500 bond. A few days later he was taken briefly from the county jail to appear as a defendant in a hearing in the federal district court, which resulted in an injunction forbidding him and nine others named, and their followers, to interfere "by acts of trespass, boycott, or picket with the free operation of the schools." On September 18 his attorney showed up with $2500 in cash and Kasper was released from the county jail. He climbed into his convertible and left immediately for Knoxville.

Little Rock dominated the news now. In that city soldiers stood guard around a high school with instructions from Governor Faubus to prevent the entry of Negro pupils whom a federal court had ordered to be admitted. While John Kasper was fretting in the Davidson County jail, the governor of Arkansas and the President of the United States were conferring tensely in Newport, Rhode Island, in a historic collision of state and federal authority. Withdrawal of the forces under the command of the governor would be followed by uncontrolled rioting and the arrival of a detachment of the United States Army to restore peace and insure compliance with the orders of federal courts. But before we move to that exciting theater, let us observe the evolution of the Nashville Plan, which would be widely studied and copied; and to look ahead briefly to the progress under it that would keep Nashville in the forefront of Southern cities in the elimination of segregation in public schools.

The Nashville school board was under a federal district court order to submit by December 31, 1957, a plan for abolishing segregation in the remaining eleven grades. Under heavy local pressure, the board attempted to abandon the grade-a-year desegregation principle and submitted a plan based largely on the state's School Preference Law, which had already been declared unconstitutional. At the same time the Negro plaintiffs in the original Nashville school-desegregation suit petitioned the court to order an end to segregation in all grades the following year. In January 1958 the court rejected the latest school-board proposal, and in April the board committed itself formally to a program of desegregating one higher grade each year until all segregation should be eliminated. This plan was allowed by the federal courts to stand.

The schools opened in September 1958—with both first and second grades desegregated, in complete tranquillity. Only a handful of Negro pupils accepted their assignments to mixed schools during the first two years, then a concerted movement in the Negro community caused a dramatic increase in the number of Negroes in school with whites. During six years the year-by-year totals of Negro pupils in predominantly white schools were: 1958, 34 in two grades; 1959, 41 in three grades; 1960, 183 in four grades; 1961, 270 in five grades; 1962, 490 in six grades; and 1963, 773 in seven grades.*

* In addition to these totals, approximately 530 Negro children were enrolled in an elementary school with one white pupil in 1960. No whites were enrolled in this school in 1963.

Chapter 10

LITTLE ROCK

The events of September 1957 in Little Rock, Arkansas, made the name of that city familiar to all the world. For many months afterward, when the United States was mentioned among ordinary folk in Bombay, Nairobi, or Singapore, the city that came first to mind was not Washington or New York, but Little Rock. Informed foreign observers were concerned over the constitutional crisis in the most powerful nation on earth; millions of people overseas received impressions of Negro children being first barred by soldiers from a public school and later escorted through a hostile mob into that school by other soldiers, and of Negroes being beaten by white men on the streets of an American city.

A state governor persisted for eighteen days in preventing by military force the execution of an order of a federal court for the desegregation of a public high school, affording abundant time for publicity and debate over that posture from every conceivable angle; a tense week-end and a day of rioting followed withdrawal of the state force; then troops of the United States Army arrived on the scene. There were twenty-two days of suspense before the constitutional issue was thunderously decided in favor of federal authority. It is easy to observe in retrospect that the journalistic output on Little Rock would have been less overwhelming—and much grievous damage would have been averted—if events had moved with greater dispatch.

The task of the historian would certainly be easier if the source material were less massive and discordant. However, subsequent events and a marked change in the Southern temper in the six years since the crisis have joined with a quieter sifting of evidence to make for clarity and concensus in our appraisal of what happened at Little Rock. The possibility of peaceful integration of public schools has been demonstrated, at least on a token scale, in scores of Southern cities; resistance sentiment has markedly subsided; and many erstwhile defenders of the Arkansas governor have withdrawn from that side of the debate.

An elementary fact that needs to be borne in mind in any examination of the Little Rock events is that the National Guard detachment which was called into service by the governor of Arkansas, was at the time a *state,* rather than a national, military force. The National Guard is a reserve component of the United States Army and is supported mainly by the federal government; but, except when it is formally called into federal service, it retains the status of state militia and is under the command of the governors of the states. It is normally, and properly, called upon by state governors when the public order is seriously threatened. From this distance detached observers generally agree that the danger in Little Rock at the beginning of September 1957 was not sufficient to justify Governor Orval Faubus in calling out the National Guard as a public safety precaution. But it is also apparent, since the smoke has cleared away, that the questions of calling out the National Guard and withdrawing the National Guard— to which so much passionate argument was directed—were irrelevant to the central issue. Deploying Guardsmen around Central High School may have been, and probably was, unnecessary; but it was constitutionally correct. The impropriety, or the rebellion, lay in the orders the troops were given to carry out.

If the Guardsmen had been used to protect the school and its pupils in their attempt to comply with federal court orders, as the governor of Tennessee had used the National Guard at Clinton, a totally different chapter of history could have been written. It is interesting, if fruitless, to dwell on the hypothetical consequences of this "if": the Little Rock experience would surely have been recorded as one more instance of orderly adjustment to the Brown ruling; and elsewhere in the South, instead of a stiffening of resistance, we would probably have witnessed some acceleration of the movement toward school desegregation.

When the Arkansas National Guard blocked the execution of a federal court mandate, Harry S. Ashmore, a distinguished author, then editor of the Little Rock *Arkansas Gazette,* urged that it be promptly federalized and its orders changed—a remedy that would have placed a minimum of onus upon Governor Faubus. This move was considered in Washington, but, as Congressman Brooks Hays, who played an active mediatory role throughout the crisis, has recalled in his book *A Southern Moderate Speaks,*[1] Presidential Assistant Sherman Adams was "not convinced that federalizing the National Guard was the

answer." The Guard was federalized only after the withdrawal of the
detachment sent by Faubus, and the subsequent explosion, along with
the dispatch of regular Army troops—as a final act in the drama. Often
obscured in the talk about a governor's duty to preserve order, the
paramount question in Little Rock was whether military force could
be used by a state to nullify the law of the land.

The issue was further clouded by the impression widely given by
the deployment of federal troops that "bayonets" were being used to
"ram integration down the throat of the South." It was inevitable that
this interpretation would be given it in many quarters; but it was made
more emphatic by the circumstance that action to assert federal authority was taken only after—and ostensibly inspired by—a riotous
popular demonstration of opposition to school integration. The troop
action appeared to be directed against the populace rather than
against a rebellious governor.

The Little Rock move was not a "breakthrough" from a state point
of view. Negroes had already been admitted to previously all-white
public schools in five Arkansas districts without incident, except for
minor disturbances in the town of Hoxie. All state-supported institutions of higher learning in Arkansas were open to Negroes. The Little
Rock school board had announced its decision to comply with the
Brown ruling in May 1954, six days after the decision was handed
down. A year later it had adopted a plan of gradual integration, under
which senior high-school grades would be desegregated in September
1957. The remaining classes would be desegregated during a six-year
period thereafter, with the lower classes the last to be affected. Students assigned to schools in which they might be in a racial minority
were to be permitted to transfer. Twenty-seven Negroes who applied
for admission to white schools ahead of the schedule, in 1956, were
rejected; when NAACP attorneys complained, federal courts upheld
the Little Rock school-board plan.

The emotional climate of Little Rock with respect to the segregation question before the pyrotechnics of September 1957 was comparable to that in the four other Upper South cities whose experiences
were related in the previous chapter. Similar agitation had taken place
in Little Rock on both sides of the segregation question, but it had
involved a somewhat smaller fraction of the community and was less
heated, for instance, than that in Nashville. In the March school-
board election Little Rock voters had elected two supporters of the

desegregation plan by 2-to-1 majorities over two opponents of it. John Kasper, who had considerable talent for detecting potential trouble centers, had not found the prospects of turmoil in Little Rock sufficiently promising to draw him away from Nashville; nor had the Ku Klux Klan appeared. The most disturbing incident had been a visit to Little Rock by Governor Marvin Griffin of Georgia, accompanied by the Citizens' Council leader, Roy Harris. Griffin addressed three hundred and fifty persons—"a courageous bunch of patriots"—at a $10-a-plate Capital Citizens' Council rally two weeks before school-opening. In a vitriolic speech the Georgia governor pointed to the "steadfast" resistance to school integration in his state, and said he would use the Highway Patrol—indeed, "enlist every white man in Georgia," if necessary—to prevent racial integration there. His speech undoubtedly did much to stimulate the mobilization of resistance elements, but at the end of August no signs of upheaval were visible.

Orval Faubus, born January 7, 1910, in Madison County in the hills of northwest Arkansas, had risen from humble beginnings, but he was by no means a "hillbilly." In 1957 he was an urbane and personable executive, with a fairly creditable record, first as state highway director, and later, for nearly three years, as governor. He was not a true segregationist from the point of view of the Deep South: he expressed acceptance of the Supreme Court ruling as the law of the land, and his criticism of desegregation moves was mainly on the score of method and timing.

The first conspicuous sign of Faubus's obsession with the danger of violence in Little Rock was on August 29 when he testified in the county chancery court in a suit brought by the segregationist "Mothers' League of Central High School" to block the admission of Negroes to that school. Predicting "violence, bloodshed, and riots" if integration should proceed as scheduled, he said he had personal knowledge of increased sales of knives and revolvers to Negro and white students. (Neither school and police officials nor newspapermen were able later to verify this.) However, Chancellor Murray J. Reed concluded: "In view of the testimony . . . and particularly in the opinion of Governor Faubus, I feel that I can only grant the injunction." [2] Chancellor Reed's ruling was nullified the next day by the federal district court, which ordered the school board to proceed with its plan of gradual integration and issued a blanket injunction against any interference.

The degree of sincerity in Faubus's attitude at this point is difficult
to measure. He had not encouraged the Georgia governor's visit—
which, he said, was "one thing that triggered" a change in sentiment;
he did not attend the Capital Citizens' Council rally, though he enter-
tained the Griffin party afterward at the governor's mansion. Faubus
was prone to seize upon a rumor that came over the telephone, or
that some unimportant individual brought to his office, and broadcast
it without investigation. Less charitable observers suspected that some
of these rumors were creatures of the governor's imagination or that
he was—as FBI Director J. Edgar Hoover in a later instance termed
the practice—"disseminating falsehoods." [3] At any rate the rumors
circulated were generally calculated to serve some purpose, and it
began to be the governor's apparent purpose to create an impression
of impending violence. As to just when Orval Faubus caught the
vision of himself as the idolized hero of Southern resistance we can
only speculate, but, from early September on, his words and actions
could not have been more skillfully designed to achieve that alluring
distinction.

Nine Negro pupils had been assigned, under federal court orders,
to Little Rock's Central High, which had an enrollment of approximately two thousand and which had been open hitherto exclusively to
white children. Classes were scheduled to begin on September 3. It
will be an aid to clarity, and bring out the salient points in the constitutional debate, if we trace the course of the crisis from here on in
day-by-day bulletins, relying for much of the story on excerpts from
the verbal exchange.

Monday, September 2

Monday night troops of the Arkansas National Guard suddenly
appeared at Central High School and surrounded it. An hour later
Governor Faubus announced this move in a radio-television speech in
which he said in part:

> Units of the National Guard have been, or are now being,
> mobilized with the mission to maintain or restore the peace and
> good order of this community. Advance units are already on duty
> on the grounds of Central High School. . . .
>
> The mission of the state militia is to maintain or restore order
> and to protect the lives and property of citizens. They will act not

as segregationists or integrationists, but as soldiers called to active duty to carry out their assigned tasks.

But I must state here in all sincerity, that it is my opinion—yes, even a conviction—that it will not be possible to restore or to maintain order and protect the lives and property of the citizens if forcible integration is carried out tomorrow in the schools of this community. The inevitable conclusion, therefore, must be that the schools in Pulaski County, for the time being, must be operated on the same basis as they have been operated in the past.[4]

Tuesday, September 3

Monday had been a holiday, Labor Day. Acceding to a schoolboard request that they stay away for the present, no Negroes attended the school on Tuesday.

Little Rock was now in newspaper headlines throughout the world, and news and camera men were swarming there.

The mayor of Little Rock, Woodrow W. Mann, said of the governor's action:

> The governor has called out the National Guard to put down trouble when none existed. He did so without a request from those of us who are directly responsible for preservation of peace and order. The only effect of his action is to create tensions where none existed.
>
> I call the governor's attention to the fact that after almost a week of sensational developments brought about by his own action, the Little Rock police have not had a single case of interracial violence reported to them. This is clear evidence that the governor's excuse for calling out the Guard is simply a hoax.[5]

That night Federal Judge Ronald N. Davies ordered the school board to "put in effect forthwith the plan of integration. . . ."

Wednesday, September 4

The nine Negro pupils sought to enter the school and were stopped by Faubus's soldiers. The Negro children were accompanied by two Negro clergymen, the Reverend Z. Z. Driver and the Reverend Harry Bass, and two white clergymen, the Reverend Will D. Campbell of the National Council of Churches and the Reverend Dunbar Ogden, Jr., president of the Little Rock Ministerial Alliance. They were told that the Negroes were barred by order of the governor. A crowd of whites watched and jeered. However, since the troops were carrying out its wishes, only minor harassment of the retreating Negroes required the intervention of Guardsmen. The National Guard force numbered only two hundred and seventy, but, having only nine Negro children to repel, that was more than enough.

The scenes at the school were profusely photographed and reported. The first of the Negro children to be turned back was an attractive 15-year-old girl named Elizabeth Eckford. In order to find an exit from the barricaded street this dainty little miss had to walk a hundred-yard gauntlet of sneering, threatening demonstrators—before many cameras. Some of the photos resembled those of Dorothy Counts in Charlotte and rivaled them in circulation.

The day's rumors included one that federal marshals or agents of the FBI would escort Negroes into the school. If they should try to do that, State Adjutant General Sherman T. Clinger said, "a bunch of resolute boys are going to resist." But no such federal-state confrontation occurred.

Judge Davies asked the United States attorney general to order an investigation.

Governor Faubus sent a telegram to President Eisenhower which read somewhat like a message to a hostile foreign government and tended further to erect the image of himself as the embattled Southern champion of state rights. Typical Faubus "rumors" were included. The governor's telegram said in part:

> . . . The question at issue at Little Rock this moment is not integration vs. segregation. Peaceful integration has been accomplished for some time in the University of Arkansas, state-supported colleges, and in three more of our largest public schools—Fort Smith, Ozark, Van Buren. It is impossible to integrate some of our schools at this time without violence. The Supreme Court recognized that conditions in each community must be considered and I have interpreted your public statements to indicate that you are in agreement with this premise.
>
> The question now is whether or not the head of a sovereign state can exercise his constitutional powers and discretion in maintaining peace and good order within his jurisdiction, being accountable to his own conscience and to his own people. . . .

I am reliably informed that federal authorities in Little Rock have this day been discussing plans to take into custody, by force, the head of a sovereign state. This would be in complete disregard of the constitutional guarantees of the separation and independence of the three branches of government and the rights and powers of a state. As the duly elected governor and representative of the people of Arkansas, I can no more surrender these rights than you could surrender the rights of the duly elected chief executive of our nation. . . .

I have reason to believe that the telephone lines to the Arkansas executive mansion have been tapped—I suspect the federal agents. The situation in Little Rock and Arkansas grows more explosive by the hour. This is caused for the most part by the misunderstanding of our problems by a federal judge who decreed "immediate integration" of the public schools of Little Rock without hearing any evidence whatsoever as to the conditions now existing in this community. . . . As governor of Arkansas I appeal to you to use your good offices to modify the extreme stand and stop the unwarranted interference of federal agents in this area so that we may again enjoy domestic tranquillity and continue in our pursuit of ideal relations between other races. . . .[6]

Thursday, September 5

The President replied the next day:

Your telegram received, requesting my assurance of, understanding of, and co-operation in the course of action you have taken on school integration recommended by the Little Rock School Board and ordered by the United States District Court pursuant to the mandate of the United States Supreme Court.

When I became President, I took an oath to support and defend the Constitution of the United States. The only assurance I can give you is that the federal Constitution will be upheld by me by every legal means at my command.

There is no basis of fact to the statements you make in your telegram that federal authorities have been considering taking you into custody or that telephone lines to your executive mansion have been tapped by any agency of the federal government.

At the request of Judge Davies, the Department of Justice is presently collecting facts as to interference with or failure to comply with the district's court order. You and other state officials—as well as the National Guard which is, of course, uniformed, armed, and partially sustained by the government—will, I am sure, give full co-operation to the United States District Court.[7]

Saturday, September 7

The Little Rock school board went back to the federal court with a request for a temporary suspension of the order to admit the Negro pupils. Judge Davies rejected the petition with feeling. He quoted Mayor Mann's statement and said in part:

> The testimony and arguments this morning were, in my judgment, as anemic as the petition itself; and the position taken by the school directors does violence to my concept of the duty of the petitioners to adhere with resolution to its own approved plan of gradual integration in the Little Rock public schools.
>
> It must never be thought that this court has not given careful consideration to this problem and all that it entails, but it must never be forgotten that I have a constitutional duty and obligation from which I shall not shrink. . . .[8]

(According to the Associated Press, newspapers around the world were now giving space to reports and pictures of troops barring Negro children from the school in Little Rock. The *London Daily Chronicle* said "the scenes have been nauseating and pitiful." The *Tokyo News* wondered "why this problem should arise in the United States, the champion of democracy." Radio Moscow deplored "the shameful spectacle.") *

Monday, September 9

Mayor Mann was serving the last four months of his term before the inauguration of a city-manager form of government—which he had opposed—and was a controversial figure. Eight of the ten aldermen turned against him in his feud with the governor and signed a statement commending Faubus for "calling out the National Guard . . . to protect the lives and property of our people."

The governor issued a statement sharply critical of Judge Davies (who had arrived from North Dakota within the fortnight to fill a vacancy). Noting that the judge had quoted the mayor's statement,

* The foreign comment reported in this chapter did not necessarily appear on the date under which it is placed here.

he said: "Mayor Mann is a discredited, repudiated public official"; and "as proof of the grave error made by the judge," he quoted the statement of commendation from the eight aldermen and added:

> The Constitutions of the State of Arkansas and of the United States imposed upon me the duty to maintain the public peace and to use the militia if, in my judgment, it is necessary. I cannot abdicate my office and let a federal judge substitute his judgment for mine on this issue. If he has a right to substitute his judgment for mine on this issue, then he has the right to substitute his judgment on all issues involving duties imposed upon me as governor of Arkansas. . . .

On the same day Judge Davies received a report from the FBI on why the federal court order had not been carried out, and he asked the Department of Justice to institute injunction proceedings, as a friend of the court, against Faubus, Major General Sherman T. Clinger, commander of the Arkansas National Guard, and Lieutenant Colonel Marion E. Johnson, commander of the Guard detachment at Central High School.

(The *New York Times* reported from Rome that the Vatican newspaper, *Osservatore Romano,* in one of its rare comments on the situation in the United States, said that people who believe in racist theories should be banned from political life and that race discrimination "runs counter to nature, to character, to aspirations, and to the laws of the United States. . . .")

Tuesday, September 10

The Department of Justice asked the court to enjoin the governor and the two Guard commanders, "their officers, agents, servants, employees, attorneys, and all persons in active concert or participation with them" from interfering with the execution of the court's orders by "units of the Arkansas National Guard or otherwise." [9]

The date for this courtroom collision of the state's chief executive with federal authority was set for September 20.

(The *Toronto Globe and Mail* said: "The theory, assiduously spread by the Communists for decades, that the United States is the inveterate enemy of all colored people everywhere is likely to win much wider support than ever before." A cartoon in the *London Evening Standard* showed Governor Faubus hurling a guitar at a clock labeled "Progress." In Budapest, Hungary's Communist premier, Janos Kadar, said: "Those who tolerate that a people should be persecuted because of the color of their skin have no right to preach human liberty and human rights.")

Wednesday, September 11

The hearing on the Department of Justice petition for a restraining injunction against Faubus along with General Clinger and Colonel Johnson had been set for September 20 and summons had been served on the governor and the two officers.

Congressman Hays was now busy trying to arrange a meeting between Governor Faubus and President Eisenhower. He conferred frequently with Faubus and by telephone with Presidential Assistant Sherman Adams in Washington. The proposal was accepted at both ends, and it was decided that the request for the conference should come from the governor. Hays helped the governor in drafting the following telegram, which was sent to the President on September 11:

> I have accepted summons from the United States District Court, Eastern District of Arkansas, to appear before that court on September 20, to answer certain allegations in litigation affecting the high school in Little Rock. Recognizing that we jointly share great responsibility under the federal Constitution, I feel that it is advisable for us to counsel together in determining my course of action as chief executive of the State of Arkansas with reference to the responsibility placed upon me by the state and federal Constitutions.
>
> The United States District Court has already entered an order relative to the integration of the high school in Little Rock, and this order has been affirmed by the Circuit Court of Appeals.
>
> All good citizens must, of course, obey all proper orders of our courts and it is certainly my desire to comply with the order that has been issued by the district court in this case, consistent with my responsibilities under the Constitution of the United States and that of Arkansas.
>
> May I confer with you on this matter at your earliest convenience? [10]

President Eisenhower, though in constant touch with the White House, was vacationing at the time at Newport, Rhode Island—a circumstance that aroused some criticism. (Columnist Walter Lippmann wrote: "It is necessary to say . . . that during this grave business he ought not to be away from Washington, but at the center of things, where he can really keep himself informed and advised.") The President answered Faubus immediately with this brief message:

> I have your telegram in which you request a meeting with me. Would it suit your convenience to come to my office on the naval base at Newport either Friday afternoon, September 13, at 3 o'clock, or Saturday morning, the 14th at 9 o'clock? If you would let my office know your method of transportation to the Newport area, my staff will arrange to have you met and brought to the base.[11]

(The Associated Press reported: "The Soviets built a somewhat fictional radio drama around a real-life Negro schoolgirl of Little Rock and broadcast it to schoolrooms in the Soviet Union. The program was a dramatized account of racial violence terrorizing a Negro school girl named Elizabeth Eckford . . . trying to get into a desegregated school in Little Rock." The Egyptian government made heavy use of the news from Little Rock in its broadcasts to the Sudan. The *Budapest Esti Hirlap* taunted: "We would like to invite the members of the five-nation UN committee [which recommended condemnation of the Soviet Union for its actions in Hungary] to make a study trip up the Arkansas River. . . .")

Friday September 13
The Saturday hour was agreed upon for the conference. Friday, Faubus and his private secretary, accompanied by Congressman Hays, flew to Providence, Rhode Island. Hays has recalled in his book: "No one representing the governor of Rhode Island or the mayor of Providence was on hand to welcome us. There were curious crowds but no cheering. It was rather pathetic to see Governor Faubus looking vainly for some sign of enthusiasm. . . ."

Saturday, September 14
At Newport on Saturday morning President Eisenhower talked privately in his office with Governor Faubus for about fifteen minutes. Afterward the two joined Hays and Adams in the reception room for a talk that lasted nearly two hours. At the President's suggestion, Attorney General Herbert Brownell and Presidential Press Secretary James Hagerty came in for the last part of the discussion.

Among details of the conversation, revealed with the President's approval, Hays recalls that Eisenhower said to Faubus: "I do not criticize you for calling out the Guard—our only difference is that I would have given them different instructions."

Saturday afternoon the President issued this statement:

> At the request of Governor Faubus of Arkansas, I met with him this morning in a constructive discussion regarding the carrying out of the orders of the federal court in the matter of the high schools of Little Rock.
>
> The governor stated his intention to respect the decision of the United States District Court and to give his full co-operation in carrying out his responsibilities in respect to these decisions.
>
> In doing so, I recognize the inescapable responsibility resting upon the governor to preserve law and order in his state. I am gratified by his constructive and co-operative attitude at our meeting. I have assured the governor of the co-operation of federal officials. . . .
>
> I am sure it is the desire of the governor, not only to observe the supreme law of the land, but to use the influence of his office in orderly progress to the plans which are already the subject of the order of the court.[12]

And the governor of Arkansas issued this:

> The President and I have had a friendly and constructive discussion of the problem of compliance with court orders respecting the high schools of Little Rock. This trip to Newport has been worthwhile from my point of view. I recognize that the situation called for clarification and I assured the President of my desire to co-operate with him in carrying out the duties resting upon both of us under the Constitution of Arkansas with the requirements of the federal Constitution.
>
> I have never expressed any personal opinion regarding the Supreme Court decision of 1954 which voted integration. That is not relevant. That decision is the law of the land and must be obeyed.
>
> At the time, it is evident even from the language of the decision itself that changes necessitated by court orders cannot be accomplished overnight.
>
> The people of Little Rock are law-abiding and I know that they expect to obey valid court orders. In this they shall have my sup-

port. In so doing, it is my responsibility to protect the people from violence in any form.

As I interpret the President's public statement, the national administration has no thought of challenging this fact. In meeting this obligation, it is essential in proceeding to implement the orders of the court that the complexities of integration be patiently understood by all those in federal authority as well as others.

When I assure the President, as I have already done, that I expect to accept the decisions of the court, I entertain the hope that the Department of Justice and the federal judiciary will act with understanding and patience in discharging their duties.[13]

(The *Edinburgh Scotsman* said: "The duty of the President is clear. He must maintain the law. . . ." The *Sydney Morning Herald* said: "The time for compromise is clearly at an end." The *Manila Herald:* "It is a test right in America's home grounds to determine how really sincere the American people are in their avowals of equal justice and fair play—a doctrine repeatedly dinned into the ears of their allies by American leaders." The *Mexico City Novedades:* "Arkansas' Faubus is a coarse exponent of a trend that would put to shame the most backward countries on earth." The *Times* of Indonesia: "Americans should ask themselves . . . whether Governor Faubus should not be hauled before the Un-American Activities Committee for alienating half the world from the United States." And *Al-Shara* of Beirut: "America Verges on Civil Rebellion.")

Thursday, September 19

Soldiers continued on guard against the entry of Negro pupils into Central High School, although, after the first week, the patrol had been reduced to less than fifty men and demonstrators were even fewer. The governor asked Judge Davies to remove himself from the bench Thursday for the hearing on the petition for injunction against Faubus *et al.,* because of "a personal prejudice against this respondent." The motion was denied.

Friday, September 20

At the beginning of the hearing in the federal court, the governor and the Guard officers, through their attorneys, filed a motion to dismiss, declaring:

(a) The petition is in truth and in fact an attempted action against the sovereign State of Arkansas. . . .

(b) This court is wholly without jurisdiction to question the judgment or discretion of the respondent, Orval E. Faubus, the governor of Arkansas, and other respondents subordinate to him, in performing their duties made mandatory upon them by the Constitution and the laws of Arkansas. . . .[14]

When this motion was denied, the governor's attorneys stalked out of the courtroom.

As the hearing proceeded, the federal government called eight of the hundred and five witnesses it had subpoenaed, including the school superintendent, the mayor and the chief of police of Little Rock, the principal of Central High School, the president of the school board, and three of the nine Negro children. No evidence that violence was imminent came from any of these witnesses.

Judge Davies concluded that the desegregation of Central High School had "been thwarted by the governor of Arkansas by the use of National Guard troops." He said: "It is equally demonstrable from the testimony presented here today that there would have been no violence in carrying out the plan of integration, and that there has been no violence." He ordered the respondents to cease "obstructing or preventing . . . the attendance of Negro students" at the high school.[15]

Three hours later Faubus ordered the Guardsmen to leave the school. In a broadcast that evening the governor said in part:

I have tried to follow a course that would preserve and maintain the peace and order in Little Rock and in the state. The calling out of the Guard and every order to its commander was designed to achieve that purpose. Now that a federal court, however, has chosen to substitute its judgment for mine as to how the peace and order should be preserved, I must temporarily at least abide and therefore I have issued orders that all units of the Arkansas National Guard stationed at the high schools in Little Rock be removed therefrom as soon as this can be accomplished. . . .

If by their own volition the Negroes would refrain from seizing upon that [court-declared] right to [attend the school] until such time as there is assurance that it can be accomplished in a peaceful manner as it has been in other sections of the state it would be an act of prudence and good judgment that would be applauded by a vast majority of the people. . . .

I appeal now for reason and clear thinking and good order. . . .
The public peace will be preserved. . . .[16]

Saturday, September 21

Commenting in Washington, President Eisenhower called the National Guard withdrawal "a necessary step in the right direction" and expressed confidence that the federal court orders would be executed promptly and without disorder. The *New York Times* had said on September 8 in "The News of the Week in Review": "If he [Faubus] withdraws the National Guard so that the Negro students can enter the high school, the battle will be over."

But with the tension and unrest that had been generated by this time the withdrawal of the Guard left a dangerous law-enforcement vacuum in Little Rock. Having noted earlier rumors of a possible troop withdrawal, Mayor Mann had asked the governor to notify him "twenty-four hours before such withdrawal is effected" in order that "proper preparations" might be made. Now, without warning, the responsibility for keeping the peace fell upon the mayor. Mann issued a confident statement saying that a "strong" force of police would be on hand at the high school to prevent any interference with orderly integration. Privately he expressed concern that the approximately one hundred city police available might not be able to cope with the situation.

Governor Faubus left by plane to attend a Southern Governors' Conference at Sea Island, Georgia. Stopping over in Atlanta, he attended a football game, along with several other governors, as a guest of Governor Griffin. When Faubus was introduced over the public-address system at Grant Field, the crowd rose and cheered—the hero image was taking shape. Asked by a reporter if he believed there would be violence in Little Rock on Monday, the governor answered: "I think so."

Sunday, September 22

The mayor spent most of Sunday conferring with Congressman Hays, and with a larger group that included Superintendent of Schools Virgil Blossom, Chief of Police Marvin H. Potts, Assistant Chief Eugene G. Smith, editor Ashmore, former Governor Sid McMath, and Ed Dunaway (Winthrop Rockefeller's attorney), over the problem of maintaining public order when schools opened on Monday.

Among various possibilities explored was the use of United States deputy marshals, and efforts were made to secure their aid at Central High School. Many have observed that if federal marshals in plain clothes had been used instead of soldiers the spectacle would have been vastly less provocative. In later years federal marshals would in fact be used freely to enforce desegregation rulings. But Attorney General Brownell decided against it.

Monday, September 23

The soldiers assigned by the governor to prevent the admission of Negroes to Central High School having been withdrawn, a white mob accomplished the same purpose by vicious and prolonged rioting. Many received an exaggerated impression of the magnitude of that convulsion. No one was seriously wounded. Maximum estimates placed the number in the crowd around the school at one thousand, and less than half of these were active participants; a few scattered fanatics drove through the city during the day seeking Negroes to harass. But the city was not in turmoil: more than 99 per cent of the people of Little Rock went quietly about their normal occupations. It was a shocking exhibition nonetheless, and it was conveyed swiftly and voluminously to the world. Cameras played on scenes of violence for half a day, while reporters gathered material for a hundred pen pictures of personalities and incidents.

The law-enforcement contingent numbered less than a hundred and fifty. (With one hundred additional men—federal marshals, for instance—the mob could have been held in check.) The brunt of the struggle was borne by city police, many of whom had friends among the rioters and shared their feelings; one patrolman walked away from his job and turned in his badge, but most of them, led by Assistant Chief Eugene Smith, labored with stubborn courage. At one point a handful of rioters got over the wooden barricade in front of the school, but a dozen policemen slowly forced them back. Outside the barricade the mob was completely out of hand.

The crowd was beginnning to gather around the school by 7 A.M.; it increased steadily as the morning wore on and excitement mounted. Rioting started when the final buzzer sounded for school classes at 8:45. The Negro children were slipped into the school by the delivery entrance. When this was discovered, the cry went up: "The niggers are in our school!" and the mob was seized with a screaming, howling frenzy. Any Negro was attacked on sight, but "Yankee" and Negro reporters were special targets of segregationist fury—of which several correspondents of *Life* magazine and four representatives of Negro publications were conspicuous victims. The most widely circulated photos were those of Alex Wilson, Negro editor of the Memphis *Tri-State Defender,* whose stoic dignity while being beaten, knocked down, and kicked in the stomach was impressive. At 11:30 school authorities decided to remove the Negro children for safety; this was accomplished in police cars. When the announcement that the Negroes had been removed was made over a loudspeaker the tumult began to subside.

Phone calls to the White House for help had received replies which were unilluminating but tersely suggestive of impending action. That afternoon the President issued the following proclamation:

I want to make several things very clear in connection with the disgraceful occurrences of today at Central High School in the city of Little Rock: They are:

1. The federal law and orders of a United States District Court, implementing that law, cannot be flouted with impunity by any individual or any mob of extremists.

2. I will use the full power of the United States, including whatever force may be necessary to prevent any obstruction of the law and to carry out the orders of the federal court.

3. Of course, every right-thinking citizen will hope that the American sense of justice and fair play will prevail in this case. It will be a sad day for this country—both at home and abroad—if school children can safely attend their classes only under the protection of armed guards.

4. I repeat my expressed confidence that the citizens of Little Rock and of Arkansas will respect the law and will not countenance violations of law and order by extremists.

Whereas certain persons in the State of Arkansas, individually and in unlawful assemblies, combinations, and conspiracies, have willfully obstructed the enforcement of orders of the United States District Court for the Eastern District of Arkansas with respect to matters relating to enrollment and attendance at public schools, particularly at Central High School, located in Little Rock school district, Little Rock, Arkansas, and

Whereas, such willful obstruction of justice hinders the execution of the laws of that state and of the United States, and makes it impracticable to enforce such laws by the ordinary course of judicial proceedings, and

Whereas, such obstruction of justice constitutes a denial of the equal protection of the laws secured by the Constitution of the United States and impedes the course of justice under those laws;

Now, therefore, I, Dwight D. Eisenhower, President of the United States, under and by the virtue of the authority vested in me by the Constitution and statutes of the United States, including Chapter 13 of Title 10, of the United States Code, particularly Sections 332, 333 and 334 thereof, do command all persons engaged in such obstruction of justice to cease and desist therefrom, and to disperse forthwith. . . .[17]

From Sea Island, Governor Faubus grieved at "the thing I sought to prevent happening" and called upon the people of Little Rock "to do everything possible to restore calm." But Governor McKeldin of Maryland said: "Governor Faubus wrote the book, set the stage, and directed the play for today's unhappy occurrences in Arkansas." [18]

Tuesday, September 24

The Negro students stayed at home Tuesday, and in the wake of the President's proclamation only about two hundred demonstrators gathered at the school. Some of the eleven arrests made were of persons recognized as participants in the violence of the previous day.

Secretary of Defense Charles E. Wilson called the 9936 officers and men of the Arkansas National Guard into federal service and rushed one thousand men of the 101st Airborne Division of the Regular Army to Little Rock. The first group of five hundred men flew from Fort Campbell, Kentucky, and arrived at the Little Rock Air Force Base near the city in midafternoon. At nightfall twenty-six vehicles, including trucks, half-tracks, and jeeps—filled with troops dressed in battle fatigue—drove up to Central High School.

Returning to Little Rock on Tuesday afternoon, Faubus said: "I feel like MacArthur. I have been relieved." (A few days later he would compare himself with General Robert E. Lee. An earlier reference to his "crucifixion" had suggested a more extravagant comparison.)

President Eisenhower had said in a press conference as late as

July 17: "I can't imagine any set of circumstances that would ever induce me to send federal troops into a federal court and into any area to enforce the orders of a federal court, because I believe that the common sense of America will never require it." Now, in a radio-television address to the nation, the President said in part:

> Whenever normal agencies prove inadequate to the task and it becomes necessary for the executive branch of the federal government to use its powers and authority to uphold federal courts, the President's responsibility is inescapable.
>
> In accordance with that responsibility, I have today issued an executive order directing the use of troops under federal authority to aid in the execution of federal law at Little Rock, Arkansas. This became necessary when my proclamation of yesterday was not observed, and the obstruction of justice still continues.
>
> It is important that the reasons for my action be understood by all citizens.
>
> As you know, the Supreme Court of the United States has decided that separate public educational facilities for the races are inherently unequal and therefore compulsory school segregation laws are unconstitutional.
>
> Our personal opinions about the decision have no bearing on the matter of enforcement; the responsibility and authority of the Supreme Court to interpret the Constitution are clear. Local federal courts were instructed by the Supreme Court to issue such orders and decrees as might be necessary to achieve admission to public schools without regard to race—and with all deliberate speed. . . .
>
> Proper and sensible observance of the law then demanded the respectful obedience which the nation has a right to expect from all the people. This, unfortunately, has not been the case at Little Rock. . . .
>
> At a time when we face a grave situation abroad because of the hatred that Communism bears toward a system of government based on human rights, it would be difficult to exaggerate the harm that is being done to the prestige and influence, and indeed to the safety, of our nation and the world. . . .
>
> If resistance to the federal court orders ceases at once, the further presence of federal troops will be unnecessary and the city of Little Rock will return to its normal habits of peace and order and a blot upon the fair name and high honor of our nation in the world will be removed.

Wednesday, September 25

The nine Negro children entered Central High School under troop escort. Major General Edwin A. Walker, commander of the Arkansas Military District, who directed the federal military operation, explained his mission to the press and lectured the white students before the arrival of the Negroes with fatherly sternness. (This distinguished soldier, who carried out his unpleasant assignment in Little Rock with notable efficiency, would figure in a sadly contrasting role in another desegregation crisis five years later.)

A sullen calm descended upon Little Rock.

Almost nobody was entirely happy over the use of the United States Army to enforce a school-desegregation order. The South seethed with indignation. The rest of the nation reacted in the main with a somber feeling of relief that the President had finally acted. There were divergent views of Eisenhower's performance during the earlier stages of the crisis, but a remarkable degree of unity in approving the use of military force in the situation which had developed on September 24. Approval was expressed by the two living former presidents, Hoover and Truman, by President Eisenhower's recent Democratic opponent, Adlai Stevenson, by many other public figures of both political parties, and by most of the press.

In foreign countries, where Little Rock had been prominent in the news since the end of August, the climactic events were followed with avid interest. Some of the earlier damage was offset by the exhibition of American military might being used to protect the rights of colored citizens. The Voice of America broadcast news of the troop intervention and President Eisenhower's radio-television speech in forty-three languages. The United States Information Agency sent the text of the address to its seventy posts abroad for distribution.

Governor Faubus nourished the growing bitterness in Arkansas with scurrility and canard. He accused federal troops of "bludgeoning innocent bystanders, with bayonets in the backs of little girls and the warm, red blood of patriotic American citizens staining the cold, naked unsheathed knives"; he charged that teen-aged schoolgirls had been taken by the FBI "and held incommunicado for hours of questioning." He addressed—and gave to the press—a letter to General Walker saying that he had "received a number of complaints from parents, mostly mothers, about your troops accompanying the girl students into their dressing rooms." The charges were hotly denied.

There was a universal desire, in which the administration expressly joined, to see the federal troops withdrawn from Little Rock at the earliest safe date. The Southern Governors' Conference appointed five of its members to negotiate with Faubus and the President to this end. One of the five, Griffin of Georgia—who applauded Faubus's performance—did not serve. The four others reached an understanding with Faubus and the President under which the former would give certain public assurances, after which the latter would order the troop withdrawal. On October 1 the White House issued the following statement:

> The President today met with four members of the committee representing the Southern Governors' Conference. These members were Governor LeRoy Collins of Florida, Governor Luther Hodges of North Carolina, Governor Theodore McKeldin of Maryland, and Governor Frank Clement of Tennessee.
>
> At the meeting the governors informed the President that the governor of Arkansas had authorized them to state that he is prepared to assume full responsibility for maintaining law and order in Little Rock, and, in connection therewith, will not obstruct the orders of the federal courts.
>
> The President stated that upon a declaration on the part of the governor of Arkansas that he will not obstruct the orders of the federal courts and will, in connection therewith, maintain law and order in Little Rock, the President will direct the Secretary of Defense to return the command of the Arkansas National Guard to the governor. Thereupon, as soon as practicable, all federal troops will be withdrawn.

Within two hours Governor Faubus issued this statement:

> At a meeting of a committee representing the Southern Governors' Conference this afternoon at the White House, the President was informed at my request that it has never been my intention to obstruct the orders of the federal courts, that the orders of the federal courts will not be obstructed by me, and that I am prepared, as I have always been, to assume full responsibility for maintaining law and order in Little Rock.
>
> This has been consistently my stand and viewpoint throughout the controversy.

On the basis of this assurance, the President has declared that the Arkansas National Guard will be returned to my command and thereafter as soon as practicable all federal troops will be withdrawn.

I now declare, that upon withdrawal of federal troops, I will again assume full responsibility, in co-operation with local authorities, for the maintenance of law and order, and that the orders of the federal courts will not be obstructed by me.[19]

President Eisenhower found this statement unsatisfactory. The four governors said that the wording had been changed from the text previously agreed upon. Governor McKeldin termed it "ignominious doublecrossing." The precise changes were never fully revealed (to avoid embarrassment in further efforts which might be made), but the President said in a press conference on October 3: "The message that came back must be read as a whole, and you will find that all the way through it says, 'As I have intended from the beginning,' meaning that anything stated in the telegram merely took the situation back to where it was before the federal troops arrived."

The President then issued this statement:

The statement issued this evening by the governor of Arkansas does not constitute in my opinion the assurance that he intends to use his full powers as governor to prevent the obstruction of the orders of the United States District Court.

Under the circumstances the President of the United States has no recourse at the present time except to maintain federal surveillance of the situation.

I want to commend the governors representing the Southern Conference for their co-operative attitude at their meeting today. I hope they will continue their efforts, as will the federal government, to bring about a basis for the withdrawal of the federal forces in Little Rock and for the orderly carrying out of the orders of the district court.[20]

A wave of sympathy with Faubus spread over the South, rising to boundless acclaim in extreme segregationist circles. The governor's soaring popularity in Arkansas would be attested by unprecedented majorities in coming elections. Southern bitterness toward President Eisenhower went beyond verbal fulminations: in Arkansas a United States Savings Bond Committee chairman and several Selective Service Board members resigned; Governor Timmerman of South Carolina resigned his commission as a member of the United States Naval Reserve. Thoughtful segregationist leaders in most of the South drew from Little Rock the salutary lesson—which would have a quiet effect upon future decisions—that all the power of the federal government stood behind the rulings of federal courts; and the counsel, "Remember Little Rock"—though it only aroused anger now—would within a few years be found a cogent argument for proceeding with court-ordered school desegregation. But the immediate effect was to embarrass or silence "moderates," increase race tension, and strengthen the position of the advocates of resistance in every political situation.

By the end of October the Negro pupils were attending Central High School without escort, and on November 27 the last Regular Army troops were withdrawn from Little Rock. A progressively shrinking detachment of the federalized National Guard continued its surveillance until the school year ended on May 27, 1958. Eight Negro children remained in school throughout the year, and one of them graduated with his class.

Chapter 11

THE SCHOOL-CLOSING
EXPERIMENT

The year 1958 was a year of virtual standstill in the movement to end public-school segregation in the South. Even the scattered desegregation initiatives in western Texas came to a halt before an obstruction erected by the legislature of that state in 1957. The Texas legislature prescribed that school funds would be withheld from any district in which desegregation should be undertaken without a prior expression of approval by a majority of the voters in a referendum election. In Little Rock and in three Virginia cities, schools serving approximately sixteen thousand pupils were closed to prevent the admission of Negroes to them. The action in Virginia was part of a bold program of so-called "massive resistance," the manifestations of which—between violent outbreaks elsewhere—had dominated the news from the South for long periods.

There was no violence over the school issue in Virginia—a fact which citizens of that state of all shades of opinion on the segregation issue recall with justifiable pride. Virginia went through the cycle of, first, hesitant acceptance of the Brown decision, then fierce defiance of the ruling, and, finally, substantial compliance with it, entirely without serious disorder. There was never a riot or a bombing, not even a fisticuff, in this connection in the Old Dominion. Yet Virginia during the first four years after the 1954 decision was probably more influential than any other state in setting the South upon a course of resistance; anguish, other than physical, was also suffered by many Virginians during that experience.

With Kilpatrick's interposition and Byrd's Southern Manifesto, Virginia threw down the gauntlet; and, as if in response, the initial pressure for enforcement of the desegregation ruling was focused mainly on that state. The NAACP was more active and had a larger membership in Virginia than in any other Southern state, and far more desegregation suits were in litigation there. In both the legal and the dialectic

146

sphere, Richmond, the Southern Confederacy's capital, and Virginia, the native state of General Robert E. Lee, became once more the battleground in a struggle between North and South. The nostalgic implications of Virginia's position as the northernmost bastion of this twentieth-century Southern rebellion gave a sentimental stimulus to its own political leaders and a certain authority to the Virginia example in the eyes of other Southern states. "If Virginia surrenders," Senator Byrd declared, "if the Virginia line is broken, the rest of the South will go down too." [1]

It is interesting that one Southern state, Virginia's contiguous neighbor North Carolina, was little impressed. A contrast in the general attitudes of those two traditional rivals has been noted by many observers, including Arnold Toynbee. [2] For example, North Carolina has made liberal use of the state's credit in developing highways and other public improvements, while Virginians have clung to a "pay-as-you-go" policy and have warned that North Carolina was moving down a primrose path to fiscal bonfire. Similarly North Carolina approached the problems posed by the Brown decision in a spirit disdainfully out of harmony with Virginia's "massive resistance." North Carolina adopted no interposition resolution, and local option—anathema to the massive-resistance proponents—was the cornerstone of the North Carolina plan.

In the South as a whole Virginia enjoyed a unique prestige—due perhaps to Virginia leadership in its diminished present as much as to its illustrious past. The Old Dominion had long been ruled by a genteel, respected line of politicians, and Harry Byrd was a Southern favorite, fondly put forward from time to time as a possible candidate for President of the United States. When the leaders of sedate, conservative Virginia defied the United States Supreme Court, other Southerners felt more comfortable in doing so too.

Resistance to the Brown decision was a natural impulse of many in the South, but the precise thing called "massive resistance" was both in name and concept a Virginia product. In its broadest reach it aimed at establishing a united front among the eleven former Confederate states. Senator Byrd regarded the Southern Manifesto as "a part of the plan of massive resistance we've been working on," and he envisioned the possibility "that some form of action" could "be accepted as a pattern for all." [3]

Another connotation of massive resistance—one that had a greater impact upon the course of events—was the concept of *total* resistance, or a united front, *within each state*. Paradoxically, the foremost champions of local option at the state level sought to extinguish local option at the level of smaller governmental subdivisions. Even before local option was suppressed by Virginia legislation, any county or city that showed signs of moving toward adjustment to the desegregation ruling incurred wrathful criticism and cries of "betrayal." When near the end of 1955 the school board of Arlington County drew up a tentative plan for desegregation of its public schools, the state legislature punished it by taking away the county's privilege of electing its school board by popular vote. A dozen counties in western Virginia, where the small Negro population presented only a minor problem, were thinking in terms of compliance with the desegregation ruling until the heavy hand of massive resistance descended upon them. A similar compulsion to conform to the lowest common denominator of race prejudice in the state prevented many other such communities in the South from clearing their comparatively easy desegregation hurdles; it has remained a major obstacle to beginnings of compliance in Alabama and Mississippi.

Local option on school desegregation was contemplated briefly in Virginia. The catalyst in that state's transition to the massive-resistance posture was an ambiguous proposition called the "Gray Plan." A commission set up by Governor Stanley, under the chairmanship of State Senator Garland Gray, to study the school problem labored fourteen months and produced in November 1955 two significant recommendations: a plan for issuing state tuition grants to enable pupils to escape racial integration by attending private schools; and a locally administered pupil-assignment law. Only the tuition-grant plan, which required a constitutional amendment, needed to be submitted to popular vote, but many moderates voted for the Gray Plan on the assumption that the principle of local option would be followed in the other legislation. Even so, the proposal met with strong opposition at first, but an unprecedented mobilization of segregationists and members of the Byrd organization resulted in a substantial victory at the polls. The campaign had raised resistance sentiment to a high pitch, and the outcome was hailed by the victors as a resounding expression of Virginia's determination to retain segregation. Interposition held the stage next, and local option was scuttled—buried so deep that it would not be resurrected until the courts struck down massive resistance four years later.

The tuition-grant plan and many other segregationist proposals were written into law—into twenty-three laws, to be specific—in a special session of the legislature convened for that purpose in September 1956. After a year of mounting fulminations, in which moderate voices were almost silenced, a majority of the legislators came prepared to vote for almost any bill thrown into the hopper designed to prevent desegregation or to harass the NAACP. The majority did not prove to be an impressive one in the initial test. House Bill No. 1, a proposal of Governor Stanley, had received the bulk of the advance publicity; it cut off state school funds from any district in which any Negro child should be admitted to a white school. This key bill received 61 to 37 votes in the House of Delegates, but it passed the Senate by only 21 to 17, and an eighteenth opposing senator, who was ill, let it be known that he would have attended the session if his vote should have been decisive. Nevertheless, it was evident that the massive-resistance faction was in firm control and little opposition was offered to the remaining twenty-two bills.

It is interesting in passing to examine the vote at the test which cleared the track for the massive-resistance legislation. The twenty-one senators voting for House Bill No. 1 represented districts containing little more than one million of the state's 2,581,555 white inhabitants (by the 1950 census); Virginia Negroes opposed the legislation with practical unanimity. With a more equitable pattern of legislative apportionment, which a Supreme Court ruling has since required, the massive-resistance aberration might conceivably have gone no further.

There is, indeed, much evidence to support the speculation that adjustment to the Brown decision would have been easier in Virginia than elsewhere in the South if the ruling political organization had decided to point the state in that direction. Catholic parochial schools and state institutions of higher learning in Virginia were desegregated without incident; Negroes represented only 22.2 per cent of the state's population, and in twenty-one counties and three cities Negro residents ranged from none at all to 5 per cent of the total population; and across the borders in Maryland, West Virginia, and the District of Columbia compliance had begun promptly after the Brown decision was handed down. A large element—and by far the most articulate element—of Virginians rallied to the banner of massive resistance with enthusiasm; but there is reason to believe that the reckless adventure was not favored by a majority of the people.

The twenty-three bills in the package passed in September 1956 included sixteen enactments dealing directly with the school-segregation problem, and seven aimed at the NAACP. One of the former was actually more drastic than House Bill No. 1: it would block school integration before the point of withholding funds could be reached. This Senate Bill No. 56 contained many complicated provisions which no one clearly understood, but the heart of it was the blunt command that in the event of the enrollment of any child of another race, "such school is closed and removed from the public-school system." Another measure established a single three-member board with the responsibility for assigning all pupils to public schools throughout the state. Against the event that somehow some white children might still find themselves with only integrated public schools to attend, the compulsory school-attendance law was repealed. The plan first adopted to help finance private-school education with tuition grants from public funds was to run into legal difficulties that would prevent the grants from being available to meet the need for which they were intended when public schools were closed.

During the next two years Virginians watched—nervously in the communities involved but with only casual interest in much of the state—while NAACP lawyers pushed doggedly on with litigation in federal courts for desegregation of schools in five Virginia districts. In November 1957 State Attorney General J. Lindsay Almond, Jr. was elected to succeed Stanley as governor. Committed to "oppose with every faculty at our command, and every ounce of our energy, the attempt to mix white and Negro children in our classrooms" [4]—and aided by the furor over Little Rock—Almond received 63 per cent of the popular vote; his Republican opponent was Ted Dalton, an enemy of massive resistance.

Opposition to the school-closing legislation was voiced by a few thoughtful leaders, including former Governor Colgate W. Darden, but the sentiment publicly expressed continued to be overwhelmingly in support of it. No major newspaper except the *Norfolk Virginian-Pilot* spoke out boldly against it. Yet few really believed that schools would be closed: most people felt that something—no one could say what—would happen to avert that calamity. In a glibly vague way, champions of massive resistance contemplated resort to private schools, but no significant steps were taken to expand the state's private-school facilities. Although the Defenders of State Sovereignty and Individual Liberties (the Virginia version of Citizens' Councils) was instrumental in the setting up in May 1958 of an organization, called the Virginia Education Fund, for promoting private-school projects, the initiative aroused little public interest and its fund solicitations brought only a meager response.

By the summer of 1958 the litigation in the Norfolk, Charlottesville, and Arlington County cases seemed clearly headed for final, unappealable court orders to desegregate schools come September. Moderates had been largely silenced or driven underground, but Arlington County, in the metropolitan area of Washington, D.C., had been conspicuously cold toward massive resistance, and it now became aroused. An Arlington Committee to Preserve Public Schools appeared and quickly rallied several thousand members. (It was the nucleus of a statewide organization which would develop after school-closing began.) There was talk of plans for massive demonstrations, even a taxpayers' strike, if Arlington schools should be closed by the state. But to the vast relief of the massive-resistance leaders, an Arlington explosion was averted by a district court ruling of September 17 allowing that county to postpone desegregation until mid-term. (A suit for the desegregation of schools in Newport News had been complicated and delayed by the merger of that city with the neighboring city of Warwick.)

The showdown came first in an unexpected quarter. In little Warren County in northwest Virginia, court action on a suit for school desegregation was consummated with a dispatch which remains a record for the South. Twenty-two Negro pupils applied for admission to Warren County High School in July; when their applications were rejected by the State Pupil Placement Board on August 29, NAACP lawyers filed suit in the federal district court in their behalf the same day; on September 8 Judge John Paul granted an injunction requiring the plaintiffs' admission to the school; and on September 12, just two weeks after the suit was filed, the order was made effective immediately by a refusal of stay by Judge Simon E. Sobeloff of the Circuit Court of Appeals. (The action was affirmed by the full Appeals court on September 27.) The Negro students were immediately enrolled in Warren High School effective Monday, September 15.

A few hours later lightning struck. That Friday evening, September 12, at 8:30 P.M., reporters were handed copies of the following notice which Governor Almond had sent to Superintendent Q. D. Gasque and the Warren County school board:

> Under compulsion of an order issued by the United States District Court for the Western District of Virginia, both white and colored children have been enrolled effective September 15, 1958, in the Warren County High School, located in the county of Warren.
>
> Pursuant to the provisions of Chapter 9.1 of the Code of Virginia, the Warren County High School is closed and is removed from the public-school system, effective September 15, 1958, and all authority, power, and control over such school, its principal, teachers, other employees, and all pupils now enrolled or ordered to be enrolled, will thereupon be vested in the Commonwealth of Virginia, to be exercised by the governor.
>
> Accordingly, by virtue of the authority vested in me as chief executive of the Commonwealth of Virginia, I will thereupon assume all power and control over such school and hereby request all local officials and all citizens to co-operate with the Department of State Police and local law-enforcement officers in the protection of public property and the security of public peace and order.
>
> You are requested to forthwith notify all teachers and other personnel connected with such school, and all parents and other persons having the custody and care of all pupils enrolled or ordered to be enrolled in such school, of this action.[5]

One thousand Warren County children were left with no school to attend. Meanwhile, the legal machinery ground inexorably on to desegregation orders and the harsh implementation of massive resistance in Charlottesville and Norfolk. On September 19, Governor Almond paraphrased his message to the Warren County school authorities and closed two Charlottesville schools, locking out over seventeen hundred pupils; on September 27 he closed Norfolk's six white high schools with an aggregate enrollment of approximately ten thousand.

These schools, be it noted, were not closed at the instance of the pupils or the parents involved, but in pursuance of an act of the Virginia legislature. The parents now set about frantically to find schools for their children to attend. Some who could afford the expense placed them in regular Virginia private schools, but the few dozen vacancies in these were quickly filled. Displaced Virginia students were sent to private or public schools as far away as Connecticut and California; exiles from Norfolk schools were scattered over twenty-nine states. (Ironically, some of the displaced white students from Virginia were accommodated in racially integrated schools!) The emergency was met most efficiently in Charlottesville, where two alert civic organizations organized classes in a new private school and in churches, homes, and miscellaneous vacant buildings, for more than thirteen hundred pupils. But by mid-October less than half of Norfolk's ten thousand displaced pupils had found schooling, and in Warren County only a hundred sixty-two of the schoolless children had been accommodated in improvised classes.

The liquidation of the public-school system, which massive-resistance enthusiasts had held out as an acceptable alternative to racial integration, had begun; presumably it might go on district by district as Negro plaintiffs and federal courts moved. But the showdown, when it came, revealed how largely the massive-resistance furor had been an emotional outlet rather than a matter of realistic planning. The state was not prepared for any substantial changeover to private schools. Where, for instance, were the private schools? It would take many years and hundreds of millions of dollars to provide private schools for Virginia's eight hundred thousand school children. Millions would be needed to provide adequately even for the students now locked out of public schools.

At 4:30 P.M. on that Friday evening, September 12, several hours before Governor Almond framed his notice to the Warren County school board, Governor Faubus signed a proclamation closing the four high schools of Little Rock. School doors were shut to 3698 pupils by the 1958–59 registration—2071 at Central High School, 731 at Hall, 717 at Horace Mann, and 179 at the Technical High School. Unlike the Virginia action, Faubus's order affected Negroes as well as whites: Horace Mann High School was a segregated school for Negroes.

The Little Rock move differed from the long-premeditated operation in Virginia in other ways. Faubus found his authorization in a bill which the Arkansas legislature had passed in a special session the previous month; it had lain on his desk until he signed it into law on that same fateful Friday, September 12. His immediate provocation was a refusal of the Supreme Court to allow a two-and-a-half-year suspension of racial integration at Central High School, which a federal district court had granted earlier.

The year's experience had far from reconciled the Little Rock populace to the mixing of white and Negro school children. In seeking the court's permission to withdraw the Negro students and postpone integration, the school authorities reported "chaos, bedlam, and turmoil" at Central during the past year; they testified that there had been thirty "nuisance fires" in the school building; that search parties had been organized on twenty-three occasions to look for hidden bombs; that firecracker explosions had been a constant distraction; and that two hundred pupils had been suspended and three expelled. They attributed the public hostility largely to the attitude of the governor and the legislature. (School-board chairman Wayne Upton testified that a consideration of the board in proposing January 1961 as the date for resumption of integration was the belief that by that time Governor Faubus would no longer be in office!)

The Arkansas statute required that school-closing be followed within thirty days by a referendum on the question of school integration. In the election, which was held on September 27, only the five polling places in Negro neighborhoods showed majorities for integration; the vote was 19,470 "against" and 7561 "for."

The governor said that "feelings" were "more intense" than when federal troops surrounded Central High School; that, if the troops should return, "they would be met this year by the cold fury of the people. . . ." Faubus, running in the August primary for an unprecedented third term, had received more votes than any other candidate for governor in the history of Arkansas—264,346 out of a total of 383,904 votes cast.

Little Rock delayed longer than the Virginia cities in settling down to private-school improvisations because of faith in an illusory scheme for simply transferring the high schools from public to private operation. In two broadcasts urging a vote against integration in the September 27 referendum, Governor Faubus had assured his hearers that this simple changeover plan was "sound and workable" and one to which "the advocates of the so-called 'law of the land' can have no objection." Accordingly, two days after the September 27 referendum, the school board signed a contract leasing the school properties to a newly formed "Little Rock Private School Corporation." But the United States Circuit Court of Appeals quickly issued an order blocking the transfer. Uncertainty existed for another six weeks—although hopes faded under repeated extensions of the restraining order—until the Appeals court on November 10 issued a formal decree enjoining the school board from "taking any further steps or action, without the approval of the district court, to transfer possession, control, or operation, whether directly or indirectly, of any of the senior high schools or any other property or facilities of the Little Rock School District, to any organization or person, for carrying on any segregated school operations of any nature. . . ."

However, due to greater public excitement and the fame which Faubus and the city had achieved the year before, Little Rock was somewhat more fortunate than the Virginia cities in raising outside funds to get private schools started. A fund-raising campaign was conducted by mail from the governor's office and contributions were received from sympathizers far and near: checks for $11,100 and $18,071 respectively were sent by two groups in Louisiana; a number of Mississippi communities sent smaller sums; $18.15 came from persons in Johannesburg, South Africa. By the end of October about $150,000 had been collected. Arkansas was also able, after some delay, to make tuition grants available to displaced students at the rate of $172.66 per year per pupil, according to a specified formula; the state began sending out payments late in November.

On October 21 the Little Rock Private School Corporation started classes for seniors in a building purchased from the University of Arkansas by a wealthy friend of Faubus for $50,900; some juniors and sophomores were accommodated later in two hurriedly purchased warehouses, bringing the corporation's total enrollment to about eight hundred and fifty. Protestant churches—Baptist, Episcopal, Methodist, and Presbyterian—carried a similar pupil load; the Baptist High School, meeting in two churches, enrolled about four hundred. Approximately six hundred and fifty white students attended schools outside the city, including four hundred and forty-nine in nearby county schools. By the end of October two-thirds of the white students were in classes of some kind. As for the Negro high-school students, about two hundred were able to enroll in segregated county schools, but nearly all of the remaining five hundred were left without schooling of any kind. Of the original nine Negro pupils who had attended Central High School, the five remaining in the city took the correspondence courses offered to high-school pupils by the University of Arkansas.

The thought of resort to segregated private schools as an ultimate recourse when federal court desegregation orders could no longer be warded off had been harbored by many in all sections of the South. Florida, Georgia, Louisiana, Mississippi, North Carolina and South Carolina, as well as Virginia and Arkansas, had legislation which could be used to close public schools in which racial integration might be imminent or might have taken place. (After the occurrences of September 1957, Florida, Texas, and Virginia adopted further so-called "Little Rock laws," requiring the closing of any schools patrolled by federal troops.)

Much of the school-closing legislation elsewhere was patterned after Virginia's, and Virginia was the first to carry into effect a state-wide plan. The Virginia experiment, therefore, was watched with particular interest. During the initial hysteria in that state some enthusiasm had been expressed over the move, even by the students and parents affected, but dissatisfaction mounted as the novelty of improvised classes wore off. The few private schools and all the makeshift arrangements fell far short of meeting the emergency. Little Warren County, though late getting started, in the end came nearest to finding classes for all of its displaced pupils; a single organization, launched in the spirit of a civic enterprise—and with much outside help—succeeded in setting up a segregated "Mosby Academy" and was providing schooling for nearly eight hundred pupils by the end of the year. But in Norfolk, Virginia's largest city, three thousand children were deprived of any schooling at all, and over four thousand were attending loosely organized tutoring classes, meeting in twenty-seven churches and synagogues and in basements, attics, living rooms, and the like. Many classes had been organized simply by groups of mothers, who would bring together a dozen or two dozen children, then find a teacher and a classroom for them. There was no evidence that the state, or even, for the most part, the communities affected, were grappling realistically with the stupendous problem of establishing private schools for masses of children.

A few enthusiasts, like the *Richmond News Leader,* argued that a proliferation of private schools, with their release from uniformity of curriculum and philosophy, was a desirable end even apart from the aim of preserving racial segregation, and they suggested that the South eventually might have this crisis to thank for an educational advance. Out of the confusion following the closing of public schools several more or less permanent private schools did emerge in the Virginia districts affected. But they served only a fraction of the local school population, and no broad trend developed. The Little Rock Private School Corporation dissolved after the 1958–59 school term. Elsewhere in the South there was no rush to private schools. The *Southern School News,* in its edition of November 1959, published the results of a survey which showed a steady, but not a sensational, growth of private-school enrollment in the South over the previous five years. The recent opening of a few new private schools in the Atlanta metropolitan area and in Montgomery, Alabama, was attributed in part to a fear of racial integration—or a fear of closed public schools —but reports from most Southern states indicated that such increase in private-school enrollment as had taken place had not been significantly affected by the segregation controversy.

The school litigation in Little Rock—which had raised hopes of a suspension of integration, then dashed them with the order which triggered school-closing—ripened in a stern and sweeping opinion of the Supreme Court of the United States. Designated *Cooper v. Aaron* (after William G. Cooper, a school-board member, and John Aaron, a Negro student), it was the most important pronouncement of the high tribunal on public-school desegregation next to the Brown rulings of 1954 and 1955.[6]

Incidentally, the Department of Justice—where Brownell had been succeeded by Attorney General William P. Rogers—was prepared to use federal marshals in the Little Rock school crisis in the fall of 1958. Over a hundred were on hand in early September to help insure an orderly operation if Faubus had allowed Central High School to reopen with the Negroes in attendance.

The Eighth Circuit Court of Appeals had reversed the district court's decision [7] allowing a "temporary delay" of integration at Central High School, and the case had gone to the Supreme Court on further appeal. After a lengthy review of the whole Central High School integration story, the Appeals court said: "We say the time has not yet come in these United States when an order of a federal

court must be whittled away, watered down, or shamefully withdrawn
in the face of violent and unlawful acts of individual citizens in opposition thereto." [8]

The Supreme Court order of September 12 was a simple affirmation
of the Appeals court decision, with the promise: "The expression of
the views supporting our judgment will be prepared and announced in
due course."

The opinion which the Supreme Court handed down September 29,
three times the length of the original Brown decision, reviewed the
whole school-desegregation attempt in Little Rock and then strength-
ened and amplified the Court's earlier rulings with the broad picture
of Southern resistance plainly in view. As for the predicament of the
Little Rock school board, the Court said:

> One may well sympathize with the position of the board in the
> face of the frustrating conditions which have confronted it, but
> regardless of the board's good faith, the actions of the other state
> agencies responsible for those conditions compel us to reject the
> board's legal position. . . .
>
> The constitutional rights of respondents are not to be sacrificed
> or yielded to the violence and disorder which have followed upon
> the actions of the governor and legislature.

The gentle tone of the 1954 and 1955 rulings was gone now, along
with some vagueness. To an armful of Southern plans for circumven-
tion of the desegregation ruling the Court struck a crushing blow:

> In short, the constitutional rights of children not to be discrimi-
> nated against in school admission on grounds of race or color de-
> clared by this Court in the Brown case can neither be nullified
> openly and directly by state legislators or state executive or judicial
> officers, nor nullified indirectly by them through evasive schemes for
> segregation whether attempted "ingeniously or ingenuously." . . .

Since the 1954 decision, John Marshall Harlan, William J. Brennan,
Jr., and Charles Evans Whittaker had been appointed to fill Supreme
Court vacancies. The opinion was signed by each member of the
Court, an unprecedented move to emphasize the justices' unanimity
and determination, and the Court observed:

> The basic decision in *Brown* was unanimously reached by this
> Court only after the case had been briefed and twice argued and
> the issues had been given the most serious consideration. Since the

first Brown opinion, three new justices have come to the Court. They are at one with the justices still on the Court who participated in that basic decision as to its correctness, and that decision is now unanimously reaffirmed. . . .

Justice Felix Frankfurter, "while unreservedly participating with my brethren in our joint opinion," appended an individual concurring opinion, from which several of the dicta of this sage and erudite jurist are excerpted below:

> Violent resistance to law cannot be made a legal reason for its suspension without loosening the fabric of our society.
> Local customs, however hardened by time, are not decreed in heaven.
> Compliance with decisions of this Court, as the constitutional organ of the supreme law of the land, has often, throughout our history, depended on active support by state and local authorities. It presupposes such support. To withhold it, and indeed to use political power to try to paralyze the supreme law, precludes the maintenance of our federal system as we have known and cherished it for one hundred and seventy years.

Representative Hays, who had labored to avert the Little Rock explosion in September 1957, was rewarded for his moderate attitude, in 1958, by defeat at the polls. A veteran congressman of extraordinary popularity in the nation, and hitherto in his district, which included Little Rock, Hays survived the Democratic primary but lost by a few votes in the November election to a write-in candidate and an uncompromising segregationist, Dr. Dale Alford.

Chapter 12

THE AGONY OF THE SOUTH

The gesture of abandoning public education testified no less than the rioting to the depth of the emotions which the Brown decision had aroused in the South. But neither gave more than an inkling of the sinister malaise which had seized a gallant and gracious people.

The outbreaks of domestic violence that attended school desegregation were not the bloodiest the nation had seen even in the twentieth century. (No one as yet had been fatally injured.) *Freedom to the Free,* the report of the Civil Rights Commission on the one hundredth anniversary of the Emancipation Proclamation recalled: ". . . During the last six months of 1919, there were some twenty-five race riots. During July there were three days of violence in the Nation's Capital. Later in the month, Chicago fell victim to thirteen days of lawlessness. The state militia was called out on the fourth day of the rioting. The Chicago death toll was thirty-eight—fifteen whites and twenty-three Negroes. . . ."

But the Southern challenge to federal authority in the 1950s was graver than any that had arisen since the Civil War; and with this kind of rebellion a fever spread over the disaffected region, a fever of conformity to a single line of thought and purpose and intolerance of dissent, which was reminiscent of its pre-Civil War reaction to the Abolitionist movement. A deterioration, not of public schools but of public enlightenment in a broader sense, and a popular distortion of human values were accompanying afflictions.

That liberties were taken daily with history, sociology, anthropology, theology, and current news to prove the segregationist thesis was not alarming in itself. There are controversial areas in which views on one side, even extreme views, of course, are properly to be heard. But unless the other side is allowed equal opportunity for expression, an intellectual imbalance results and inaccuracies of fact remain uncorrected. In the South in the late 1950s speakers opposed to racial segregation, however learned or distinguished, were scorned and seldom permitted to be heard; books which challenged racist theories were removed from school libraries; and teachers who questioned the wisdom of defying the Supreme Court's desegregation ruling were silenced or dismissed. In human relations, kindness and brotherly behavior, if they crossed the racial line, came to be regarded, not as virtues, but as transgressions; segregationists even found clergymen to support the assertion that "the so-called Fatherhood of God and brotherhood of man was repudiated by Christ. . . ." [1] The words "liberal" and even "moderate" became terms of reproach.

Meanwhile, anyone, white or colored, who protested against these things was persecuted in a variety of ways. The sickness was most pervasive in 1958 and early 1959; a cleansing breeze began to blow across the northern marches and headed southward in 1959, but the malady lingered and worsened for several more years in the Deep South, and in large areas it is present in a malignant form today.

Hodding Carter said in an address in Nashville, Tennessee, in May 1957: "The First Amendment to our Constitution is probably in more danger in the South today than are either our white or Negro children." Those who spoke out against resistance to the Supreme Court decision, or even called for constructive discussion of the problem, found themselves in uncomfortable situations, sometimes in physical danger. A dissenter from the segregationist line often found former friends unwilling to associate with him; even if privately sympathetic, they feared the consequences of this identification. An outspoken dissenter was likely to be harassed by insulting phone calls and might find rocks thrown in his window or garbage piled on his doorstep; in some instances hostility was expressed in dynamite explosions.

In a decision invalidating three of Virginia's "anti-NAACP laws" a federal court described the situation existing in that state in 1958 in the following language:

> . . . The agitation involved in the widespread discussion of the subject, and the passage of the statutes by the legislature, have had a marked effect upon the public mind, which has been reflected in hostility to the activities of the plaintiffs in these cases. This has been shown not only by the falling off of [NAACP] revenues, indicated above, but also by manifestations of ill will toward white and colored citizens who are known to be sympathetic with the aspirations of the colored people for equal treatment, particularly in the field of public education. A number of white people who attempted

to give aid to the movement by speaking out on behalf of the colored people, or by taking membership in the Association, or joining the complainants in school suits, have been subjected to various kinds of annoyance. When their names appeared in the public press in connection with these activities, they were besieged day and night by telephone calls which were obscene, threatening, abusive, or merely silent interruptions to the peace and comfort of their homes. Letters and telegrams of like nature were also received. Some of these persons found themselves cut off by their friends and made unwelcome where they had formerly been received with kindness and respect. Two crosses were burned near the homes of two of them; an effigy was hung in the yard of a white plaintiff in a school case, and a hearse was sent to the home of the colored president of the Norfolk branch of the Association during his absence "to pick up his body." [2]

Many agencies were working against race discrimination in the South now. Among the militant organizations, in addition to the NAACP, the Congress on Racial Equality, or CORE, established in 1942, was expanding its activities and would soon be in the forefront of campaigns to end segregation in transportation facilities and places of public accommodation. The National Urban League, which had fought against discrimination in the United States since 1910, placed its major emphasis upon securing equal employment opportunities for Negroes. Another mainly Negro organization, the Southern Christian Leadership Conference, devoted to the philosophy of nonviolent protest preached by its founder, the Reverend Martin Luther King, had grown out of the bus boycott in Montgomery, Alabama.

Apart from the predominantly Negro groups, a score of organizations, generally bi-racial but in which white people, many of them Southerners, took a leading part, had offices in the region and were engaged in combating race discrimination. These received their funds from membership dues and individual contributions, from churches and trade unions, and above all from the philanthropy of national foundations. Only a small fraction of their financial support came directly from the South.

The Southern Regional Council was, by name and charter, strictly Southern: its officers and the eighty members of its bi-racial board, as well as nearly all of its full-time staff, then of about fifteen, were from the South. Affiliated with it were nine bi-racial Councils on Human Relations in various Southern states.

Two of the national organizations which concerned themselves most with the Southern problem were the Anti-Defamation League of B'nai B'rith and the American Friends Service Committee. The Quakers had been known for their efforts on behalf of the Negro for a century and a half; in this crisis they labored systematically to ease tensions and prepare communities for the abandonment of segregation. The Anti-Defamation League, with offices in Richmond, Atlanta, Miami, New Orleans, and Houston, engaged in much valuable research and campaigned unceasingly against racial injustice. The American Jewish Committee was active in the quiet mobilization of influential community leaders in support of social change.

A number of denominational religious organizations had departments, committees, or societies devoted to work in this field. The Department of Racial and Cultural Relations of the National Council of Churches of Christ contributed to the cause in many ways, particularly through its chief Southern representative, the Reverend Will D. Campbell, a man of rare ability and dedication.

Jewish organizations had a twofold concern over the segregationist furor in the South. Anti-Semitism was officially disavowed by the Citizens' Councils, but it was preached by many racist individuals and publications. Mysterious dynamite explosions damaged Jewish community centers in Miami and Nashville in March 1958 and wrecked a Jewish temple in Atlanta the following October.

The number of these reformers was still minute in comparison with the multitude of aggressive segregationists, but they crusaded openly and they were subjected to criticism and harassment in varying degrees. Many were vilified or derided in segregationist publications; they had difficulty sometimes in obtaining office space; some were arrested on trumped-up charges and briefly imprisoned.

Apart from the active personnel of organizations committed to the fight, many men of moderate or liberal views in the South wrestled with the dilemma of whether to speak out and take the consequences or to compromise and remain silent in the hope of being able to exert a salutary influence in private or at some later stage of the crisis. Newspaper editors feared loss of circulation, politicians feared loss of votes, clergymen feared loss of communicants, if they deviated from segregationist orthodoxy. And these were not entirely selfish considerations: readers, voters, and hearers were needed if they were to retain any influence.

No group suffered more anguish than the white Christian ministers. Many felt when public-school segregation was outlawed by the Supreme Court that a problem partaking so much of morals and conscience, and so rooted in the hearts of men, was logically one for the clergy, and that the pastors of churches should lead in preparing Southerners for the change. It seemed at the outset that the clergy might assume that responsibility. Two days after the appearance of the Brown decision on May 19, 1954, the General Board of the National Council of Churches of Christ in the United States of America hailed the Supreme Court's pronouncement as offering the "promise of further steps for translating into reality Christian and Democratic ideals." In June the Southern Baptist Convention recognized that the decision was "in harmony with the constitutional guarantee of equal freedom to all citizens, and with the Christian principles of equal justice and love for all men." The General Assembly of the Presbyterian Church in the United States (Southern) affirmed that "enforced segregation of the races is discrimination, which is out of harmony with Christian theology and ethics and that the church . . . should lead rather than follow." [3] Episcopalians, Lutherans, Congregationalists—virtually all major Protestant denominations—took similar positions at the administrative level.

The Roman Catholic hierarchy strongly supported the Brown decision, and steps were taken to accelerate the removal of racial barriers in the remaining all-white Catholic hospitals and parochial schools. The desegregation of the huge parochial system of New Orleans would be delayed until 1962, but Archbishop Joseph Francis Rummel began early to prepare that archdiocese, declaring in 1956 that "racial segregation is morally wrong and sinful." In November 1958 the Catholic Bishops of the United States expressed the earnest and prayerful hope "that responsible and sober-minded Americans of all religious faiths, in all areas of our land, will seize the mantle of leadership from the agitator and the racist. . . ." [4]

Jewish leadership and all major Jewish organizations vigorously supported the Brown decision.

But Southerners were not easily to be led in this matter, not even by their spiritual leaders. The Charleston, South Carolina, Presbytery, representing thirty Presbyterian churches in the area, withheld its financial support from the National Council of Churches and urged the Presbyterian General Assembly to withdraw from it. More or less similar action was taken by a number of Baptist, Methodist, and Presbyterian Churches in the South. Some repudiated the stand taken by the national church bodies of their own denomination; many Baptist churches disassociated themselves from the pronouncement of the Southern Baptist Convention. Striking out in other directions, a South Carolina Methodist Men's Club applauded the actions of Governor Faubus and Governor Almond "against the un-Christian and evil forces of the Supreme Court and the federal government . . ."; [5] and the Carolina Baptist Fellowship, an organization of ministers, took Evangelist Billy Graham to task for his pro-integration leanings.[6]

A number of ministers, though a tiny minority of the Southern clergy, joined the segregationist chorus. The Right Reverend Albert S. Thomas, retired Episcopal bishop of South Carolina, was among those defending segregation,[7] and the Reverend James P. Dees, pastor of the Statesville Episcopal Church, headed North Carolina's principal segregationist organization.[8] Important meetings of Citizens' Councils and like groups were rarely without a clergyman to invoke God's blessing on their deliberations.

Some ministers championed segregation fervently and with apparent conviction. The obsolescent myth that God, through Noah, through Ham, through Canaan, had put a curse upon the Negro race—so widely used to defend slavery in the South before the Civil War—was brought out now and then; the Tower of Babel story and a collection of New Testament passages were more popular: did not St. Paul himself say that "God hath made of one blood all nations of all men . . . and determined . . . the bounds of their habitations"? Other ministers used more mundane arguments or merely decried the desegregation movement itself as being a source of contention and strife.

Many clergymen in the late 1950s admitted privately that segregation was morally wrong, took that position freely in meetings of known moderates, and joined fellow clergymen in public pronouncements condemning it—yet avoided mention of the subject from their own pulpits. They contributed to the impressive lists of signers of ministerial pleas for sanity which came forth in Richmond, Atlanta, Dallas, and other Southern cities. Apart from personal considerations, these ministers endured what the Reverend Robert Paul Sessions described as the "dreaded agony . . . of having to choose between protecting the organized church we love and proclaiming the universal gospel we believe." For, as this Arkansas pastor observed: "There are places in the South where a clergyman's forthright advocacy of even gradual integration might mean not only his own dismissal but the wholesale withdrawal of members from his church." [9]

At the same time the South abounded in examples of ministers who preached the gospel of interracial brotherhood with saintly, and often heroic, dedication; and of clergymen who labored openly in organized efforts to combat race prejudice. In the infinite variety of local situations many such ministers were able to hold their congregations; but many others were forced to seek pastorates elsewhere, generally outside the South. A Methodist minister in Alabama, Presbyterian, Baptist, and Episcopal ministers in Georgia, a Presbyterian minister in Mississippi, Baptist ministers in Arkansas and Virginia, indicated disapproval of segregation and were forced out of their pastorates in well-publicized incidents. The approach to the subject in these instances generally had been mild: one pastor had opposed the circulation of segregationist literature at a laymen's meeting; another had written an article advocating a "creative contact between leaders of both races," and one had proposed a panel discussion of the segregation problem at a joint meeting of white and Negro ministerial associations. Other liberal clergymen aroused antagonism among their congregations that necessitated their "voluntary" resignation; many were separated from their pastorates as being "ineffective" or "doctrinally unsound" when the dissatisfactions arose from their failure to uphold racial segregation.

The persecution or the ouster of the pastor was often due to an aggressive element, not a majority, of the congregation. Writing in the *New York Times Magazine* of September 27, 1959, Ralph McGill had sharp words for these rebellious laymen and their prompters:

> . . . These all-out segregationists unhesitatingly put the separation of the races ahead of Christian teaching, law, or moral principle.
>
> With an example before them of public officials' defiance of the courts on school integration, they find it easier to bomb churches and schools, to defy Christian teaching and church policies, and to make life miserable, if not impossible, for any minister who seeks to follow his conscience, secular law, and church policy. Publications by extremist states' rights groups and White Citizens' Councils repeatedly urge that "weak-kneed preachers" be "whipped into

line" by the withholding of contributions. They sneer at the clergy of all faiths, saying, "Money talks and they all listen."

In an address to a Southern Presbyterian Men's Convention, held in Miami in mid-October of 1957, Governor Collins of Florida unburdened himself in a manner rare for a Southern political leader of this period:

> Last spring in our state legislature a resolution was introduced in the heat of all this racial controversy. It was a resolution that struck at the very vital concept of law and government. It was anarchistic in its very nature. It defied all those things that we as patriots have tried to preach and practice over the years. I took the position that passage of that sort of legislation would stultify our state. I so hoped that some bar association, lawyers who knew better, in our state or somewhere, would say, "Don't do that!" But the mob was howling, so they washed their hands of it and they said, "See to it yourself."
>
> Months back in one of our towns here in Florida we had a woman doctor, one of our public health doctors who served three towns. She needed to have a conference with the Negro nurse who worked under her supervision. All of her day was filled with appointments and she couldn't find the time for that conference, so she asked the Negro nurse to meet her in the back of an eating place downtown where they could have a sandwich and discuss their work. And they did meet and they ate a sandwich together as they discussed professional matters.
>
> The people heard about it and the mob gathered. Citizens went down to the county commissioners of the town and of the other two counties and cried, "Fire her! She has violated the traditions and customs of the Southland. Fire her!"
>
> Where in that situation were our Presbyterians? Where were our Methodists? Our Episcopalians? Where were all of our churchmen? Where were all of our people who are dedicated to this proposition of *All for Christ?* Did they go before these county commissioners and say, "Don't! This is wrong!"? No, they called for the bowl, and they washed their hands, and they said, just as Pontius Pilate said, "The blood of this innocent, righteous person won't be on my hands. See to it yourself." And she was fired, to the everlasting shame of our citizens.[10]

We have already seen how largely hostility to the Brown decision dominated the business of government in the eleven Southern States.

Here the evasion and chicanery of respected leaders were symptomatic of the general malaise. With a disingenuousness which became routine, innumerable plans were advanced for excluding Negroes from white schools "for reasons other than race." The sophistry that race segregation was not in fact practiced—to which even university presidents lent themselves—was sometimes used to defend the status quo in federal court litigation.

In electoral contests the issue of race segregation was paramount; and the question generally was not whether a candidate was for or against segregation, but which candidate was most blatantly and uncompromisingly prepared to cling to segregation at all costs. The expression "niggering" was used in some sections of the Deep South to denote the kind of appeal to race prejudice which a lower order of politicians found effective in getting votes. At more respectable levels the execrations were focused on the NAACP, the Supreme Court, "liberals and do-gooders," and, in 1957–58, the federal troops at Little Rock. It might be said that the fiery, anti-integration fulminations which politicians felt were necessary must have been a reflection of voter sentiment. But that is not an entirely accurate assumption. Unquestionably a majority of white Southerners preferred segregation; how many were prepared to flout federal court orders, however, and go to reckless lengths to prevent the admission of any Negro to any white school nobody knew. What concerned the politician was the fact that it was the aggressive extremists who made the most noise— and brought the most voters to the polls. The harassed moderate was likely to cast only his single, silent vote.

The diligence of segregationists in fostering race prejudice and stifling dissent oppressed Southern education from the grammar school to the university level.

The professor faced a dilemma similar to that of the clergyman. Many members of university and college faculties who abhorred the prevailing hysteria felt they could serve best by exercising caution and continuing in their jobs; but many others resigned, and some were dismissed. To teach history, sociology, political economy, or law with fidelity both to truth and to the Citizens' Council syndrome was patently impossible. The *Southern School News* reported fifteen instances of white professors leaving Southern universities apparently because of their liberal views. These were only the most publicized cases; a large number with liberal views on the race question left the South without announcing their reason for doing so. It was not hard for professors to find employment in a freer atmosphere. Jim Hall, writing in the *Montgomery Advertiser* of August 26, 1957, attributed "the loss of some thirty or more top-notch educators" from the faculty of the University of Alabama following the Autherine Lucy incident in part to "the letters and telegrams students and faculty get signed by the Ku Klux Klan and persons claiming membership in the White Citizens' Councils; the midnight threats and voices who identify themselves as members of the KKK; the numerous letters 'threatening' the school if it ever integrated," and "the many meetings the Klan held menacingly close to the university campus, at which university professors and students were denounced as 'pinko,' 'red,' 'brainwashed,' and 'Communist.' "

Following the resignations in 1956 of Dr. Douglas S. Ward, acting dean, and Dr. B. J. Chandler, associate professor, of the School of Education at the University of Virginia—two who had openly advocated gradual desegregation of Virginia's public schools—Colgate W. Darden, Jr., the university's president and a former governor of the state, said: ". . . If I were a non-Virginian, I don't think I'd want to come in here for the next ten or fifteen years. I don't blame these men." [11]

A number of professors were forced to leave when their liberal leanings on the segregation issue were revealed in an article written for publication in a magazine or in a lecture delivered at some distant place. Yet it is not to be inferred that many college presidents, or even trustees, willingly sacrificed liberal professors or yielded without a struggle to extremist pressure. In the Deep South, where most of the oustings occurred, some university officials fought stubbornly and with much diplomacy in unpublicized battles with politicians and leaders of segregationist groups to defend the intellectual integrity of their institutions. As a result, some valued professors were able to stay with their classes even though they persisted in voicing liberal convictions.

Liberal initiative on the part of students met with cautious reprimand from university authorities and harsh reprisals off the campus. A minority, but in some colleges a very substantial number, did not share the segregationist craze, and some of them threw aside restraint. Raymond L. Morton, a 23-year-old English major, wrote in the *Game-*

cock, the student newspaper at the University of South Carolina: "Speak we must, else the throat choke and burst with silent truths. . . . Unconsciously, we have been smothered and strangled with tradition, the so-called 'Southern' tradition, a backward-looking and odious attitude. . . . For several years I have been a page in the state legislature. . . . Arrested by the decision of 'nine old men' on the United States Supreme Court, they are intent on circumventing. . . ." He was quickly fired from his job as a page in the state legislature.[12]

A frequent source of faculty and student resentment was the canceling by university authorities, under extremist pressure, of the speaking engagements of lecturers when their disapproval of race segregation was discovered. The Reverend Albert Kershaw, a noted Episcopal divine from Ohio, was invited to speak during "Religious Emphasis Week" of 1955 at the University of Mississippi. When it was learned that the clergyman, who had won $32,000 on a television quiz program, had donated the sum to the NAACP, the invitation was withdrawn. The student newspaper, *The Mississippian,* reflecting a spirit of independence still present among the students of "Ole Miss," protested: ". . . Students attend a university to increase their knowledge, gather information through freedom of speech and inquiry, and formulate their own opinions. How is this possible when they are coddled like children? . . ." But in the state capital the *Jackson Daily News* called the young editors to order, saying: "The Citizens' Council of Mississippi has asked that the invitation be withdrawn because it sincerely believes that any man who gives aid or comfort to the NAACP is an open enemy of the Southern way of life and is arrayed in opposition to the things we hold near and dear. . . . There is no escape from the logic of that reasoning." [13]

The intimidation of administrators and teachers in white public schools was almost complete. A few teachers were dismissed or "not rehired" at the end of the term; state law in some cases required the dismissal of any teacher advocating integration. A white-haired, 64-year-old schoolteacher in Georgia was dismissed (although reinstated after an outcry over such treatment of a beloved figure) for allowing a white lad to ride home on a bus with Negro children after the bus carrying white children had left! After the dominant attitude hardened, it was rare indeed that any murmur against the prevailing trend was heard among white public-school personnel. Most of these public servants, who could not well do without their generally modest teacher salaries, were careful to avoid any mention of the subject; though those who upheld race segregation, of course, were unmolested.

Intimidation of Negro educators focused on preventing school personnel and college faculty members from joining the NAACP or participating in other pro-integration activities. A number of teachers were dismissed because of their refusal to sign statements inquiring as to NAACP membership. Some lost their jobs because members of their families had signed petitions seeking admission to white schools.

Many school libraries were investigated and "purged" by governmental agencies and private organizations to see that children did not have access to "subversive" literature. Books expressing views liberal on the subject of race relations or critical of "the Southern way of life"—even views generally accepted outside the South—were considered "subversive." The Georgia Board of Education rejected a textbook on sociology which had been recommended by its professional textbook committee because, according to the newspaper report, it taught "that the white people are unfair to the Negroes in elections, in school facilities, and in recreation facilities." The banned book was *Our Changing Social Order,* by Ruth Wood Gavian, H. A. Gray, and Ernest Groves.[14] The two houses of the South Carolina legislature adopted a concurrent resolution asking the State Library Board to take out of circulation "certain books, such as *The Swimming Hole, . . .* that are inimical to the traditions and customs of our state." *The Swimming Hole* is an illustrated children's book which depicts white and colored boys swimming together. In supporting the resolution, State Senator L. Marion Gressette said such books "only confuse and warp the thinking of our young people." Asked if the resolution would "cover magazines and newspapers," Gressette replied: "As for myself, I stopped subscribing to the *Saturday Evening Post, Time, Life,* and other publications" favoring compliance with the Brown decision.[15] *Time, Life,* and *Look* were banned from high-school libraries in several Louisiana parishes. A New Orleans Citizens' Council warned parents that a history textbook was being prepared for use in the eighth grade in which "Booker T. Washington and George Washington Carver are hailed as heroes and saviors of the South, but evidently the author could find no whites worthy of mentioning." The school board announced that the book in question

(*The United States—Story of a Free People,* by Samuel Steinburg) would not be considered.[16] Even in Virginia, the South's northernmost state, pressure was exerted on school authorities to keep library offerings "pure." On March 14, 1958, the PTAs of the Staunton River District, comprising five Virginia counties, adopted what the segregationist magazine *The Virginian* termed "a set of constructive resolutions which should serve as a model to similar groups throughout the nation." The resolutions exhorted parents to:

> Read carefully all textbooks being taught in high school and grades for any instances of author depreciation of Southern heritage or its past and present leaders. . . .
>
> Search into the background, aims, and goals of all youth or young people's movements and organizations, directly or indirectly associated with education, which attempt to destroy Southern social customs.

Under Citizens' Council pressure, the Mississippi Board of Education in October 1959 withdrew from circulation a film on tolerance, which had been used by the audio-visual division for six years. The film, entitled "The High Wall," was made by the Anti-Defamation League and donated by the state B'nai B'rith. The latter's president, Robert Besser, commented: "No one found anything objectionable in the film when we presented it to the state six years ago, but, of course, that was before the Citizens' Councils were organized." [17]

As for television, commercial stations withheld many national programs dealing with segregation and the race problem from Southern viewers.

The Citizens' Council, the official organ of the Citizens' Councils of America prepared "A Manual for Southerners," which appeared serially during 1957 in that publication. This instruction was addressed to school children. Installments were introduced with an editorial note such as: "The portion appearing in this issue is for use in grades 3 and 4. However, there are many adults who might benefit from a review of these fundamental truths." Or: "The purpose of this series is to impart to our children (and some adults too) a true understanding of their origins and the reasons for our bi-racial society."

After several installments of the series, *The Citizens' Council* said in its May 1957 issue:

> Public reaction to "A Manual for Southerners" has been both keen and widespread, indicating great concern with this long-neglected field of education.
>
> If you want your local Citizens' Council to undertake a project that will get some real results, why not suggest that copies of your official paper containing sections of "A Manual for Southerners" be requested from this office for distribution, with permission of the teachers of course, to elementary school pupils in your community?
>
> Some Councils have since last fall made it a project to mail copies of *The Citizens' Council* to the high-school seniors in their counties during their senior year.
>
> Several teachers are requesting bundles of *The Citizens' Council* for classroom discussion as monthly current events assignments.

The authors of the "Manual" had difficulty in stretching a limited number of "truths" over so lengthy a series, and the little nuggets of racist doctrine, which appeared about twenty-five to an issue, were endlessly redundant. A few selected paragraphs, which give the gist of this indoctrination, are quoted below. They are of interest as indicating in simple language the thinking of many thousands of white Southerners and the kind of instruction imparted—more at home than at school—to their children.

> God put the white people off by themselves. He put the yellow, red, and black people by themselves. God wanted the white people to live alone. And He wanted the colored people to live alone. That is why He put them off by themselves.
>
> God made so many different things. He must like for things to be different. And we must keep things as God made them. Races of men are different colors. Some people do not think God made men different. But we know God did make men different.
>
> You do not go to the same schools. You do not swim in the same swimming pools. Negroes use their own bathrooms. They do not use the white people's bathroom. The two races do not sit together on the city bus. If you are white, you go to a white man's show. A Negro goes to his own show. We do not live side by side. The Negro has his own part of town to live in. This is the Southern Way of

Life. This is the way Negroes and whites can live in the same land. We do not live together.

"Why do some people want us to live together?" you will ask. They want to make our country weak. If we are not happy, our strong and free country will grow weak. Did you know our country will grow weak if we mix our races? It will.

One thing that made the Americans so mad at England was her terrible idea of slaves. English merchants wanted to make money. They bought Negro slaves from Negro masters in Africa and brought them to America to sell them. The Americans said, "We do not want black men in our country. They will not be happy among white people, and we will not be happy among them." But King George wanted his merchants to make money. So the Americans were made to buy the Negro slaves.

Many white parents saw that Ike's government is going to force the races to mix in Washington. So these parents took their unhappy children and moved out of Washington, D.C. And Negroes are moving to our nation's capital by the thousands. Before the races were mixed, Washington schools had many more white students. Now that the races are mixed, our capital's schools are mostly black. Do you blame the white people for moving away from a city where they were forced to go to school with Negroes?

But the Race-Mixers are forcing us to mix our races in America. Most of the people don't want to mix the races. So you see, the Race-Mixers are like the Communists. They are a few men who want to make the rest of our people be slave to them and do as they say. These people are trying to change our way of life. They know we will be unhappy if we change. Then our country will not be strong.

Some of you have been told that you are not a Christian if you don't want to mix with another race. This is not true, either. The Bible teaches you to keep the races pure. In Acts 17:26 you can read God's plan about the races. It says that God segregated (separated) the races by putting them in different part of the world.

The first civilized nation in the world that we know about was Egypt. The Egyptian people of that time were pure white people. So you see that the white people built the first civilization on earth. These Egyptian white people were careful to build a strong nation they could be proud of. Even today we are surprised at some of the wonderful things they did.

But about the time the Egyptians had built a wonderful country, they brought Negro slaves among them. It was not long before the Race-Mixers of those days began saying the slaves should be set free among the white Egyptians. And finally the Egyptians set the Negro free, cleaned him up, and taught him in their schools.

Now you can already guess what happened to the Egyptian nation. Since the races were mixed, the people began marrying one another. Then the Egyptian race was no longer pure, and their nation was no longer strong. A mixed race is weak and all confused, and this makes the country weak, as we have already learned.

Let's look at another very great civilization in the early world. This civilization grew in India. But the people were white people just as you and I are. They were not the Indians you see in India today. They were called Hindus.

The Hindus built a very beautiful, high civilization and a strong nation. They kept themselves segregated from the negroid natives who lived around them. But just as always, the Race-Mixers got busy and said the negroid natives ought to be free among the white Hindus. So finally the white Hindus let the natives go free among them, cleaned them up, and educated them in their white schools.

You can surely guess by now what happened to the High civilization of the white Hindu. He began to marry the cleaned and educated native, and so his race was mixed. What happens to a race when it mixes with another race? Well, the Hindu race became weak, and the nation was no longer strong and beautiful.

If this is not enough to show that Race-Mixing is not good for us, let's look at still another great white nation that fell because it mixed its people. This civilization was Greece. Again the white man built a civilization that could not be beaten. Again the Race-Mixers got busy. And again the white people set the slaves free among them, cleaned them up, and educated them in their schools.

You understand now why the races should not mix and why we Southerners want to keep our own Way of Life. And you must learn your lessons well so that you can help keep your race and nation pure. As long as we are pure, we can keep a strong nation which we can be proud of. We can enjoy the nation George Washington, Jefferson, Madison, and many other Southerners helped to build for us to live in. We do not want the Race-Mixers and Communists to take our country from us.

Not only was the South separated in many ways from the mainstream of national life and thought, but there was in varying degrees an atmosphere of actual alienation from the rest of the country, particularly as it was represented in "the government in Washington." A non-Southerner sojourning in Mississippi or Alabama often felt as if he were in a foreign land. The federal government, under both Republican and Democratic administrations, was referred to by many Southern politicians as if it were a foreign power. Perhaps it would be closer to the precise concept to say that segregationist agitators pictured the South as still a component of the American Union, but standing firm, alone, against a nefarious and largely foreign conspiracy that had seized control of the nation. Many actually believed the frequent assertions "that the enemy has taken over completely in Washington, D.C., and that we are right now living under the Communist Revolutionary Government." [18]

In 1959 *The Citizens' Council* undertook to identify the composite "enemy" of the South. Under the heading "HERE IS THE ENEMY," in its November issue, it listed seventy-four national organizations and agencies, public and private; the following August, under the heading "HERE IS THE ENEMY—PART II," it listed thirty-three. The first was described as "the official list of organizations appearing in House and Senate committee records as favoring 'civil rights' and anti-South force legislation during 1957 and 1959." The organizations in the second list were said to have been "the source of the 'civil rights' planks in both the Democratic and Republican platforms." Allowing for some repetition, the aggregate comprised nearly one hundred national groups. Organizations primarily concerned with civil rights were cited of course, but the list as a whole was a startling revelation of how largely the Citizens' Councils had assumed an attitude of belligerency toward the government and people of the United States.

Blacklisted were twenty-seven national Protestant, Catholic, and Jewish church and religious organizations. The National Council of Churches was included; "The Methodist Church" was listed as such.

Thirteen labor unions were listed; also the National Newspaper Publishers' Association and the Benevolent and Protective Order of Elks!

The Government of the United States was represented in the camp of the "enemy" by the following: Commission on Civil Rights; Department of the Air Force; Department of Health, Education and Welfare; Department of Justice; Department of Labor; Department of the Treasury; General Services Administration; Housing and Home Finance Agency; Interstate Commerce Commission; President's Committee on Government Contracts. The enemy status of the Supreme Court and the federal judiciary was apparently taken for granted.

Chapter 13

RIFTS IN THE CLOUDS

Though the extent of actual school desegregation was still microscopic, 1959, the fifth year after the Brown decision, marked a turning point in Southern resistance. In Virginia, which had been a conspicuous bellwether, the attitude of both government and public underwent a dramatic change. From this year onward the state that had led the parade of defiance was to set an example to the rest of the South of quiet but progressive—though still only token—compliance. Little Rock resigned itself in 1959, with relatively minor disorder, to the admission of Negroes to two white high schools; and the walls of public-school segregation were breached in another Southern state, Florida. More convulsions were still to come in the Deep South; but the nerving image of Virginia in the vanguard of a solid seven-state front was shattered, and the ultimate futility of resistance was brought home to an ever-increasing number of thoughtful Southerners.

As for closing schools, the intolerable situation resulting from this expedient led to vigorous and steadily growing popular protest both in Little Rock and in Virginia. The movement in the former city was spearheaded by a Women's Emergency Committee to Open Public Schools, that in Virginia by a league of Committees for Public Schools which grew out of the Arlington County initiative. These organizations, composed of white citizens, favored compliance with federal court orders in preference to closed schools; but their range of support was greatly expanded by their insistence upon standing "neither for integration nor for segregation."

Public pressure and court action converged to bring the climax first in Virginia.[1] Committees for Public Schools were formed in Charlottesville, Norfolk, and Warren. The Charlottesville Committee quickly reached a membership of one thousand and that in Norfolk enrolled sixty-five hundred. Then alarmed citizens elsewhere in the state rallied to the movement, and early in December a Virginia Committee for Public Schools was set up with an office and staff in Richmond. Dr. J. L. Blair Buck—a former official of the state Department

178

of Education, who had retired in 1956 with a denunciation of massive resistance—was appointed co-ordinator of the statewide organization.

Other organizations joined in the fight. Groups of clergymen in the affected districts protested, also two liberal statewide organizations, the Virginia branches of the American Association of University Women and the League of Women Voters. The influential white Parent-Teacher Associations approached the issue, which so directly concerned them, with temerity and mixed sentiments. Some of their most articulate leaders approved of the school-closing escape from racial integration. Moreover, Virginia PTAs were traditionally loyal to state policy and rarely expressed themselves on controversial matters outside their own school districts. Nevertheless, when the PTAs met in their annual convention October 20, they listened to a fiery clarion call to massive resistance from the governor, then rejected a resolution in support of his program and adopted one urging local option—albeit with close votes in each case. The white schoolteachers went further; meeting ten days later in the convention of the Virginia Education Association, they adopted by overwhelming voice vote a resolution expressing "grave concern" and calling for continued operation of the public schools.

The moderates were coming out from underground, and no group was in a better position to sense the fact than the Virginia press. Somewhat abruptly and in seeming concert, during October and early November most of the state's leading newspapers turned against the massive-resistance program. The *Lynchburg News* and the *Lynchburg Advance* became aggressively critical; the *Roanoke Times* and the *Roanoke World News* declared the time had come for a change; the Norfolk afternoon *Ledger-Dispatch,* which, unlike its morning colleague, had supported massive resistance, and the *Charlottesville Daily Progress* joined the procession. On November 11 the editor of the *Richmond News Leader,* whose paper had beaten the drums of massive resistance more loudly than any other, sounded a call to retreat. In an address to the Richmond Rotary Club, Kilpatrick said: "I believe that new laws must be devised—speedily devised—if educational opportunities are to be preserved and social calamity is to be averted." The *Richmond Times-Dispatch* and the *News Leader* followed through editorially the next day in the same tenor.

Not all the agitation was on one side. A large element that feverish autumn still supported the school-closing program. In Norfolk the issue was disputed with particular acrimony. Countering the propaganda of the Committee for Public Schools, the racist Defenders of State Sovereignty, in the words of the *Ledger-Dispatch,* were "saturating Norfolk residents with a barrage of home-delivered literature." The mayor and city council of Norfolk, staunch massive-resisters, decided to submit the school question to popular vote. The proposition they presented to the voters was not an attractive one: it warned that if the closed schools were reopened with Negroes enrolled, state financial support would be forfeited and all school patrons in the city would have to pay "substantial tuition." Only some 22,000 of the city's 300,000 inhabitants went to the polls. Nevertheless, the results were arresting; approximately 60 per cent of the votes were cast against reopening the schools.

One powerful element of the body politic in Southern states, the financiers and corporation executives, tried anxiously to avoid the desegregation nettle; but they followed the controversy privately with no little interest. Events in Virginia aroused grave concern in this quarter. Whatever the views of Virginia businessmen on the question of race segregation, massive resistance from an economic point of view was proving the rankest folly. The state was paying $172,000 a month in Norfolk, for instance, for idle teachers and other costs of *closed* schools. Talk of a more extensive abandonment of public education raised acutely disturbing questions relative to school properties and several hundred million dollars' worth of school bonds. Meanwhile, the confusion and uncertainty were frightening new industry away from Virginia, while North Carolina, with all schools in normal operation, was enjoying an unprecedented industrial boom. Early in December twenty-nine of the state's most powerful business magnates expressed themselves at a quietly arranged dinner conference with the governor, the lieutenant governor, and the state attorney general. The incident was not publicized until long afterward, never in detail. The businessmen warned that massive resistance was leading the state toward catastrophe; and Governor Almond, though stubbornly non-committal, was unmistakably impressed.

Actually, a step taken earlier by his administration suggested that Almond may have foreseen the failure of massive resistance from the beginning of school-closing. It was a move which in the excite-

ment of early September attracted little attention. State Attorney
General A. E. S. Harrison, the governor's closest adviser, filed a suit
requesting the State Supreme Court of Appeals to require State Comp-
troller Sidney C. Day, Jr., to issue warrants for payment of tuition
grants under the massive-resistance legislation. The attorney general
explained that "the proceeding will test the validity of what is commonly known as the 'school-closing law' and the 'fund cut-off law,'
for under both of these enactments tuition payments . . . are envisioned." The dubious legislation was thus placed at the mercy of
the state court. When the time came, it would be easier to abandon
massive resistance on a signal from Virginia's own highest tribunal
than in obedience to federal court orders!

Six weeks later federal legal action against the school-closing laws
was also set in motion. After a petition had been filed and withdrawn
by the attorneys for the seventeen Negro pupils in Norfolk, a group
of white citizens, prompted and financed by the Norfolk Committee
for Public Schools, filed suit in federal court declaring that closing
certain Norfolk schools while permitting other schools in the state to
remain open constituted a denial of "equal protection of the laws."
It is interesting to note that in the two litigations which would be fatal
for Virginia's stand against the desegregation of public schools neither
the NAACP nor any Negro had a direct part.

The two crucial suits moved along through the briefs and hearings
of litigation more or less simultaneously in state and federal tribunals.
Meanwhile, a desegregation move in another city and a further school-
closing initiative in Norfolk also engaged the attention of federal
courts. NAACP attorneys had filed suit on September 5, seeking the
admission of fourteen Negro pupils to five white schools in the city
of Alexandria. In a hearing in January, Judge Albert V. Bryan directed the Alexandria school board to go ahead and act on the Negro
applications without discrimination.

In Norfolk on January 13, the jaundiced city council voted to withhold funds for the operation of any public-school grades above the
sixth. This move would have added nearly two thousand to the ten
thousand already displaced white pupils; its unconcealed object was
to bar five thousand Negro children from public schools. "Seventeen
Negro children," Mayor W. Fred Duckworth said, "are keeping ten
thousand white children out of school!" On a petition filed by the

Norfolk Committee for Public Schools on behalf of both the whites and the Negroes affected, Federal District Judge Walter E. Hoffman quickly put an end to this proceeding.[2]

The state and federal courts weighing the school-closing legislation delivered their opinions on the same day, January 19. (It is of casual historic interest that this crucial day in a maneuver of state resistance to national authority was the birthday of the great Confederate leader, General Robert E. Lee.) Rumors had circulated for several weeks that January 19 would be the day, and public suspense was at its peak.

The Supreme Court of Appeals delivered its judgment at 10:30 A.M.: the petition was denied. The massive-resistance legislation was invalidated! School-closing, cutting off funds from integrated schools, and tuition grants were all declared unconstitutional—and the judgment was that of the state's own supreme court. Virginia was depicted by a *Washington Evening Star* cartoonist as exclaiming: "Et tu, Brute!"

The state court, having concluded that "certain provisions of the acts . . . violate the Constitution of Virginia," found it unnecessary to "consider the questions whether these acts likewise violate the provisions of the Fourteenth Amendment to the federal Constitution as interpreted by the recent decisions of the Supreme Court of the United States. . . ." It held that the requirement of the Virginia Constitution for the state to "maintain an efficient system of free public schools throughout the state" meant "that the state must support such free public schools in that state as are necessary to an efficient system, including those in which the pupils of both races are compelled to be enrolled and taught together, however unfortunate that situation may be."

Later the same day federal authorities spoke. The three-judge federal district court in Norfolk listed the school-closing statutes and the governor's Norfolk school-closing order and declared them all "in violation of the Fourteenth Amendment to the Constitution of the United States and therefore void."

It remained for Governor Almond to face the state legislature and tell it that the massive-resistance posture could no longer be maintained. But first he made one unfortunate further gesture of belligerency—a mistake from every point of view. In a fiery radio-television speech on the evening of January 20 the governor thundered: ". . . To those who would . . . embrace a new moral code declared by nine men in Washington . . . , to those who would substitute strife, bitterness, turmoil, and chaos for the tranquillity and happiness of an ordered society . . . , to all of these and their confederates, comrades and allies, let me make it abundantly clear for the record now and hereafter, as governor of this state, I will not yield to that which I know to be wrong. . . ."

What caused the unhappy governor to make such a speech at this juncture is a question for psychologists. Almond himself said apologetically a year later it was the fact that he "was tired—harassed and under strain. . . ." [3] To the many who were hoping to hear that the war was over the broadcast was a heartbreaking disappointment; those who wanted to keep up the fight were crudely unprepared for the coming disillusionment. In the opinion of the *Richmond News Leader* the speech "removed any doubt that his administration might shift from the massive-resistance stand."

Though he had added immensely to the difficulty and embarrassment of his task, Almond's performance when the General Assembly met in special session January 28 was a masterpiece of extrication from an impossible situation. The drama was enhanced by the suspense with which the legislators—many of them eager to fight on—waited upon his words. It was not known up to this moment which way the governor would turn. But all doubt was removed when he read slowly and clearly from his written text: "It is not enough for gentlemen to cry unto you and me: 'Don't give up the ship! Stop them! It must not happen.' Or, 'It can be prevented.' If any of them knows the way through the dark maze of judicial aberration and constitutional exploitation, I call upon them to shed the light for which Virginia stands in dire need in this her dark and agonizing hour. No fair-minded person would be so unreasonable as to seek to hold me responsible for failure to exercise powers which the state is powerless to bestow."

A majority of the two chambers welcomed the governor's decision to retreat. His recommendations for immediate action, which were adopted with near unanimity, appealed to both sides: repeal of the compulsory school-attendance law, a law making bombing threats a felony, and a tuition-grant plan independent of school appropriations, which would start payments flowing at last. A spate of proposals from diehards designed still to halt school desegregation were easily beaten down. Almond announced his intention to appoint a commission to study a new approach to the school problem and asked the General Assembly to recess until that commission should be ready to report.

Though this business was attended to before the week-end, nervous legislators insisted upon staying in session through Monday, February 1—just in case. The first public-school integration was scheduled to take place on that day, and "violence and bloodshed" had been incessantly predicted. Four Negro children were to be admitted to Stratford Junior High School in Arlington (where no schools had been closed), and the six closed high schools in Norfolk were to be reopened with seventeen Negroes in attendance. The event proved anti-climactic. Although elaborate police precautions were taken, no crowds gathered, the Negro children entered school with their white classmates in both cities without interference or disorder. Massive resistance had come to an end. When eleven Negro children quietly entered schools with whites in Alexandria nine days later it attracted little attention.

In the Charlottesville and Warren County situations the denouement was delayed until the beginning of the next school term. In the former, the school board had voted on January 26 to reopen the closed schools and desegregate them whenever required by the federal courts, and a co-operative city council had endorsed the school board's action. Impressed by this spontaneous demonstration of good faith, Judge Simon E. Sobeloff permitted that city to reopen the schools and to wait until September before inaugurating its desegregation plan.

In Warren County the federal court was less considerate and a sensational "boycott" resulted. There nearly all the displaced high-school pupils were pursuing their courses in a respectable private-school system; the opposition of the white community to a changeover in mid-term was almost unanimous. When the Warren County High School was ordered reopened notwithstanding, only the twenty-two Negro applicants enrolled. Segregationists made much of this incident. The white parents who refused to transfer their children to the school were hailed as heroes far and wide. The legislature of Alabama applauded their "courageous action"; the *Richmond Times-Dispatch* found "Warren's stonewall refusal to surrender . . . a bright spot . . . in the gloomy annals of the five-year constitutional crisis." But four hundred white pupils were to return to Warren High School, and the

Negroes were to enter white schools in Charlottesville, without incident, in September.

A change in the atmosphere in Virginia was apparent as spring came. A feeling of relief had been suggested by the results of a newspaper poll conducted after Almond's address to the legislature: two out of three expressed approval of his new stand. The Virginia Committee for Public Schools now boasted a membership of over twenty-two thousand and its advice and aid were sought by politicians. People who had felt massive resistance to be a mistake were no longer afraid to say so. Many felt that a great load had been lifted and were glad to turn their thoughts to other things.

But there was to be one more struggle over the issue in the General Assembly. When that body recessed on February 1, the members of the old guard of massive resistance, the hard core of the Byrd machine, left the chambers with lamentations. "There's a sickness in my heart," one said. But they came back when the legislature reconvened March 31 determined to act the drama out to the end. If massive resistance could not be resuscitated, they would at least die with their boots on. The result was a tumultuous and inconclusive session. One bastion of massive resistance was still intact, the State Pupil Placement Board, responsible for the assignment of all pupils in the state to their public schools. In practice this duty had been discharged by merely stamping thousands of assignment forms submitted by local school authorities, with a sharp eye to see that no Negro by any possible chance was placed in a white school. The board had never assigned a Negro to a white school, and, of its own volition, it never would. To frustrate this reliable device with local option was viewed by the diehards as a horrendous proposal, and here the battered massive-resistance bloc rallied for its last stand. In the minds of some it was another last stand for an embattled South. At one point in the debate two massive-resisters—one of them was State Senator Harry Byrd, Jr.—displayed a large painting of Robert E. Lee!

Local option was one of the recommendations of the forty-member study commission set up by Governor Almond; it was called the "Perrow Commission," after its chairman, State Senator Mosby G. Perrow, Jr. Its proposal was mild in the first place: a cumbersome procedure to enable localities to withdraw from the jurisdiction of the Pupil

Placement Board. Yet this passed the Senate only by a vote of 20 to 19, and the opposition was successful in securing a postponement of the date for its coming into effect to March 1, 1960 (in the hope that the provision might be repealed in the meantime). The other recommendations, a more elaborate tuition-grant plan and further aids to private schools, were readily adopted. All these together were proclaimed the "Freedom of Choice Plan." Any pupil who objected to attending his public school would be free to choose a private school and receive a sum of money toward his expenses.

But, as the months went by, the action of federal courts and the march of events were to leave any resistance mechanism by the wayside. Members of the Pupil Placement Board told a federal court in Norfolk in September that they could not conceive of a situation in which they would assign a Negro to a white school; Judge Hoffman angrily ordered them to do so forthwith. Three months later he issued an order relieving the Norfolk school board of any responsibility for dealing with the Pupil Placement Board. When the latter's segregation watchdogs finally gave up and resigned, Governor Almond reconstituted the board with three members who proceeded voluntarily to assign a few Negroes to white schools. From then on the Pupil Placement Board performed only a limited regulatory function in a continuing process of public-school desegregation.

Freedom of choice was epitomized—and, hopefully, constitutional objections were circumvented—by the tuition-grant plan as it emerged from the April session. A "scholarship," or tuition-grant, roughly equal to the per-pupil public-school cost, was made available to any pupil who chose to attend a qualified nonsectarian school anywhere in preference to a public school of his district. Many private-school pupils collected the grants even when the public schools which they could have attended were completely segregated. Some actually used the money to attend private bi-racial schools. In 1962, 8518 Virginia children were receiving "scholarships" at a total annual cost—divided between the state and the localities—of $2,074,690. In some situations the program tended to siphon off from integrated public schools, and to mollify, hostile elements; but it became more and more expensive and less and less related to the segregation problem—and increasingly unpopular—as the years went by.

Senator Byrd said in September 1959, when his famous policy was in process of relentless liquidation: "I stand now as I stood when I first urged massive resistance. . . ." He continued to stand there year after year. But in the mystic governance of the Byrd machine the chief's attitude in this particular was no longer one his followers were expected to emulate. Massive resistance disappeared from newspaper headlines and from political debate. The very words "massive resistance" dropped out of common parlance except as critics of that adventure recalled it with ridicule. The admission of Negroes to an additional white school somewhere in the state scarcely made front-page news any more. Local enactments brought compulsory school attendance back in fifty-seven districts.

Tiny though the figures were in comparison with Virginia's total school enrollment, the number of Negroes in previously all-white public schools approximately doubled each year thereafter. Beginning with 51 admitted during the 1958–59 school term, the number grew throughout the state as follows: 1959–60, 103; 1960–61, 208; 1961–62, 533; 1962–63, 1230; and 1963–64, 3721.

Nevertheless, in one small Virginia county a long-inflamed boil of hostility burst in 1959 and festered on for five tragic and scandalous years.

In the summer of 1959 Prince Edward County abandoned public education completely. In many ways the Prince Edward saga is separate from, and out of time with, the larger Virginia story. During the first two years after the 1954 Supreme Court decision the belief that school integration was imminent in that county contributed to the hysteria in the state, and the action of the Prince Edward governing board in holding up public-school funds in 1955 was loudly applauded by Virginia extremists. But that county's schools continued in full operation throughout the massive-resistance period, and the public-school system in the state as a whole was returning to normal when Prince Edward took its melancholy plunge.

In 1959 the school controversy in some form was more than ten years old there, and the county had been involved in federal court litigation since 1951. By the time the Supreme Court decision was handed down, a new Negro high school—the earlier Negro objective—had been erected at a cost of over $800,000; by 1959 all the plaintiffs in the desegregation suit had graduated long since or left school. Prince Edward, it will be remembered, was one of the five original Brown cases. The other Southern case was that of Clarendon County,

South Carolina. Both these counties lay in the heart of the rural Black Belt. In any schedule of selective gradualism they would have been among the last places in the South in which to expect adjustment to the anti-segregation ruling.

The private-school organization that was formed when the Prince Edward board of supervisors balked at appropriating public-school funds in 1955 had remained intact, holding its collections of some $12,000 in cash and $200,000 in pledges. The county's resolution to operate no racially mixed schools had, if anything, hardened further while the case went back and forth between the district court and the court of appeals. District Court Judge Sterling Hutcheson implemented the Supreme Court ruling with orders to end public-school segregation; but, as a native of a neighboring Black Belt county which had a more heavily Negro population than Prince Edward, deeply conscious of the difficulties of the situation, he was inclined to allow much time before the change was required to be effected. Finally, on May 5, 1959, the Fourth Circuit Court of Appeals directed that the district court order the Prince Edward school board "to take immediate steps . . . to permit the entrance of qualified persons into the white schools in the term beginning September 1959." [4]

Without waiting for the district court orders (which were not issued until nearly a year later), the county leaders took out their private-school-system blueprint and launched upon the long-contemplated program of evasion. The board of supervisors cut off funds for public-school operation and reduced the county tax rate by 53 per cent. Public education in Prince Edward came to an end.

For most of the county's Negro children it was the end of schooling of any kind. For the white children, the Prince Edward Educational Foundation opened two private high schools and six private grade schools in a score of miscellaneous buildings scattered over the county—stores, churches, Sunday-school rooms, private homes, etc., and used a motion-picture theater for assemblies. Employing sixty-six teachers, most of them from the closed public schools, they accommodated 1475 of a former white public-school enrollment of 1562. "No Trespassing" signs were tacked up on the walls and grounds of the twenty public schools. Upward of two hundred Negro children were sent to schools outside the county, and crude "training centers" were operated spasmodically by the Negro community for some of those who remained. Public education, or the default of public education, would follow substantially that pattern for the next four years.

Anxious to avoid a court challenge, the county shied away from the tuition grants during the 1959-60 school term, but before the next term began it went to the aid of the financially hard-pressed private schools not only with tuition grants, but with provision for tax credits up to 25 per cent of tax obligations for amounts contributed to the private-school fund (which brought $56,000 into the organization's coffers). However, in view of the fact that public schools were closed, and the purpose was the perpetuation of segregated schooling, both these devices were struck down by the federal court before the 1961–62 school term. In the meantime the Prince Edward Educational Foundation erected an attractive little private high-school building— at a cost of some $200,000, plus donations in kind—which increased the vested interest and tended to give a permanent character to the private-school venture.

The population of Prince Edward County, where the economy is largely rural, with a high percentage of homeowners even among the Negroes, was not very mobile. It had increased 3.2 per cent from 1940 to 1950. But the 1960 census showed a decline in the population from 15,398 to 14,120. Nearly all of the loss was in the non-white population, which fell from 6860 to 5631; the non-white proportion of the total fell from 44.6 to 39.9 per cent. In November 1961 the Prince Edward school board reported to the federal district court the results of a school census, which showed that the number of school-age children residing in the county had declined by 449 since 1955, leaving 1455 whites and 1573 Negroes. Of these, 1224 whites were still in the private schools and 289 Negro children were in schools scattered widely across the nation.

The Prince Edward County affair has been the subject of a stream of news dispatches, of many articles and a few books. Many, including some foreign observers, wondered how an American county could be left entirely without public education. The Virginia Constitution required the state to maintain public schools but, as stipulated in detail, only on a meager scale. The state circuit court found nothing there to compel either the state or the county to appropriate the necessary funds.[5] In the state house, Albertis Harrison, who had succeeded Almond as governor, was an apostle of "harmony," loath to throw the Prince Edward problem into the lap of the legislature and see the segregation issue raised in state politics again. And the problem was infinitely complicated. Responsibility for public-school administration was vested in the local school board. Without new legislation the state could not move in and operate Prince Edward County's schools. The only group which seemed to have a clear-cut plan was the governing board of the county and the sponsors of its private-school system; these were determined to stand fast to the end.

The performance of the federal district court, where Judge Hutcheson had been succeeded by Judge Oren R. Lewis, was cautious, dilatory, and indecisive where prompt and forceful action was indicated. In 1962 Judge Lewis finally came to the point of ordering the public schools reopened, though failing to fix a time limit for compliance. A year later the Fourth Circuit Court of Appeals vacated Judge Lewis's order on the ground that the state supreme court should first make an interpretation of the relevant provisions of the Virginia Constitution. The state's high tribunal made its interpretation on December 2, 1963: it ruled that the closing of public schools in Prince Edward was not a violation of the Constitution or any law of Virginia. It was a six-to-one decision; Chief Justice John W. Eggleston in a sharply worded dissent warned that the ruling was "a clear invitation to the federal courts to step in and enforce" the rights of the county's citizens.

However, in August 1963 Governor Harrison announced that a non-profit corporation known as the Prince Edward Free School Association had been formed to operate a system of schools open to all in that county for the 1963–64 school term. The Association would use public-school buildings under lease for a token fee and would rely on financial support from individuals and foundations. The board of trustees, composed of prominent Virginia educators of both races, was headed by Colgate W. Darden, now a member of the state Board of Education.

Governor Harrison expressed his conviction that Prince Edward's public schools would be reopened at least by September 1964. In the meantime, in the fall of 1963, the county's Negro children returned to school at last after four years in the educational desert.

Whites in another Virginia county resorted to private schools to escape public-school integration in September 1963. In little Surry County, where Negroes represent approximately 65 per cent of the total population of 6200, the school board decided not to open the one white school when the state Pupil Placement Board assigned seven Negro children to it. Private classes were arranged for 431 white pupils, with their 22 former public-school teachers. They used two former public-school buildings which had been declared surplus two years earlier, and two churches. Tuition grants from public funds covered most of the expense, but each pupil was required to pay a fee of $125 above the amount of the grant. The two public schools for the county's 1200 Negro pupils continued to operate as usual.

In Little Rock the long crisis that began in 1957 came to an end in August 1959. The extremist groups in that city, though reduced in number, continued to be voluble and virulent for many months; fanatics and hoodlums expressed their resentment in bombings and harassment of "integrationists." The initial admission of Negroes to schools with whites in 1959 was on a meager scale (only six Negro pupils), and the further progress of desegregation would be painfully slow. But public order and stability were restored; the gradual elimination of school segregation was accepted by most as inevitable; and Little Rock returned to the normal activities and concerns of an American city. In a few years' time much of the bitterness also faded and moderation rose in public esteem. Orval Faubus himself veered toward a course that alienated some of the extreme segregationist groups. When he ran for the Democratic nomination for a fifth term in 1962 the segregation issue was subordinated, and he attributed his victory to the people's desire "not to wander in the thickets of extremism."

Unlike the Virginia cities, Little Rock bore with the private substitutes for public schools—and the considerable education vacuum—to the end of the 1958–59 school year. The Arkansas Supreme Court upheld the state's school-closing law. It ruled in April 1959 that the legislature's duty to "protect the safety and welfare of the people" overrode the constitutional requirement for maintaining public schools.[6] The federal court order invalidating that law and ordering the Little Rock school board to proceed with its integration plan came only in June.[7] By that time a popular demand for return to the public high schools was unmistakable, and it had the resolute backing of the economic power structure of the city. This development was the more remarkable in view of the relentless opposition, not only of the segregationist organizations, but of Governor Faubus, who denounced every constructive initiative and vilified its proponents.

The Women's Emergency Committee to Reopen Our Schools (its membership grew to some twelve hundred) marched in the front line of the crusade from beginning to end. It was joined by most of the Parent-Teacher Associations and later by a proliferation of newly formed organizations, but most importantly by the Little Rock Chamber of Commerce. In the return of moderate elements to control of the city, the business community—which so often has remained aloof from the school controversy in the South—played an active and, in a sense, a decisive part. As Frank Cantrell, manager of the state Chamber of Commerce reminded a Rotary Club audience in October 1958, Little Rock's industrial program, which had had bright prospects before September 1957, had been brought "practically to a standstill." Though eight new plants with a total value of over three million dollars had opened during the first eight months of 1957, not a single new industry had come to Little Rock since. Businessmen gave early support to the Women's Emergency Committee and some went to work individually in the cause.

In January the newly elected president of the Little Rock Chamber of Commerce, E. Grainger Williams, urged consideration of the "cost of public education and the cost of the lack of education," and the chamber began to move as a body. A mild resolution urging that a way be found to reopen the high schools and pointing to the need for better interracial communication brought a barrage of criticism and abuse, and a few members resigned. But the chamber proceeded to take a stronger stand. In March it recommended reopening the high schools under a pupil-placement plan and declared: "The decision of the Supreme Court of the United States, however much we dislike it, is the declared law and is binding upon us. . . ."

The private-school undertaking in Little Rock proved entirely transitory. During the summer of 1959, even before the reopening of the public high schools was an accomplished fact, all the improvisations passed out of existence. When it graduated twenty-eight seniors on July 10, the Baptist High School announced that it would be converted into a permanent Christian academy if as many as seventy-five students enrolled on this basis; ten days later, when only twenty-two had registered and paid the $250 tuition fee, the plan was given up and the money returned. The vestry of Trinity Episcopal Cathedral announced July 20 that its Trinity Interim Academy would continue inactive and recommended that its pupils enroll in public schools. The announcement by the Little Rock Private School Corporation in August came as a general surprise; its T. J. Raney High School, zealously aided by Governor Faubus and much publicized, was the largest and proudest exhibit of the private-school proponents. Although in the midst of adding twenty-eight classrooms to its building, and with an enrollment of 1226 pupils, the corporation suddenly declared that it was insolvent. The school would not operate during the ensuing year. Its president, Dr. T. J. Raney himself, broke the news.

A survey made in the spring by Little Rock's school Superintendent, Terrell E. Powell, showed what had happened to the 3665 pupils who were locked out of the public high schools. Of the 2915 white students, 643 were not in any school (though 405 of these were taking correspondence courses provided by the University of Arkansas); the remaining 2272 were attending miscellaneous schools as follows: T. J. Raney High School, 714; Baptist High School, 296; special high-school classes at Conway Baptist College, 42; special high-school classes in a Little Rock kindergarten, 38; Trinity Interim Academy, 30; schools outside Arkansas, 275; and public schools in 124 Arkansas districts, 877. Of the 750 Negro pupils, 376 were not in any school (though an estimated 35 of them were taking correspondence courses), 283 were attending other schools in Arkansas, and 91 had been placed in schools outside the state. The total, white and Negro, who remained without any school was 1019.

The focal point of the drama and of the controversy, which raged without respite from school-closing in 1958 to school-opening in 1959, was the Little Rock school board. Fluctuations of public sentiment were registered in the reaction to the moves and pyrotechnics of this body and in the successive changes in its composition through elections, recall elections, and appointments. Two months after the closing of the public high schools in 1958, the segregationist Mothers' League of Central High School, angry at the school board's submission to federal court orders, launched a movement for the recall of five of its six members. The favored exception was the ultra-segregationist Dale Alford, who was campaigning to unseat Representative Brooks Hays. Upon Alford's election to Congress, the other five members promptly resigned to give the voters an opportunity to elect an entirely new school board. Emerging victorious in the election of December were three moderates from a five-man "businessmen's slate" —which Governor Faubus had denounced—and three of the extremists put forward by the Citizens' Council and favored by the governor. One of the "businessmen's" candidates elected was Everett Tucker, Jr., manager of the industrial department of the Chamber of Commerce. Tucker, who was elected vice-president, and later president, of the board, was to be largely responsible for engineering the return of the high schools to normal operation.

Virgil T. Blossom had been separated from the position of superintendent of schools, which he had held for the previous six years. Blossom had attracted national attention as early as 1955 by his promising plan for the integration of Little Rock schools; he had been in the center of the maelstrom of the past two years; he was now the target of bitter segregationist criticism and abuse. Fred Graham, the assistant superintendent, and Bill Hemstead, business manager of the school system, resigned—Graham said, "to preserve my health, which has been impaired by the strain and tension of the past two years." Terrell E. Powell, principal of Hall High School, was promoted to succeed Blossom.

The new school board, evenly divided in two opposing factions, moved inevitably into confusion and stalemate. Amid rumors of a contemplated "purge" of moderate school personnel, an effort was made to break the tie by enlarging the board; a bill was introduced in the state legislature to authorize the governor to appoint three new members. Little Rock PTAs now came vigorously into the fight and joined the Women's Emergency Committee in opposing this bill, and it was defeated.

Only highlights of the months of incessant school-board wrangling can be touched upon here, but a fateful crisis was reached May 5. After a deadlocked morning session that day, the "businessmen" trio withdrew, assuming that they were leaving no quorum for further business. However, the pro-Faubus trio came back in the afternoon and, declaring that the quorum established in the morning still existed, proceeded to indulge in an orgy of extravagant moves. They voted to replace Superintendent Powell with T. H. Alford, father of the Alford who had been elected to Congress, and to dismiss forty-four high-

school administrators and teachers who were alleged to have "integrationist tendencies." (Though the schools were closed, the teachers
and principals were still carried on the payroll.)

A law passed by the 1958 special session of the legislature provided
for the recall of school-board members by popular vote. Opposing
groups petitioned for the recall of both factions, and an election was
called for May 25. The ensuing campaign brought the issue of moderation squarely before the voters. It also put the influence of Faubus,
who backed the extremist trio, to a crucial test. Joining the now militant PTAs and the Women's Emergency Committee, a hundred and
seventy-nine downtown business and civic leaders formed a "Committee to Stop This Outrageous Purge," which acquired the handier
nickname "STOP." On the other side, the Citizens' Council, Mothers'
League, and States' Rights Council rallied in a "Committee to Retain
Our Segregated Schools," or "CROSS." In the election the three
Faubus-backed members were removed by a margin of approximately
two thousand votes in each case, and by a closer vote the three
moderate members were retained. Observers agreed that the Little
Rock problem was not yet resolved, but the results of this election
were widely hailed as a major setback for the advocates of reckless
resistance; the *Miami Herald* said it "might well mark a turning point
in the struggle over school segregation in the South."

Of the three Little Rock replacements appointed by the Pulaski
County Board of Education in June, two were prepared to co-operate
with the moderate incumbents. (The third was found disqualified and
this vacancy was not immediately filled.) Then a harmonious school
board of five members promptly expunged from the record all the
actions of the May 5 three-member meeting and proceeded to plan
for the reopening of the high schools in a manner acceptable to the
federal court.

On August 1, after a July registration, the school board announced
the assignment of three Negroes each to Hall and Central High
Schools. A major defect of the earlier plan had been the failure to
assign any colored pupils to Hall High School, a "silk-stocking" school,
where race prejudice was less rampant than at Central (and which
was attended by children of school-board members). Three days later
it was suddenly announced that Little Rock high schools would open
August 12, nearly a month earlier than usual. The surprise move

foiled any plans of Governor Faubus for calling a special session of the legislature.

When the day came, no difficulty was experienced at Hall; that school opened quietly at 9:30 A.M. with the Negroes in attendance. Obstructionist attention was focused on Central, which opened at 1 P.M. After a rally on the capitol steps and a speech by Governor Faubus, approximately two hundred pro-segregation fanatics marched toward Central High School, but they were stopped a block away from it and repulsed in a sharp twenty-minute scuffle with city police. Twenty-one members of the crowd were arrested, twelve of them teenagers. Two Negro children walked into the school, and no further violence occurred.

In July, Governor Faubus had declared that if Little Rock high schools were desegregated for the coming term it would be done with federal force, "using live ammunition." In a broadcast the night before school-opening and in haranguing the crowd in the morning, he had continued his fulminations, though he said to the crowd on the capitol steps: "I see no reason for you to be beaten over the head today by the forces in the field or to be jailed. That should be faced only as a last resort, and where there is much to be gained. Honestly, I do not think that should be faced today."

That night, after the schools had been reopened, speaking at a fish fry in the country near Little Rock, Faubus once more denounced the "integrationists, puppets, and hypocrites" and made scathing references to the school-board president and to the chief of police, Eugene G. Smith. As assistant chief, Smith had led the forlorn attempt of the city police force to quell the riot of September 23, 1957; now chief of police, his firm and efficient performance at Central High School on this reopening day won national applause. Faubus compared him to Janos Kadar, the Hungarian puppet of the Russians.

During the night of Labor Day 1959, the second anniversary of the appearance of National Guardsmen at Central High, three dynamite explosions were set off—one in the driveway of the home of the chief of the Fire Department (whose firemen had aided the police on May 12 by spraying demonstrators); another in front of the building which housed the mayor's private office; and a third at an office of the public-school administration. The swift public indignation completed the discrediting of Little Rock's pro-segregation extremists. The Chamber of Commerce offered a $25,000 reward for arrest of the dynamiters.

Within eleven days five suspects were arrested; one was tried, pleaded guilty, and was given a five-year prison term. The other four were eventually given three- or five-year prison sentences, though the sentence of one was suspended because of his "material assistance to the state." Testimony revealed that the dynamitings had been planned at a Ku Klux Klan meeting.

In terms of school districts desegregated the dent made in 1959 in public-school segregation in the South was minute. In addition to the five situations in which race barriers were breached in Virginia, and the recovery in Little Rock, token integration was effected in four more North Carolina districts, High Point and Durham, and Craven and Wayne counties; sixteen children of Negro Air Force personnel were admitted with whites to a Rutherford County public school in Tennessee; and two public schools were integrated in Miami, Florida. But the breakdown of resistance in Virginia and Little Rock had a far-reaching impact, and the admission of Negro children—though only a handful—to public schools with whites in Florida for the first time removed one more from the list of totally resisting states.

In Florida school authorities did not have to contend with an obstructionist governor or with an official posture of massive resistance; local option was emphasized in that state. Nevertheless, the small beginning made in one district marked a signal turning point, and further ventures were encouraged by the tranquillity and ease with which this hurdle was cleared. It is notable also that the step was taken voluntarily. NAACP attention had focused on a protracted, and finally successful, suit to secure the admission of Negroes to the University of Florida. The first public-school desegregation suit was filed only in June 1956, and in 1959 no such suit had reached the point of definite federal district court orders.

The popular image of Florida as a fast-growing resort state with a highly cosmopolitan population led many to expect earlier compliance with the broad Supreme Court command to end public-school segregation. But native Floridians were steeped in Southern tradition and politically powerful; nor was race prejudice uncommon among the multitude which had more recently made Florida its home. The northern section, bordering on Georgia and Alabama and including the capital city of Tallahassee, was in many respects a typical part of the Deep South. Clouding the picture further, an obsolete and fantastically inequitable system of apportionment enabled a handful of representatives from old and strongly prejudiced communities to dominate the state legislature. That body, in a spirit of hostility and defiance, enacted a series of anti-integration laws, including a local option pupil-assignment law, and set up an investigating committee which harassed the NAACP and other groups favoring compliance with the Supreme Court ruling (though it investigated the Ku Klux Klan also). But the Florida law-makers stopped short of any general school-closing legislation; Governor Collins urged them "never, never, never to set up any plan or device by which our public schools can be closed."

Citizens' Councils flourished for several years in northern Florida and the Tampa area (aided, incidentally, by John Kasper), but they failed to enlist a large membership or to take permanent hold. At least seven separate, and often feuding, Ku Klux Klan groups operated at times. The Association of Florida Ku Klux Klans disbanded, revived, and disbanded again; W. T. Griffin, its "grand dragon," finally expressed disgust at "intimidations, parades, cross-burnings, mask-wearing, and all other public exhibitions to confuse and frighten innocent people." Much hate literature was circulated, and some of the newspapers were inflammatory in their hostility. A number of revolting instances of undercover violence were reported. Negro protests in areas other than public education resulted in some rioting in Tallahassee and Jacksonville. But Florida saw no spectacular disorder related to the admission of Negroes to schools with white children. In spite of wide dissemination of germs of racist fanaticism, the singular restraint which attended school desegregation when it came indicated that the bulk of the populace had escaped infection.

The nine-year fight by Virgil Hawkins, a 50-year-old Negro, to enter the University of Florida succeeded in 1958 in breaking the racial barrier for the first time in a state institution of higher learning, though the long-persevering Hawkins failed at last to pass the entrance examinations. Another Negro, George H. Starke, Jr., who applied in 1958, was accepted as a law student. Starke was dropped in February 1960 because of academic deficiency, but yet another Negro was then in attendance, Miss Ester M. Langston, a Phi Beta Kappa from Fisk University, and more Negro students would follow. The admission of Starke to classes in 1958 was without disorder of any kind. When his low marks finally necessitated his withdrawal he said: "The law school and its professors were eminently fair," and a professor said there had "never been as much as two minutes' trouble because of him."

After 1956 Governor Collins discouraged any further legislation related to segregation. In 1958 he began to hint that "we must be prepared to accept some desegregation." In December of that year he invited public-school officials from five counties to a private conference at the governor's mansion in Tallahassee to discuss the possibility of "limited integration." Collins complained afterward that "no school board was willing to proceed voluntarily with token integration," but Dade County (Miami) school officials who had attended the conference said they would continue to study the proposal.

The Dade school board did in fact proceed. It voted unanimously two months later to admit four Negroes come September to Orchard Villa, an elementary school previously for whites only. The four Negro children had completed all the procedures required under the pupil-assignment law, and they resided within two blocks of the school. It was one of the situations where rejection of the Negro applications would have been least defensible. At the same time it was an embarrassing place for a pilot operation: the neighborhood for several years had been steadily changing from white to Negro, and the trend would now be accelerated. By the summer it was estimated that fewer than seventy children would register for the 450-pupil school, and how long any whites would remain was a matter of speculation. In the meantime, almost unnoticed by the public, another situation had developed where school integration was contemplated in Dade County. A new school had been built near the Homestead Air Force Base to serve the children of military personnel and other children within its district. The school board, welcoming an opportunity to establish an integration exhibit where it would stick, announced that the new school would open with both white and Negro children in attendance.

As in other cities approaching the first public-school desegregation, but involving perhaps a smaller fraction of the public, controversy and apprehension mounted in Miami. At Orchard Villa, where trouble was most feared, the teaching staff had been carefully selected and an ex-Marine, Erwin Marshall, had been chosen to provide a "strong man" as principal. Extra precautions were taken by the police when school opened in September. But the event was another anticlimax: there were no disturbances at either school. However, only eight white children and four Negroes enrolled at that school. A few days later these were joined by three more white children, bringing the total enrollment there to fifteen. At the Air Force Base school, 741 white and 21 Negro children enrolled without incident.

In October 1959 the school board assigned 379 more Negro children to Orchard Villa; in December that school, now with an all-Negro faculty, was serving 468 Negro and 9 white children. The school building was enlarged by the addition of ten new classrooms. In September 1960, when the Negro enrollment exceeded a thousand, the last remaining white pupil withdrew—her parents moved to another neighborhood. However, the school board gingerly extended desegregation to two more white schools, admitting one Negro child to each.

In the fall of 1961 four more Florida counties began token public-school desegregation, and in Dade County 513 Negro children were attending classes with whites in ten schools. In the fall of 1962, 1168 Negro children were attending fifty-five formerly all-white public schools in ten Florida counties; and for the 1963–64 term, 3650 Negroes were enrolled with whites in Florida schools.

Chapter 14

THE BANISHMENT
OF UNCLE TOM

The year 1960 is memorable as marking a massive awakening of Negroes in the South with a new-found resolve to fight against all forms of discrimination against them. Initial inroads were made with sensational speed upon the pattern of segregation beyond the field of public education. The path led through stubborn and sometimes violent opposition, and on toward a nationwide upsurge. The new spirit was to spread also through the Negro minority in the rest of the United States and—though affected only slightly in the first instance by developments overseas and devoted to nonviolent expression—would become a part of the rising tide of belligerence among colored races throughout the world.

The militant element before 1960 had embraced only a small fraction of the nearly ten million Negroes in the eleven Southern states. The incessant assertions of Southern whites in the 1950s that the Negroes preferred segregation, that "90 per cent" or "99 per cent" of them were not interested in racial integration, was an exaggerated, but in many cases a superficially honest, appraisal. Few white people ever heard Negroes express a desire to see their children mingle with white children in public schools, and many heard Negro domestics say that integration would only cause trouble. Centuries of meek dependency had taught most ordinary Negroes to say to white people what they thought white people wanted to hear.

And there were indeed thousands of Negroes among whom the Supreme Court decision caused no rejoicing. Those of little education or contact with the larger world were slow to grasp its significance, and many who did feared that efforts to secure its enforcement would lead only to grief. Some well-educated Negroes held this view. The statements of Negro "segregationists" were so widely quoted by white propagandists as to give an impression that these Negroes were prominent and substantial in number, but they were in fact rare and generally little-known individuals. One Negro intellectual, the novelist Zora Neale Hurston, achieved momentary fame among a Southern public not generally aware of the existence of Negro literati when she said in a letter to the *Orlando* (Florida) *Sentinel* in 1955 that she was "not delighted" over the Brown decision. "It is well known," the late Miss Hurston wrote, "that I have no sympathy nor respect for the 'tragedy of color' school of thought among us, whose fountainhead is the pressure group concerned in this court ruling. . . ." [1] The philosophy of accommodation and reliance upon the good will of whites for a gradual Negro advance had many thoughtful adherents among the older generation, even though they did not approve of segregation in principle.

J. C. Furnas in his *Goodbye to Uncle Tom,* published in 1956, noted that American Negroes had made the name of the titular hero of *Uncle Tom's Cabin* "a hissing and a byword." In its odious connotation the label was unfair both to Mrs. Stowe's loyal paragon of Christian virtues and to many to whom it was lightly applied after the Brown decision. Brash young Negro crusaders used it to express their impatience with many of their elders—including indiscriminately Negro educators, who were almost invariably sympathetic and often unostentatiously helpful in the civil rights cause. Negroes in public education at all levels were state employees and were dependent upon white politicians not only for their jobs, but for appropriations and a variety of help needed to carry on the education of Negro youth— which included the training of future leaders in the fight for Negro rights. Presidents of private Negro universities and colleges needed the support of white trustees and benefactors, and on their high pedestals they were under the watchful eyes of politicians and segregationist organizations. Some Negro college presidents of prestige and statesmanlike diplomacy were able, nevertheless, quietly to render inestimable service directly in the fight against race discrimination; their advice was often sought by liberals of both races and in the highest official and political circles of the nation. Rufus E. Clement of Atlanta University, Albert W. Dent of Dillard University, Luther H. Foster of Tuskegee Institute, Benjamin E. Mays of Morehouse College, and Stephen J. Wright of Fisk University were distinguished members of this group.

What came to be generally regarded as "Uncle Tomism" was most conspicuous in Mississippi. "White men are still in charge in Mississippi," Percy Greene, the leading "Uncle Tom," often reminded his brethren, counseling that "a friendly relation with white people is still the greatest asset of the Mississippi Negro." In the atmosphere of heavy-handed repression which prevailed in that state, the argument was not without a certain myopic merit. Dr. J. H. White, president of the Negro Mississippi Vocational College, told a Negro gathering at Mound Bayou: "I don't believe you are going to throw away your churches, schools, hospitals, businesses, insurances, newspapers . . . just to sit, eat, and ride with a white person." [2]

Greene became the most persistent, the most famous, and the most hated of all the "Uncle Toms." Editor of the weekly *Jackson Advocate* and chairman of the Mississippi Association of Negro Democratic Clubs, he was a rugged, hard-bitten veteran of many battles for Negro causes. He suggested in 1955 that the NAACP "show a willingness to support a formula that will enable the moderate to start a working solution of the problems posed by its hard-won decision," declaring that no solution could be found "in an atmosphere of vituperation, vindictiveness, finger-pointing, name-calling, and threats of retaliation." [3] "Uncle Tom Percy Greene," as he did not hesitate to call himself, continued to attack the NAACP and in return became a pariah in militant Negro circles. He insisted that "the Southern Negroes do not want public-school integration," and he became a favorite exhibit of the Citizens' Councils and the segregationist press in support of that contention. Greene's position, and that of some lesser "Uncle Toms," was not unlike that of collaborationists in France under the German occupation.

In the South as a whole the "Uncle Toms" were gradually submerged in the rising tide of Negro awareness. A Gallup poll in 1957 found 69 per cent of Southern Negroes in favor of enforcement of the school-desegregation ruling and only 13 per cent opposed. Although only a bold few were willing to affront the whites with desegregation moves, within the Negro community opposition to segregation had become the only respectable attitude. Indeed, the odium that descended upon the Negro dissenter was not unlike that suffered by the white moderate in an ultra-segregationist milieu. Leaders in the desegregation movement became popular heroes. The pupils who braved the storm of insult and harassment in the pioneer marches across the segregation line in Clinton, Little Rock, and elsewhere were a source of deep pride to the Negro public—a feeling which the dignity and fortitude of those children inspired in all unbiased observers.

By 1960 the masses of Negro Southerners were conscious of the injustice and degradation of segregation in all of its manifestations. Moreover, they were no longer resigned to relying for relief entirely upon the NAACP and the federal courts, far less upon white benevolence and the slow processes of time. The Uncle Tom of servility and submission was making his farewell appearance. Yet Negroes generally were still quiescent, as if waiting for a signal. Then the signal came from four Negro college boys in North Carolina.

The inception of the student protest movement was sudden, spontaneous, and not without an element of romance. It had been talked and dreamed about for three months in dormitory huddles among four freshmen at the Negro Agricultural and Technical College in Greensboro. The young conspirators—Ezell Blair, David Richmond, Joseph McNeil, and Franklin McLain—were all students in good standing. The plan had been divulged to no one off the campus. The NAACP was to aid, and CORE was to embrace, the movement in due course, but they were taken by surprise at its spectacular beginning.

At 4:30 P.M. on February 1, 1960, the four boys took seats at a lunch counter of a Woolworth department store, ordered coffee, and waited until the store closed at 6:30. They were not served. Negroes were not served at white lunch counters in the South—not yet. But the idea spread with sensational rapidity. The next day seventy-five students from A. and T. "sat-in" at Woolworth's, and the performance was repeated daily by growing numbers. Within a week Negroes were staging lunch-counter "sit-ins" in Durham, Winston-Salem, Elizabeth City, Fayetteville, Charlotte, and High Point; by the end of the month, in Virginia, South Carolina, Maryland, Tennessee, Alabama, Kentucky, and Florida.

Avoidance of provocation to violence and even decorum were emphasized by the Negro students who dominated the movement. The writer talked at an early stage with the four boys who started it. They were voluble on the subject of Thomas Jefferson and Patrick Henry and only vaguely familiar with Mahatma Gandhi; they insisted that demonstrators be sober, well-groomed (wearing coats and ties), and nonviolent. Fellow students were told: "If you can't take insult and injury, stay away." A Tennessee group published a code to govern sit-ins, which read in part:

> Don't strike back or curse if abused. . . .
> Don't block entrances to stores and aisles.
> Show yourself courteous and friendly at all times.
> Sit straight and always face the counter.[4]

Southern whites reacted with shock, and anger in many quarters, at these extraordinary performances. And yet an astonishing number were favorably impressed. An elderly lady of segregationist background, seeing Negro students rebuffed at a lunch counter in Raleigh, exclaimed: "How can they refuse to serve such nice, polite young people?" The segregationist editor of the *Richmond News Leader* said, on February 22, of a sit-in in that city: "Here were the colored students, in coats, white shirts, ties, and one of them reading Goethe and one was taking notes from a biology text. And here, on the sidewalk outside, was a gang of white boys come to heckle, a ragtail rabble, slack-jawed, black-jacketed, grinning fit to kill, and some of them, God save the mark, were waving the proud flag of the Southern states in the last war fought by gentlemen . . . !' "

As the sit-ins multiplied, they were supported increasingly by parades and picket lines. Apart from the demonstration of Negro intelligence and good manners, the movement had a profound effect upon the thinking of white Southerners. Many of them had really believed that "our Negroes" were contented with their lot, that all the agitation was the work of outsiders. Here was unmistakable evidence to the contrary. White student groups and religious bodies, a few in the South and many in the nation, expressed sympathy with the student crusade. At the same time the spectacle of sit-ins and picket lines tended to frighten regular customers away from trading centers and caused substantial loss to white merchants, while the task of maintaining public order taxed the resources of municipal authorities. Bi-racial "mayor's committees" and similar bodies were set up in many cities to seek a solution of the problems—or, expressed more realistically, to induce merchants to open their lunch counters to Negroes. White clergymen were in the forefront of this work of adjustment.

Governor Collins of Florida in a broadcast on March 20 expressed his opinion that "if a man has a department store and he invites the public generally to come into his department store and trade, then it is morally wrong to single out one department and say he does not want or will not allow Negroes to patronize that one department." In the atmosphere of tension which sit-ins precipitated in Florida, Collins moved forthwith to set up a state commission on race relations —the only such body in the South—which worked diligently through the remaining eight months of his administration. Significant also was the formation in April of the Student Nonviolent Co-ordinating Committee, a mainly Negro organization, which would become a permanent and dynamic addition to the militant organizations in the field.

The desegregation of lunch counters in response to the sit-ins was painfully slow at the start, but in the late summer the walls of Jericho came tumbling down in many places and within a year some lunch counters in over a hundred cities had dropped race barriers.

When the advance in this area ran into the more difficult strongholds of segregation and the pace slackened, the movement itself only gathered momentum. It broadened its objectives. Segregation and discrimination were challenged in restaurants, theaters, churches, public parks and swimming pools, courtrooms, libraries, museums, art galleries, laundromats, on the beaches and in voter registration, employment, and transportation. Economic boycotts were added to the pressure upon merchants practicing race discrimination in service or employment. There was much scattered disorder and some rioting; several thousand arrests were made. But in relation to the provocative nature and the vast sweep of the movement, the amount of serious violence was small—except in an attack upon segregation in interstate bus transportation.

In this undertaking, audacious forays into Alabama and Mississippi —two fierce citadels of white supremacy which the student movement had barely touched—had horrifying consequences. In May 1961 the Congress of Racial Equality sponsored a bus tour of the South, or a "freedom ride," to test local segregation laws and practices in interstate transportation and terminal facilities. Although Negroes generally occupied the back seats apart from the white passengers in such buses, in most of the South this was no longer required. Segregation of passengers on buses was in violation of the principle laid down in the Brown decision. Relying specifically on that ruling, the Interstate Commerce Commission had ordered an end to segregation on interstate railroads and in their terminals. In 1956 the Supreme Court cited the Brown decision in ruling against segregation on local buses in Montgomery, Alabama; in 1962, it was to declare: "We have settled beyond question that no state may require segregation of interstate or intrastate transportation facilities." [5]

The "freedom riders," seated in front or at random in the buses, encountered no serious difficulty until they arrived in Alabama. There they experienced a week of the bloodiest racial violence in the recent history of that state. A mob attacked one contingent of "riders" at Anniston and burned the bus with an incendiary bomb. White toughs met another contingent at Birmingham and assailed both the "riders" and the gathering newsmen. In the capital city of Montgomery a replacement contingent of "riders" was met at the bus station and beaten with fists and clubs. The score of persons who were injured in several hours of rioting in Montgomery included John Seigenthaler, a Department of Justice official, who had been designated as a representative of President Kennedy; Seigenthaler was bludgeoned into semiconsciousness while attempting to save a white "rider" from the mob. A disturbing feature of the convulsions was the apparent sympathy of many of the police and other authorities with the rioters. When these failed to quell the disturbances, federal marshals were sent in; the number of federal marshals in Alabama reached a total of 666. At last on May 21 Governor Patterson called out the Alabama National Guard and order was restored.

In Mississippi similar molestation of freedom riders by the populace was prevented by heavy police precautions, including the use of the National Guard from the outset. But in that state the "riders" were subjected to harsh treatment by the law-enforcement authorities, and their "ride" for the most part ended in Jackson jails or in the state prison farm. As contingent after contingent arrived in Jackson, more than three hundred were arrested and convicted—generally on the charge of "breach of the peace" when they refused to obey police orders to "move on" after entering segregated terminal facilities.

The freedom rides aroused both criticism and sympathy in national liberal circles. They drew some distinguished white participation. A party which arrived in Montgomery on May 24—whose members were arrested the following day—included the Reverend William S. Coffin, Jr., Yale University chaplain and a member of the Peace Corps Advisory Council; the Reverend Gaylord B. Noyce, assistant professor

of religion at the Yale Divinity School; and Dr. David E. Swift and
Dr. John D. Maguire, professor and assistant professor of religion at
Wesleyan University. A bi-racial group of Episcopal ministers, headed
by the Reverend John B. Morris, executive director of the Episcopal
Society for Cultural and Racial Unity, joined the freedom riders in
Jackson and spent some time in jail there.

The sound and fury of the Alabama violence and the Mississippi
jailings echoed through the world's press and radio; there were protest and sarcasm and grave warnings of Communist gains in the
damage to American prestige. Secretary of State Dean Rusk supported
a petition of Attorney General Robert F. Kennedy to the Interstate
Commerce Commission to adopt more stringent regulations against
segregation. The immediate gains of the freedom riders in practice
were meager and tenuous, but on September 22, 1961, the Interstate
Commerce Commission prescribed new rules prohibiting discrimination in seating on interstate buses and requiring each bus to display a
sign to that effect. Similar action was taken with respect to bus
terminals.

A detailed account of the fast-spreading protest movement of the
1960s and its development into a massive revolt of Negro Americans
against the incubus of race discrimination would be beyond the com-
pass of this book. The Brown decision was a mighty precursor, but it
may have been more a cushion than a causal factor. A stage had been
reached in history and in the enlightenment of our Negro minority
when it is hard to see how a rebellion could have been postponed.
The Supreme Court opinion in the Brown cases told Negroes that
their resentment of segregation was supported by the Constitution of
the United States and made their aspirations a part of what we like to
call the "American dream." The great decision pointed to the possibilities of relief through processes of law when, to many zealots, more
dangerous methods might have suggested themselves. It encouraged
continued recourse to federal courts, and the greatest of Negro organizations, the National Association for the Advancement of Colored
People, moved within this channel.

A further fortunate circumstance was the fact that the Southern
Christian Leadership Conference, the Congress on Racial Equality,
and the student organizations, though going beyond court action, were
devoted to nonviolent methods. Martin Luther King was the most

conspicuous personality in the Negro protest movement. This gentle clergyman with an iron will exasperated many Southern whites. Demonstrations that he inspired, however nonviolent in themselves, were regarded as an incitement to strife and violence and became a nightmare for Southern municipal and police authorities. Liberals also often criticized his strategy and timing. But King's primacy in the eyes of the Negro public was never challenged, and the wave of insurgence was dominated by his philosophy. To this he gave lofty expression in a frequently repeated message to the whites:

> We will match your capacity to inflict suffering with our capacity to endure suffering. We will meet your physical force with soul force. We will not hate you, but we cannot in good conscience obey your unjust laws. . . . We will soon wear you down by our capacity to suffer. And in winning our freedom we will so appeal to your heart and conscience that we will win you in the process.[6]

It was not to be expected that a clash on so vast a scale of concepts, mores, and local laws would be free from turmoil. But thanks to King's philosophy and a disposition on the part of the federal judiciary —shared increasingly by the federal executive—to extend to the Negro minority "the equal protection of the laws," the convulsions have been mild in comparison with those which often have attended the rise of oppressed peoples.

Chapter 15

THE BEGINNING OF A
MOVEMENT OF COMPLIANCE

In statistical analyses and forecasts of the region's approach to "all deliberate speed" in its compliance with the Brown decision, the year 1960 should be taken as the point at which the South began to move. The earlier school-desegregation initiatives—outside of Texas—however significant psychologically, had been meager and more or less isolated. During the years 1960 and 1961 the number of Negroes in school with whites in Texas increased, in approximate figures, from 3300 to 5000. In the ten other Southern states, the number increased from less than 350 to more than 2600, and the number of school districts desegregated rose from twenty-six to sixty.[1]

Some observers, on the eighth anniversary of the Brown decision, divided the total number of Negroes attending classes with whites in Southern public schools by eight—ignoring progressive acceleration— and came forward with dismal and misleading calculations. James Graham Cook began his book *The Segregationists* with a chapter entitled "1. Introduction—The 7288-Year Integration Plan"! This author calculated that on the basis of the average annual rate of desegregation for eight years it would take 7288 years to bring the 2,482,170 Negro school children in ten states into public schools with whites![2] Actually it was not until 1960 that anything like an annual rate of desegregation was discernible, and it would accelerate dramatically from year to year. The admission of several thousand Negro pupils in the sixth and seventh years after Brown was still a dilatory and feeble response to the desegregation mandate, but it was far from being as hopeless as this extravagant arithmetic suggested.

The breaking down of resistance postures in 1960 and 1961 was more impressive than the count of integrated pupils. The wall of segregation was breached in two more states, leaving only Alabama, Mississippi, and South Carolina on the totally recalcitrant list. Over the great urban centers, within the limits of token adjustment, the winds of change blew briskly. Negroes were admitted to schools with whites for the first time in five of the six largest cities in the South—Houston and New Orleans in 1960 and Dallas, Atlanta, and Memphis in 1961; in the sixth, San Antonio, two hundred Negro children had been admitted to previously all-white schools in 1955. Miami, which ranks among the South's largest cities when its populous metropolitan area is taken into account, had begun desegregation in 1959. (Another sprawling metropolis, Birmingham, was to be among the last bitter strongholds of resistance.) In a somewhat lower population bracket, public schools were desegregated in Raleigh, North Carolina (Durham had moved in 1959), Knoxville, Tennessee, and Richmond and Roanoke, Virginia, in 1960; in Tampa, Florida, and Galveston, Texas, in 1961. Incidentally, in all these cities the travail of Little Rock and the economic penalties that city still suffered—"We must not have another Little Rock"—was a potent influence for orderly adjustment. Violence in this area of Negro advance largely subsided. New Orleans was torn with ugly turmoil, but elsewhere the change was made in unbroken public order and tranquillity.

Most impressive of all was the growing recognition of the inevitability of change in the broad field of interracial relations. In the fall of 1958 a Gallup poll had asked the question: "Do you think the day will ever come in the South when whites and Negroes will be going to the same schools, eating in the same restaurants, and generally sharing the same public accommodations?" Only 53 per cent of the Southerners queried had answered "Yes." When the same question was put to Southerners in January 1961, 76 per cent answered in the affirmative.

The year 1960 was a presidential election year in the United States. Both major political parties promised vigorous support of public-school desegregation and civil rights. The anti-segregation plank in the Democratic platform was adopted over angry Southern protests, with ten Southern delegations issuing a dissenting minority report. At the Republican national convention the fight was between a regular subcommittee, which proposed a milder stand, and two powerful leaders, Vice-President Richard M. Nixon and Governor Nelson Rockefeller of New York, who demanded and secured the strong plank. Each party expressed a determination to end public-school segregation, proposed legislation to empower the attorney general to initiate desegregation suits, and greeted the Negro students' sit-in movement with expressions of approval of "peaceful demonstrations" or "peaceful assembly" in support of their aims.

Senator John F. Kennedy and Vice-President Nixon, who emerged as the Democratic and Republican nominees for President, and Henry Cabot Lodge, the Republican candidate for Vice-President, all took fervently liberal positions on the race question in the ensuing contest; Senator Lyndon B. Johnson, Kennedy's running mate—himself a Southerner—was more guarded on the subject. In spite of Negro loathing for the Democratic politicians who ruled the South, faith in the liberalism of the party as a whole and in its candidate—aided during the campaign by gestures of sympathy for Martin Luther King, who was in a Georgia jail at the time—appeared to have won a preponderance of the Negro vote for Kennedy.

The Civil Rights Act of 1957 had been the first such act in eighty-two years, or since the Reconstruction era. A second was passed in 1960. Both bills were limited in scope and were further emasculated before passage over stubborn Southern opposition. In 1960 the issue monopolized the attention of Congress from February 15 until the bill's final passage on April 8, and Southern Senators broke previous filibuster records with a continuous 125-hour performance. The act which emerged was a disappointment to liberal leaders in both houses. Two provisions which had been recommended by President Eisenhower were rejected: one would have given statutory authority to the President's committee seeking to eliminate discrimination in employment by government-contract firms; the other would have provided federal aid for communities struggling with the problem of desegregating their public schools and would have stated that the Brown decision was the law of the land. Like its 1957 predecessor, the Civil Rights Act of 1960 was mainly concerned with protecting the voting rights of Negroes. The former gave the attorney general the power to defend Negro voting rights in court; the latter authorized the appointment by federal judges of referees to register qualified Negro voters in situations where registration was denied them.

The Eisenhower Administration further altered its hands-off policy in its closing days in office by permitting Attorney General William P. Rogers to take over major responsibility for enforcing federal court decrees in the vexing New Orleans school crisis. As successive waves of defiant legislation flowed from the Louisiana legislature, the Justice

Department took the initiative in obtaining injunctive relief from this kind of interference. Within a few weeks the task was inherited by the Kennedy Administration, and thereafter federal energies were increasingly devoted to guaranteeing the efficacy of federal court desegregation orders, at New Orleans and elsewhere.

The inauguration of President Kennedy in January 1961 ushered in a new era of recognition of the Negro and of sympathy with his aspirations on the part of the federal government. A number of Negroes were appointed to high office. Robert Weaver was named Administrator of the Housing and Home Finance Agency, a position with responsibilities comparable to those of a cabinet member. Other Negro appointees included two federal district judges and one judge of a United States Court of Appeals, two ambassadors, an Assistant Secretary of Labor, two federal district attorneys, Deputy Assistant Secretaries of State and of the Department of Health, Education and Welfare, a Deputy Assistant Postmaster General, a Commissioner of the District of Columbia, and a White House Associate Press Secretary. The President's attitude was one of positive support of the Brown decision and of equal opportunity for Negroes in a broad field—an attitude which, though by-passing Southern members of Congress, began to pervade the official atmosphere of Washington.

We have now observed enough Southern cities in the throes of first adjustment to bi-racial public schools to have established a certain pattern. In the hostile manifestations of elements who were determined to preserve segregation at all costs, in the tireless labors of citizens who were prepared to accept inevitable desegregation and who strove to preserve public education, in the threats of fanatics and the apprehensions of law-enforcement authorities—and in the relaxation of tensions after the fact of desegregation—the experience of cities little and big was remarkably similar. Interminable federal court litigation was often, but not always, a part of the ordeal. Crises differed in the degree and timeliness of recognition by the business community of its interest in public stability. The opposition varied in vehemence and in the proportion of the populace involved. Where violence and rioting occurred, we saw the hand of uncannily effective racist agitators, as in Clinton, or an inflammatory performance by state authorities, as in Little Rock. Both these phenomena plagued New Orleans.

The 1960–61 desegregation saw the development in the two most difficult situations, those of New Orleans and Atlanta, of save-the-public-schools organizations patterned after those of Virginia and Little Rock. These organizations, avoiding the segregation issue as such, were able to arouse broad opposition to closing the schools as an alternative to desegregation. Groups in Dallas and elsewhere used a similar approach. When the point of desegregation was reached, a gradual schedule of admitting Negroes to white schools in the first grade only at the outset and to the next higher grade each year thereafter was widely favored. Although this plan was frowned upon by federal courts in some school districts where desegregation had already begun or where no serious emotional problem existed, New Orleans, Houston, Dallas, Galveston, Memphis, and Knoxville began by integrating only the first grade with the approval, or upon the suggestion, of federal district judges. (The two Tennessee cities were later ordered to move faster than one grade a year.) The business community of Dallas exerted itself vigorously on the side of law and order and public education; that in Atlanta moved belatedly but with wholesome effect; the businessmen of New Orleans were tragically too late.

Texas, after the early fumbling in Mansfield, was not again a scene of sensational disorder in public-school desegregation, and so large a part of the state had adjusted early to the Supreme Court ruling that many observers classed Texas with the border states in this respect. Before the legislature put a brake on the movement in 1957 by requiring previous approval by popular vote if state school funds were not to be withheld, 123 out of 722 Texas school districts had removed racial barriers. Although desegregation was extended in school districts which had already taken the first step and referendum approval for initial desegregation was secured in two districts, this enactment largely put a stop to voluntary action. The Galveston school board, for instance, suspended a plan for desegregation which had been scheduled to begin in September 1957. An important result of the Houston crisis in 1960 was a ruling by State Attorney General Will Wilson removing this statutory handicap when desegregation was ordered by federal courts.

In spite of the degree of emotional stability on the issue at which Texas had arrived, and which the events of 1960–61 would attest, the approach of the change in the eastern section with its heavy Negro population aroused considerable apprehension. The event was nervously awaited in the great metropolises of Houston and Dallas, the two largest cities in the nation where public-school segregation still prevailed. In both those cities and in Galveston the familiar controversy and protests raged. But Negro first-graders were admitted to classes with whites—twenty-one in Houston, eighteen in Dallas, and thirty-seven in Galveston—quietly and without incident. In Dallas the work of businessmen in a "Dallas Citizens' Council"—with objectives more or less the opposite of those of organizations elsewhere of similar name—aided by associations of ministers, lawyers, and physicians, was largely responsible for making the initial desegregation what many observers, including NAACP officials, called "a model operation." [3] Dallas had also responded to the student protest movement with the desegregation of forty restaurants and lunch counters.

That city's earlier experience with the school problem was made particularly noteworthy—and disturbing with respect to the efficiency of the federal judicial system—by the bizarre performance of two superannuated district judges, volubly out of sympathy with the Supreme Court's decision, who presided over six years of litigation there. After balking through three district court hearings and four interventions by the court of appeals, Judge William H. Atwell, eighty-eight years of age, at last issued a desegregation order. But in apparent pique, without waiting for a plan to be submitted, he ordered Dallas to desegregate all its schools by the beginning of the next semester, in January 1958. The court of appeals vacated this command, and the NAACP attorneys did not press the matter again until the summer of 1959, when it asked the court to require the school board to submit a plan.

By now, however, Judge Atwell had retired. The case was assigned to Judge T. Whitfield Davidson, eighty-two years of age, who a year later, under unequivocal instructions from the court of appeals, ordered the school board to submit a desegregation plan. The school board produced a one-grade-a-year program to begin in 1961. This the aged jurist rejected. Instead he offered his own plan: it was the scheme, which had been put forward in Alabama and Tennessee, for keeping all the schools segregated except one or two for such pupils as might voluntarily choose interracial mingling. The court of appeals then reversed the court in Dallas for the sixth time and directed Judge Davidson to approve substantially the school board's plan.[4]

New Orleans and Atlanta—each was the first redoubt of public-school segregation to fall in a state that in 1960 was still mobilized for total resistance. Their problem presented greater difficulty, and the event had greater significance, on that account. It was evident by 1960 from the course of federal court litigation in both cities that peremptory orders to end public-school segregation could not be held off much longer. Atlanta was grappling with all aspects of the question, but New Orleans and Louisiana were engaged mainly in stifling free debate and in raising higher the ramparts of resistance which would have to be toppled over.

Atlanta—sophisticated, enterprising, bustling with progress—was a symbol of the "New South" that its own Henry W. Grady had proclaimed three-quarters of a century before; it was one of the nation's great industrial and financial centers. Yet the capital city and metropolis of Georgia, with approximately one-eighth of the state's total population, was a feeble force in state affairs. The county unit system of elections and an obsolete pattern of legislative districts, which gave many times as much representation to rural districts, left Atlanta almost powerless by electoral processes to alter the state's political course.

We have seen many manifestations in these pages of the aggressive hostility of Georgia's legislature and its Governors Talmadge and Griffin to any departure from the South's rule of race segregation. Griffin's successor, Governor Ernest Vandiver took a similarly adamant stand.

Atlanta's leadership was far more constructive. The city enjoyed the rare advantage of having in key positions of influence two individuals who rank high among the leaders of the South in this whole difficult period: Ralph McGill, editor of the *Atlanta Constitution,* and William B. Hartsfield, the city's sagacious and indomitable veteran mayor. The Negro element, approximately 30 per cent of the city's population, included a group of wealthy and distinguished individuals who gave Atlanta a view of the Negro that white people in most Southern cities never saw; a Negro held elective office as a member of the city school board. Though the suit which brought desegregation to Atlanta was filed only in January 1958, by 1960, 311 clergymen, 419 physicians, two-thirds of the faculty of Emory University, and a number of Parent-Teacher Associations had declared themselves publicly in favor of continued operation of the public schools with acceptance of desegregation, and a dynamic organization, Help Our Public Education, Inc., or "HOPE," had been in operation for over a year. At the same time race prejudice was deeply rooted in a large element of the Atlanta populace and the opposition to desegregation had busy promoters and virulent spokesmen.

Federal District Judge Frank A. Hooper, himself a former Georgia legislator, persevered in the express hope that the state's school-closing legislation would be repealed. In January 1960 he gave the legislature a clear-cut choice: accept gradual integration or be prepared to close, not only Atlanta schools, but all the public schools in the state. In February the legislature acted to the extent of setting up a nineteen-member commission to study the problem. Headed by John A. Sibley, a 71-year-old Atlanta banker, the commission conducted a whirlwind month of hearings—hearing eighteen hundred witnesses—in Georgia's ten congressional districts. The commission's report, rendered April 28 and signed by eleven of its nineteen members, recommended local option on the issue—the indicated retreat from massive resistance. Judge Hooper, in a May hearing, gave the legislature what he described as a "last chance" and fixed May 1, 1961, as the deadline for Atlanta school desegregation, to be effective upon the opening of schools for the next term.

New Orleans had been under a school-desegregation order since 1956. The suit, *Bush v. Orleans Parish School Board,** was filed in 1952, suspended pending disposition of the Brown cases, which were then on their way to the Supreme Court, and reactivated after the Supreme Court's 1955 ruling. In a decision of February 15, 1956, Federal District Judge J. Skelly Wright ordered the desegregation of public schools "with all deliberate speed," but he pointed out that this did not mean that desegregation must be completed "overnight, or even in a year or more." [5] His opinion concluded with a paragraph which has been widely quoted as one of the philosophic gems of this crisis in the South:

> The problem of changing a people's mores, particularly those with an emotional overlay, is not to be taken lightly. It is a problem which will require the utmost patience, understanding, gener-

* In Louisiana the term "parish" is used for what is called a county in other states. That embracing New Orleans is Orleans Parish.

osity, and forbearance from all of us, of whatever race. But the magnitude of the problem may not nullify the principle. And that principle is that we are, all of us, freeborn Americans, with a right to make our way, unfettered by sanctions imposed by man because of the work of God.

But in the next four years the only response was continued litigation and a proliferation of laws designed to perpetuate public-school segregation.

Paradoxically, in the desegregation of institutions of higher learning Louisiana had gone farther than any other Southern state. For the 1960–61 term, 634 Negroes had been admitted to predominantly white universities supported by the state with a total aggregate enrollment of 22,565.

Louisiana has ethnic characteristics which set it apart from other states of the South, and of the Union, as a result of its background as successively a French colony, a Spanish colony, and a French colony again before its acquisition by the United States. The French influence is most apparent in the southeastern section in which New Orleans lies. About half the population of that city is of the Roman Catholic faith. In 1960 approximately fifty thousand New Orleans children were enrolled in Catholic parochial schools, and many Catholic children were among the approximately ninety-five thousand pupils in public schools. The mayor, the superintendent of public schools, and two of the five members of the public-school board were Catholics. Although the parochial schools remained segregated until 1962, Archbishop Rummel had given notice in 1956 that they were destined to be desegregated, and he had declared repeatedly that "segregation is morally wrong." Nevertheless, white Catholic laymen showed little more tolerance on the race issue than Protestant laymen. Two Catholics, Emile Wagner, a member of the public-school board, and Leander Perez, a wealthy politician, were among the foremost leaders of the extreme segregationist element. A group of Catholics took public issue with the Archbishop and appealed the question of segregation to the Pope; their communication received no acknowledgment.

Although the threat of school-closing to avoid racial integration had long hung over New Orleans, it was not until the spring of 1960 that significant voices were heard in defense of public education. Lloyd Rittiner, president of the public-school board, said: "I am a segregationist. If, however, I am faced with a choice of integrating or closing, I am already on record as favoring integration to the extent that is necessary to comply with the law"; three other board members took a similar stand. But even this degree of moderation brought down upon these school officials a flood of abuse. The movement to prevent school-closing got under way only in the early summer. It was organized in two groups, "Save Our Schools," or "SOS," and a Committee on Public Education, or "COPE." These published pamphlets, held meetings, buttonholed hesitant business and professional leaders, and succeeded in stimulating a degree of public dialogue on the question. Some groups of clergymen also spoke out.

The businessmen stayed for the most part in the large "neutral" or silent compound until actual rioting began; it was not until January 1961—after inestimable damage had been done—that a hundred business and professional leaders signed a page advertisement in the two newspapers calling for law and order. Mayor de Lesseps S. Morrison was timidly on the side of continued public education but fearful of antagonizing the extremists who were rampant in his city and the state. The local newspapers, which for several years had added to the chorus of hostility to desegregation, began only in August of 1960 to express a firm conviction that "preservation of public education at this time stands out as paramount." [6] The only medium to accept early and firmly the responsibility for community leadership was the television station WDSU-TV and the radio station WDSU. That a silent reservoir of moderate sentiment existed in New Orleans was attested when a school-board election was held on November 8, at the height of the furor; Matthew Sutherland, a member who opposed school-closing, was re-elected over three extremist opponents. But in no other city whose desegregation experience we have observed was the default of constructive leadership more apparent.

The Citizens' Council of New Orleans was feverishly active. The chief source of obstruction, however, and of incitement to turmoil, was the state capitol at Baton Rouge. Jimmy H. Davis, a writer of popular songs and a former governor, was re-elected to that office on April 19. Davis had won the Democratic nomination in the run-off primary over Mayor Morrison by gathering the ultra-segregationists into his camp. The legislature was in a mood to pass any bill aimed at preventing desegregation that was presented to it. Judge Wright's struggle with the governor and legislature of Louisiana is one of the

epics in judicial annals. He was staunchly supported by the Fifth
Circuit Court of Appeals but under a barrage of vilification and
threats.

When on May 16 Judge Wright was still unable to secure a desegregation plan from the school board, he produced one of his own.
He ordered desegregation at the opening of schools in September in
accordance with the following plan:

> "A. All children entering the first grade may attend either the
> formerly all-white public schools nearest their homes or the for-
> merly all-Negro public school nearest their homes at their option.
> "B. Children may be transferred from one school to another
> provided such transfers are not based on considerations of race."

On June 26 the court of appeals refused to grant a stay of Judge
Wright's order; [7] on July 11 Supreme Court Justice Hugo Black refused to grant a stay. On August 17 Governor Davis invoked one of
the state's portfolio of segregation laws and seized control of the Orleans Parish schools.[8] Ten days later a three-judge federal court issued
an order restraining the governor and declaring seven segregation laws
unconstitutional. Five times the governor or the legislature attempted
to take over the New Orleans schools or to strip members of its school
board of their powers.[9] In November the legislature went into a
twelve-day special session to try to block desegregation and then
launched into a thirty-day session in an effort to reverse it. Judge
Wright met every new move with restraining orders and was regularly
sustained by the higher federal courts. When November 14 was set
as the date for desegregation, the legislature declared that day a school
"holiday" and sent state police to enforce it, but the principals of the
hundred and eighteen schools stood firm and no school in New Orleans
was closed.

The explosion that ensued and the disgraceful performance of
officials and uncontrolled fanatics for weeks afterward made another
of those sensational post-Brown decision episodes which engrossed
the American press and radio-television and sent photos and stories
to the far corners of the earth. We give the picture in the following
excerpts from *The New Orleans School Crisis,* a report of the Louisiana State Advisory Committee to the United States Commission on
Civil Rights:

On Monday, November 14, four Negro girls attended first-grade classes at two previously all-white schools (the fifth child eligible for transfer was withdrawn). The schools were William Frantz Elementary and McDonogh No. 19. . . . The Negro children were accompanied to school by federal marshals. The white parents of the neighborhood, with two exceptions, withdrew their children from the schools. The Reverend Lloyd Foreman and Mrs. Daisy Gabrielle continued to send their little girls to the Frantz school. The boycott at McDonogh No. 19 was total (it was briefly broken by the children of John Thompson in late January 1961; the Thompsons braved the boycott for three days and then left town).

On November 15 William Rainach, Leander Perez, and others addressed a crowd of over five thousand at a White Citizens' Council meeting in New Orleans. Rainach advocated civil disobedience and a scorched-earth policy. Perez said, in part, "Don't wait for your daughters to be raped by these Congolese. Do something about it now." Some witnesses described the meeting as "a gathering straight out of Nazi Germany." The action suggested by the speakers was a march on the school-board building, city hall, and Judge Wright's office by protesting citizens.

On November 16 this action was forthcoming. A crowd of teen-agers and adults marched on the prescribed buildings, chanting: "Two, four, six, eight, we don't want to integrate." City police, under Superintendent Joseph Giarusso, attempted to control the mob by the use of mounted police and a few firehoses. No whites were injured, but several Negroes were hurt by flying glass as bus windows were shattered by vandals and two Negroes were severely beaten. The mob dispersed before it reached the heart of the business district. . . .

Now the legislature abandoned its legislative committee approach and took over control of the New Orleans schools itself. The legislature urged white parents at Frantz and McDonogh No. 19 to continue their boycott of the schools. . . .

A member of the Orleans Parish school staff warned that money was becoming a problem for the school board, since the state had forbidden banks to lend money to the school board and the legislature itself had refused to pay the teachers. . . .

On November 23 the legislature passed a resolution authorizing the payment of the Orleans Parish school employees, with the exception of the administrative staff and the Frantz and McDonogh teachers. An anonymous citizen loaned these teachers money to cover their earned salaries. Dr. Redmond, Mr. Rosenberg, and the administrative staff went unpaid. . . .

In mid-November the Whitney National Bank, which had honored payroll checks issued by the elected Orleans Parish school board, was removed as fiscal agent for the State. . . .

During the last days of November the Reverend Lloyd Foreman and Mrs. James Gabrielle, who had continued to take their children to the Frantz school, were subjected to abuse and physical violence by the mob in front of the school. This, coupled with the fact that several parents in the Frantz school area had appealed to SOS for help in returning their children to school, led to the organization of a volunteer "carlift," run by parents from the uptown section of New Orleans, which transported the children to school in relative safety. The "carlift" began on December 1. The car carrying Yolanda Gabrielle was stoned and manhandled by the mob. Later in the week, it was pursued for two miles by a truck which had tried to ram it. Until Wednesday, December 7, the drivers and the women who escorted the children into the school were subjected to the vilest sort of shouted abuse from the daily-assembled crowds. On December 7 the police guarding the school pushed the crowd behind barricades a full block away from the school.

The crowd then dispersed to roam the streets of the Florida Housing Project, where many of the children lived. Their parents were subjected to an organized telephone campaign of threats and abuse. Their houses and other properties were stoned, as was one of the mothers of a child at Frantz. The jobs of the fathers were threatened; four of them lost their jobs. James Gabrielle, ostracized by his fellow-workers, quit his job and took his family to Rhode Island. The volunteer drivers were threatened with death, arson, disfigurement, and other unpleasantnesses in a concerted telephone campaign. The police were unable to prevent these occurrences; and, with the exception of a couple of juveniles alleged to have stoned Mrs. Marion McKinley, no one connected with the demonstrations was arrested, nor was the mob in front of the school dispersed or told to move on.

The August 27 decision of the three-judge federal district court prohibiting implementation of segregation legislation was carried to the United States Supreme Court on appeal. This brought another rejection of the plea for a stay of the desegregation order and elicited a death blow to the doctrine of interposition which many Southern states had espoused. The high tribunal on December 12 found "without substance" the argument that the State of Louisiana had "interposed itself." Quoting from the opinion of the three-judge court, it said: "The conclusion is clear that interposition is not a constitutional doctrine. If taken seriously, it is an illegal defiance of constitutional authority . . ." [10]

New Orleans public schools returned to normal operation. The tenuous beachhead of racial integration survived the painful first year and was broadened each year thereafter. In spite of lingering scars of interracial bitterness, the aftermath resembled that in other desegregating cities. When twelve Negro children entered school with whites in September 1961, the governor and legislature were silent, even Emile Wagner advised the Citizens' Council against demonstrations, and complete order prevailed. Sixty federal marshals sent to New Orleans were not used.

In Georgia the movement against reckless resistance to desegregation had grown during 1960, but the structure of defiance and hostility was such that an explosion—some outlet for emotions, some rioting, and some demonstration of the folly of all this—seemed necessary before quiet adjustment could be achieved. Fortunately for Atlanta, the catharsis was provided at the University of Georgia at Athens.

In most Southern states the desegregation of institutions of higher learning was now no longer a major problem. State universities in six of the eleven had enrolled Negroes with whites before the Brown decision; in a seventh, Florida, the state university began to do so in 1958. In January 1961 Negroes were attending over two hundred universities and colleges in Southern and border states and the District of Columbia which before 1955 had been restricted to whites. But in four Deep South states—Mississippi, Alabama, Georgia, and South Carolina—university segregation was an outer bastion in the massive-resistance stockade. Except for the brief and stormy experience of Autherine Lucy at the University of Alabama, no Negro had been admitted to a university with whites in these states. On January 6, 1961, climaxing a litigation begun the previous August, Federal District Judge William A. Bootle ordered that two Negroes be admitted to the University of Georgia. The Negroes, Miss Charlayne A. Hunter and

Hamilton E. Holmes, were students of an exceptionally high caliber; Holmes in 1962 was to win the distinction of being elected to Phi Beta Kappa, the national honor society.

The integration of the two Negro students precipitated a week of excitement, confusion, and rioting. The disorders—in which unruly elements from the university city of Athens and from elsewhere in the state had a significant part—were not to be compared with those at the University of Alabama in 1956, but they were enough to cause widespread alarm. A degree of hysteria seized the state administration and the legislature—whose regular session had opened on the day the Negro students registered. Efforts were made to close the university and cut off its funds, but they were thwarted promptly by federal court action. The two Negroes were removed from the university for four days for their "personal safety." When they returned on January 16 the campus was calm and the crisis was over. By extension, the crisis was over in large measure for Atlanta's public schools.

What happened in the Georgia legislature during the remaining days of January was sharply reminiscent of the drama enacted in Virginia just two years earlier. Governor Vandiver in an address before a joint session of the two chambers, broadcast by radio and television, made a ringing declaration:

> We meet together to proclaim to all the world that:
> Public education will be preserved!
> Our Georgia children will be protected!
> Local administration and autonomy will be maintained!
> Grants will be authorized!

His brave rhetoric was nonetheless a retreat from massive resistance:

> Every legal means and resource to circumvent the effects of the [*Brown*] decision, yes.
> Defiance, no.

Promptly, and with near unanimity, the legislature enacted three laws which had the effect of wiping out the school-segregation laws on the Georgia statute books. The new legislation included a tuition-grant plan for pupils attending private schools similar to the one in Virginia and a clarification of appeals procedure under the pupil-assignment plan. Local option and local referendums were provided for on the question of suspension of public schools.

In Atlanta, on August 30, nine Negro students were admitted to previously all-white public schools in an atmosphere of calm—and pride of achievement. (Among half-a-dozen loiterers arrested was a youth from Arlington, Virginia, who called himself a member of the American Nazi party; he clicked his heels and shouted *"Sieg heil!"*) The city had been prepared for the event by a rare mobilization of community leadership. The Chamber of Commerce ran a full-page newspaper advertisement, saying: "The law is clear"; 850 church laymen asked school children to accept desegregation with dignity; the week-end before the move was designated "Law and Order Week-end," and Atlanta churches were asked to pray for peaceful desegregation. The "Organizations Assisting Schools in September" prepared a handbook giving background and information for reporters. Representatives of newspapers, magazines, and broadcasting services were not allowed on school grounds, but a huge news center was set up for them at City Hall, where reports from school principals and others could be heard over loudspeakers. The center was equipped with telephones, teletypes, telegraph facilities, television and radio sets, as well as typewriters and tables, and the Coca-Cola Company furnished refreshments. In the evening the mayor gave a press party and took visiting newsmen on a tour of the city in air-conditioned buses.

Atlanta's desegregation operation was reported to the nation, with justification, as the triumphant accomplishment of a great city. President Kennedy in his afternoon press conference congratulated "Governor Vandiver, Mayor Hartsfield, Chief of Police Jenkins, Superintendent of Schools Letson, and all the parents, students, and citizens of Atlanta, Georgia, for the responsible, law-abiding manner in which four high schools were desegregated today."

The success of the desegregation operations in Dallas and Atlanta in 1961 encouraged a third famous Southern metropolis, Memphis, and was a factor in a somewhat sudden decision of that city's school board. Knoxville had admitted twenty-eight Negro first-graders to classes with whites in 1960 with so little difficulty as to lead one school principal to exclaim: "This is the easiest registration day we've ever had!" Tennessee had never taken a massive-resistance stand and there was no interference from a governor or a state legislature to contend with. Nevertheless, Memphis, in the southwestern corner of the state, ten miles from ominously recalcitrant Mississippi, had been looked upon as one of the major problem cities from the standpoint of adjustment to the Brown decision.

The Mississippi River port of song and story, the great cotton market, the birthplace of W. C. Handy and the "Blues," was much identified with the traditions of the old South. Forty-six per cent of its approximately one hundred thousand school children were Negroes. But the Negro votes, since the days of "Boss" Crump,* had come to be a significant factor in local political calculations, and communications between white and Negro leaders were intact. Many changes occurred in the city during the 1960–61 period. Voter registration drives further increased the Negro's political role and were largely responsible for the appointment of a Negro member of the Memphis Transit Authority and of Negroes to a number of lesser official posts. The zoo, an art museum, an amusement park, four of the seven public golf courses, and some playgrounds were desegregated under a ten-year plan. Enforced bus segregation ceased. Although Memphis merchants were still resisting the sit-in movement a plan was to be reached during the fall for the desegregation of some lunch counters after the Christmas shopping rush.

The Memphis operation was an interesting example of initial school desegregation with a minimum of preparation or of previous notice to the public. A desegregation order had been sought by Negroes in the federal district court, which had approved the state pupil-placement law and left the matter there; the Negroes had appealed. The court of appeals was to rule nearly a year later that the pupil placement law would "not serve as a plan to convert a bi-racial system into a nonracial one" and to call for "some realistic plan." But the school board did not wait for the federal court ruling.

During September 1961 the support of the political and civic leadership and the press was secured in behind-the-scenes meetings, and brief statements conveyed the suggestion that some desegregation was in the offing. But no public announcement was made that desegregation would take place at a certain time. At a press briefing the evening before the event, the president of the school board made it clear that full coverage was desired afterward but pledged the press to withhold public announcement until the children entered school the following morning, October 3. Neither reporters nor spectators

---

* Edward Hull Crump, city and state political leader, mayor of Memphis 1910–1916 and 1940–1942.

were allowed in school areas for the first few days, but a press head-quarters set up across the street from the school-board offices was relayed information as fast as it came in from the schools and police. Thus thirteen Negro children quietly entered previously all-white public schools, the news went out to the city and the nation, and Memphis's "breakthrough" was accomplished.

Chapter 16

DELIBERATE SPEED

The year 1962 saw an extension of public-school desegregation and statistically a further acceleration of progress. In Texas some 1700 more Negro children were admitted to schools with whites, bringing the total in that state to approximately 6700. In the ten other Southern states (or seven, excluding Mississippi, Alabama, and South Carolina, which had yet to take the first step) the total number of Negro school children integrated with white pupils approximately doubled, rising from 2603 to 5517. And in May 1962, on the eighth anniversary of the Brown decision, the South's public schools had completed their first year without violence since that event. Though threats and jeering crowds accompanied desegregated school-openings in the fall in New Orleans, in Pensacola, Florida, and in Chattanooga, Tennessee, no major public disorder occurred in this phase of the civil-rights movement through the remainder of 1962.

Public-school desegregation was still a relentless objective, but it was not now the chief concern of Negro leaders or the focus of national attention in the race-relations field. An upheaval of history-making proportions occurred at the university level; the other sensational news was furnished by gestures of Negro protest, often unavailing, against discrimination in voter registration, employment, and public accommodations, and the often arrogant and violent white response. The Negro revolt was gathering momentum but still smoldering—not yet ready to blaze across the nation as it would a year later—and the gravity of the situation was sensed by only a small, though an increasing number, of observers.

The Brown decision presented an acute challenge to the Roman Catholic hierarchy in the South. Except in Louisiana and parts of Texas, Catholics were a tiny minority, and a few Negro communicants worshiped along with whites in Catholic churches in all sections. But all Catholic parochial schools—a huge school system in Southern Louisiana and scattered schools in other Southern states—had been racially segregated like the public schools. Several Southern bishops acted before the Supreme Court decision was handed down; the few Catholic schools in North Carolina (Raleigh diocese) were desegregated early in 1954, and announcement was made that those in Virginia (Richmond diocese) would be desegregated the following September. The substantial parochial school system of San Antonio, Texas, was desegregated with the 1954–55 school term. At the beginning of 1962 some Catholic school desegregation had taken place in all but the Deep South states of Louisiana, Mississippi, Alabama, and Georgia. During the fall of that year race barriers were eliminated in most of the Georgia and Louisiana parochial schools.

In the Atlanta and New Orleans dioceses the church was embarrassed by postponement after earlier announcements of forthcoming desegregation, and by the fact that action was taken in this area of morality and conscience only after the public-school authorities had already moved. The variety of apprehensions and difficulties which caused the delay included the untimely illness of the responsible prelate in each instance—Bishop Francis E. Hyland of Atlanta and the aged Archbishop Rummel of New Orleans. In 1962 two vigorous and younger men took hold: the archdiocese of Atlanta was established under Archbishop Paul J. Hallinan, and Archbishop John Patrick Cody assumed the responsibility of apostolic administrator in New Orleans. In September 1962 seventeen Negro pupils were admitted to predominantly white parochial schools in Atlanta, Marietta, and Athens, Georgia, entirely without incident.

The desegregation of the immense parochial school system of New Orleans aroused spectacular and much publicized opposition, but no violence and no major interruption in school operation. Racial distinctions were eliminated in all the 164 schools of the archdiocese; the tangible effect in September 1962 was the enrollment of 173 Negro children in thirty-five predominantly white parochial schools. (The archdiocese extends beyond Orleans Parish, so that nine of the schools, which received thirty-seven Negro children, were in neighboring parishes, or counties.) In addition to many of the difficulties that confronted public-school authorities on desegregation, the administrators of church schools were apprehensive of the effect upon Catholic loyalties and the voluntary contributions on which the costly parochial school system so much depends. However, the desegregated schools of the New Orleans archdiocese enrolled 73,433 pupils as compared with 75,796 the previous year, and church attendance and contributions were little affected.

The tension in New Orleans was increased by a drastic extension at the same time of the desegregation program in the public schools. The latter, which had integrated only twelve Negro pupils with whites the previous year, in 1962 admitted 107 Negro children to the first three grades of nineteen predominantly white schools. But, although shrill voices of opposition were heard, segregationist rallies were poorly attended, and at both public and parochial schools disorders were relatively insignificant. The city had developed a notable aversion to violence and turmoil.

The Catholic desegregation operation in New Orleans, however, was not without some widely publicized unpleasantness, and resistance in one section. Following the announcement on March 27 that segregation in the schools of the archdiocese would end the following September, vehement denunciations were heard from some Catholic segregationist leaders. Three of them, the millionaire-politician Leander H. Perez; Jackson G. Ricau, a Citizens' Council director; and Mrs. B. J. Gaillot, Jr., who headed a group called "Save Our Nation, Inc.," were excommunicated. Mrs. Gaillot, fanatic in her insistence that segregation was decreed in the Bible as the will of God, picketed Archbishop Rummel's residence, submitted that 85-year-old prelate to an embarrassing encounter, and received much attention from press and television. In September, Perez exerted economic and other pressures to frustrate the desegregation program in the area of his political control. In Jefferson Parish, scattered boycotts reduced parochial school enrollment by 1100, and one school in the town of Buras, which formerly served 340 white students, was left with no pupils at all when five Negro children withdrew.

In the matter of public-school desegregation a pattern developed in 1962 that separated eight Southern states from the other three almost as sharply as the attitude of the border states separated them from the eleven former Confederate states. In Mississippi, Alabama, and South Carolina—after school-opening for the ninth school year since the practice had been pronounced unconstitutional—public schools were still completely segregated. Moreover, these were the three states where Negroes were most numerous in proportion to total population; these accounted for 800,000 Negro school children, or one-fourth of the total in the Southern and border region combined. In South Carolina a certain mitigation of the determination to resist desegregation at all costs was discernible in 1962. But Mississippi and Alabama were firmly in the grip of hostile elements; resistance in those two states was encouraged by reckless political leaders and supported by all the machinery of public administration.

The other eight Southern states had not gone far in complying with the Supreme Court ruling, but they had reached a point on the road which was significant in several respects. In these the policy that had been called "massive resistance" had completely collapsed; resistance on the part of governors and legislatures had practically ceased; and a mass of anti-integration legislation had been repealed or invalidated by federal courts. Although a state board still went through the motions of pupil assignment in Virginia, school districts in these states were in effect free from state government restraint and each was left to deal with its own problem. District school authorities on their part sought to postpone action and hold desegregation to a minimum, but they no longer flatly resisted the change. In the eight states the public had become largely resigned to a degree of adjustment, and the admission of Negroes to a school with whites was no longer an excuse for violence or even a signal for spectacular demonstrations. Two or three Negro children, or maybe half a dozen or a score, in each case were admitted to more previously all-white schools every year; the initial integration was steadily expanded; and the process could be expected to go on and on with increasing momentum.

Yet in its larger context the scale of the whole operation was almost microscopic. The presence of less than thirteen thousand Negro pupils in schools with whites at the end of the ninth year was a feeble response to a Supreme Court ruling which required that the stigma of segregation should be lifted from the 2,803,882 Negro children in Southern schools. If the speed of school desegregation had increased, it was from that of the snail to that of the tortoise. In fact, many white Southerners, finding total segregation no longer possible, had seized upon the compromise of token integration as a means of removing federal court pressure while prolonging general segregation for an indefinite period. "Tokenism" was decried by liberals as more a frustration of the intent of the Brown decision than a stage of gradualism in compliance with it.[1]

There was evidence, too, of growing impatience on the part of federal courts. Pupil-assignment (or pupil-placement) laws, which fixed rigid criteria—not applied to whites—for Negro pupils seeking admission to predominantly white schools had been relied upon heavily to keep integration at token levels. The Sixth Circuit Court ruled in a Memphis case in March 1962: "The Pupil-Assignment Law might serve some purpose in the administration of a school system, but it will not serve to convert a bi-racial system into a non-racial one." [2] In August the Fifth Circuit Court said in a New Orleans case: "This court, like the district court, condemns the Pupil Placement Act, when, with a fanfare of trumpets, it is hailed as the instrument for carrying out a desegregation plan while all the time the entire public knows that in fact it is being used to maintain segregation by allowing a little token desegregation. . . . It is not a plan for desegregation at all." [3]

In the early national discussion of the problems posed by the Brown decision the suggestion was frequently made that bi-racial schools in the South should be segregated by sex. It was believed that placing boys and girls in separate schools would allay the fears which preyed upon so many white Southerners that school integration would result in interracial romances and marriages. Mrs. Eleanor Roosevelt was among those who advanced this proposal. Bills providing for school segregation by sex were introduced in a number of state legislatures, and one was passed by the legislature of Florida. The plan was suggested by several federal district judges, including Judge J. Skelly Wright, of New Orleans. But, except for the anomalous case of half-a-dozen first-graders during the first year of integration in New Orleans, it was nowhere put into effect. The departure from the existing coeducational system would have been onerous and costly. Most white Southerners at first were in no mood to consider so drastic a reorganization to safeguard a move they were adamantly determined not to make; when desegregation began, their chief concern was to hold it to what they considered an innocuous minimum; and after a few years of experience with Negroes and whites in school together, the fear of resulting interracial marriages tended to subside. In the border states fears on this score were never sufficiently strong to cause serious consideration to be given to pupil segregation by sex.

A comprehensive study of the problem of converting high schools to all-boy and all-girl schools was made by Superintendent O. Perry Walker and submitted without recommendation to the school board of Orleans Parish on February 12, 1963. The report noted that the change in the thirty high schools of that parish would necessitate approximately doubling attendance districts with proportionately increased transportation problems; that it would require reorganization of classes where courses were favored mainly by students of one sex, with the denial of courses to girls, or to boys, when they were too few to form a class of their own sex; that over six hundred teachers would have to be transferred; and that moving vocational shops from girls' to boys' schools and home economics equipment from boys' to girls' schools and various structural changes in schools would cost approximately $250,000. Walker's research revealed that of twenty-five thousand high schools in the United States, twenty-four are attended by boys only or girls only, and these outside the South.

Not only in the South, but in the whole broad region, including the border states, where public schools were segregated at the time of the Brown decision, the fate of the seventy-five thousand Negro schoolteachers posed a delicate and baffling problem. Teacher segregation no less than the segregation of pupils was a denial of equality under the law, but most white Southerners recoiled even more from the idea of having their children taught by Negroes than from the presence of Negro children in a schoolroom with them. In many quarters in the South the dilemma of Negro schoolteachers was hopefully expected to prevent Negroes from pressing for public-school desegregation, for it was assumed as a certainty that the change would close to thousands of educated Negroes the only remunerative and respectable career open to them. The same thought was present in a lesser degree in the border states. Even in the long-integrated public schools of the North far fewer Negro teachers were employed in proportion to the Negro pupils enrolled than in the segregated schools of the South. It is noteworthy, however, that Negro schoolteachers in the South, whose jobs were thus in jeopardy, made no significant effort to arrest the desegregation movement and, indeed, often risked reprisal to further it.

Negroes did not press for desegregation of teacher or other personnel in the earlier cases, and federal courts in the South tended to defer the question until pupil desegregation should pass the token stage. In reviewing the negative action of a federal district court on a petition for relief against discriminatory assignment of teachers, principals, and other school personnel in Escambia County, Florida, the Fifth Circuit Court of Appeals ruled, July 24, 1962, that "the district court may well decide to postpone the consideration and determination of that question until the desegregation of the pupils has either been accomplished or has made substantial progress." [4] A month later a district court ordered the Duval County school board to submit a plan for both pupil desegregation and the elimination of discrimination in teacher assignment by the following October; but the court noted that this latter problem "may well require additional study to prepare, and longer time to put into effect" [5]—an observation which has proved an understatement.

The limited pupil desegregation in the eleven Southern states— generally placing less than a dozen Negro pupils in a classroom with whites—has as yet displaced only a few Negro teachers. Most of these have been in Texas. In 1962, a hundred and twenty-five Negro teaching positions had been abolished in that state, and three in Tennessee, while only faint moves had been made toward teacher desegregation in either state. A beginning was made, however, in Arlington County, Virginia. The school board of that county by a resolution of June 6, 1963, adopted a policy "which precludes race as a consideration in all personnel actions"—including expressly "initial selection and appointment; assignment to schools and within schools. . . ."

In the District of Columbia the school authorities ceased making any distinction on account of race in the hiring or assigning of teachers at the beginning of pupil desegregation. Steps had been taken in that direction in each of the six border states, but many Negro teachers had been displaced; an estimated four hundred had lost their jobs in Oklahoma. On the other hand, in Kentucky a score of districts were employing Negroes on bi-racial faculties and the number was increasing; in Missouri the desegregated school systems of St. Louis and Kansas City were employing more Negro teachers than in 1954 and had absorbed approximately a hundred and fifty of those dismissed in smaller communities. Maryland had accomplished the desegregation of nearly all of its school districts without displacing any Negro teachers, fifteen hundred of whom were teaching on predominantly white faculties in that state.[6]

In the early 1960s the nation witnessed a new agitation in the civil rights field, which came as a surprise to most people: a campaign against racial segregation in the public schools of cities *outside the South*. The 1960 census showed that 48 per cent of the Negroes in the United States now resided outside the eleven former Confederate states. The largest concentrations of Negroes were not in Atlanta or New Orleans, but in the big cities of the North and West; New York, Chicago, Philadelphia, Detroit, Los Angeles, and Cleveland—each had a larger Negro population than any Southern city. The city of New York contained more Negroes than the state of Virginia. In these non-Southern cities public schools were nominally integrated; in most of them segregation had been prohibited by law or public policy since long before the Brown decision; in some, from time immemorial. But with the great increase in their Negro population, which was generally concentrated in Negro neighborhoods, much actual, or *de facto,* public-school segregation had developed. Beyond the residential factor, the trend had been aided by some gerrymandering of districts and arbitrary pupil assignment by school administrators.

The Commission on Civil Rights reported in 1961: "Public schools enrolling Negroes almost exclusively in some cases, and whites almost exclusively in others, are found in many cities of the North and West. . . . A 1960 report of the Board of Education of New York City reported that about one-fifth of the New York City elementary and junior high schools enrolled 85 per cent or more Negro and Puerto Rican pupils, while 48 per cent of the elementary and 44 per cent of the junior high schools enrolled 85 per cent or more white pupils. Philadelphia reported that 14 per cent of its schools had an enrollment of 99-plus per cent Negro. In Pittsburgh in 1959, half of the Negro children in public schools attended schools which had 80 per cent or more Negro enrollment. . . ." Other non-Southern cities mentioned with high racial concentrations in public schools included Los Angeles, Pasadena, Detroit, Boston, Chicago, Indianapolis, and Cleveland.[7]

In addition to the social and psychological disadvantages of segregation, the virtually Negro schools in these cities were more often overcrowded and were generally inferior to the predominantly white schools in instructional offering and physical plant. The NAACP's 1961 national convention in Philadelphia called on its branches "to

insure the end of all segregated public education in fact or by law."
The *Southern School News* of April 1962 reported that Negroes had
filed lawsuits against fourteen school districts in nine non-Southern
states, and that formal protests had been made in at least as many
more. Public demonstrations and sit-ins had also occurred on this
front.

New York City, which now contained over a million Negroes, and
where Negroes were more articulate and more powerful politically
than anywhere else in the nation, moved earliest and most drastically
in this field. The New York City Board of Education declared in December 1954 that it recognized the Supreme Court's Brown decision
"as a decision which applies not only to those cases in litigation, but
also as a challenge to boards of education throughout the nation,
in Northern as well as Southern communities, to re-examine the racial
composition of the schools within their respective systems in order to
determine whether they conform to the standards stated clearly by
that court. . . . Public education in a racially homogeneous setting
is socially unrealistic and blocks the attainment of the goals of/demo-
cratic education, whether this segregation occurs by law or by
fact. . . ." Planning remedial steps began at once, and the problem
remained a major concern of New York school authorities over the
ten-year period.[8] By 1963, 64,000 Negro children had been transferred from nearly all-Negro schools near home to schools in white
neighborhoods. Their daily transportation for the greater distance required eighty-one additional buses at an estimated annual cost of
$684,000. Yet in the context of New York's 1,053,000 pupils the
correction of racial imbalance in the public schools of that metropolis
was still insignificant.[9]

Generally, the idea of achieving a racial balance in the public
schools by transferring pupils to schools outside their residential
neighborhoods raised delicate social and legal, as well as financial,
problems. Redistribution could be accomplished at some expense by
sending Negroes away to predominantly white schools and reducing
the school plant in Negro neighborhoods. The evil could be mitigated
by having schools serve fewer grades and larger attendance areas, or
by placing schools near the border line between white and Negro
neighborhoods. But to bring large numbers of white children away
from their friends and neighbors to offset the racial imbalance in

schools of Negro neighborhoods was all but impossible; the suggestion of such a move aroused bitter white resentment.

Many voices rose in defense of the principle of the neighborhood school. A federal district court, in an opinion on January 29, 1963, in the case of *Bell v. School City of Gary* (Indiana), noted that "the financial burden of transporting 6000 students from their home neighborhood to another would be a matter of considerable concern to the administration of an already heavily taxed and indebted school district. . . . Furthermore, requiring certain students to leave their neighborhoods and friends and be transferred to another school miles away, while other students, similarly situated, remained in the neighborhood school, simply for the purpose of balancing the races in the various schools, would in my opinion be indeed a violation of the equal protection clause of the Fourteenth Amendment." [10]

The lengthy opinion in that case, in which one hundred Negro children complained of *de facto* segregation, gives an illuminating picture of the problem that had arisen in many Northern cities. Gary offered a striking example of segregation in practice in an area where segregation not only was barred by the Supreme Court decision, but had been expressly prohibited earlier by state law. Incidentally, the school board of Gary, which was in effect the defendant in the suit, was headed by a Negro, Dr. Leroy W. Bingham, and the school administration was thoroughly integrated: one of three assistant superintendents, the co-ordinator of secondary education, and several other principal executives were Negroes.

"In the school year 1961–62, 10,710 of the students enrolled in the Gary school system attended fourteen schools which were 100 per cent white; 16,242 students attended twelve schools which were populated from 99 to 100 per cent by Negroes; 6981 students attended five schools which were from 77 to 95 per cent Negro; 4066 attended four schools which had a range from 13 to 37 per cent Negro; 5465 attended five schools which had a Negro population from 1 to 5 per cent."

Thus a large majority of Gary's 23,000 Negro pupils were almost completely segregated. The total Negro population of 70,000 in Gary was concentrated in one section, comprising about one-third of the area of the city. The school administration was sorely pressed to provide schools for a city that had grown in population in ten years from 133,911 to 178,320. As the most rapid population growth was among the Negroes, schools in the Negro section were the first to be overcrowded, but more schools were being built and a number of Negro pupils had been transferred to predominantly white schools. "From a consideration of all the evidence and the record," the court could not "see that the Board of Education has deliberately or purposely segregated the Gary schools according to race." |

"The problem in Gary," Judge George N. Beamer said, "is not one of segregated schools but rather one of segregated housing. Either by choice or design, the Negro population of Gary is concentrated in the so-called central area, and as a result the schools in that area are populated by Negro students. . . ."

The first litigation to draw widespread attention to the problem of *de facto* school segregation was that of *Taylor v. Board of Education of New Rochelle* (New York), where a federal district court in 1961 found deliberate gerrymandering and ordered remedial action; the result was a plan of optional transfer of Negro pupils to schools with a larger representation of white pupils. In that case the court declared: "The neighborhood school policy certainly is not sacrosanct. It is valid only insofar as it is operated within the confines established by the Constitution. It cannot be used to confine Negroes within an area artificially delineated in the first instance by official acts." [11] In another case, that of *Branche v. Board of Education of Hempstead* (New York), a federal court ruled in April 1962 that the educational system "must deal with the inadequacy arising from adventitious segregation. . . ." [12] The question of the propriety of a public school's adherence to the segregated racial pattern of its neighborhood has not been passed upon by the Supreme Court.

Of the major Negro grievances, *de facto* school segregation was the one least understood by the general public. Many who sympathized with Negro aims in general felt that some of the pressure in this area was unreasonable or misdirected. Residential segregation was the basic evil, and any feasible measures of relief would barely scratch the surface until this larger problem had been met.

De facto school segregation was but one manifestation of the cancerous blight of the ghetto. Here was an evil—the denial of housing to Negroes outside of already established Negro districts—that cried imperatively for national attention. The rapid migration of Negroes from South to North and from country to city was crowding the urban neighborhoods that custom and prejudice had allotted to them. For a Negro to rent or purchase a home in a white residential area was often difficult if not impossible. Negro "intruders" in a white neighborhood were sometimes harassed and threatened or even attacked by mobs. An embarrassing example of the effects of this discrimination was the plight of diplomatic personnel coming to the nation's capital from African countries. The Department of State reported in 1963 that of thirty-five non-white diplomats from twenty nations who had requested its help in finding houses during eight months of the previous year, thirty-four had been turned away from houses or apartment buildings in Washington because of their color and twelve had not found suitable housing by the end of the year,

Historically, Americans of German, Irish, Italian, Polish, and other foreign origin had experienced a degree of residential segregation following waves of immigration to this country. But the condition of these Caucasian immigrants was not static; after a generation or two they moved into the mainstream of American life. Negroes were chained to the ghetto by their color; after three centuries the color of their skin was still a cruel and unrelenting barrier to assimilation. The squalid and congested ghetto caused cultural stagnation, and it became a breeding place for vice and crime as well as racial discontent.

In employment, discrimination against the Negro was to be found virtually everywhere, except in some categories of government jobs. More than one out of every ten Negro workers in the United States was unemployed; among white workers only one out of twenty was without a job. Some labor unions, notably in the building trades, excluded Negroes from membership, thus barring them completely in "closed shop" situations from work. Large categories of the higher and better-paid positions were practically closed to Negroes regardless of their competence.

Humiliation and oppression of the Negro, of course, were not new, despite some modern variations. The picture had been familiar to Negro Americans all their lives, and to their fathers before them. It was not out of a sudden desperation that the protest of the 1960s arose. What was discernible among Negroes in the sit-ins and freedom rides, the parades and picket lines, the youths huddled in patrol wagons on their way to jail, singing "We Shall Overcome," was the beginning of a powerful awakening of the human spirit, with incalculable possibilities for both the near term and the long future. White Americans still saw the picture only dimly; comparatively few would have admitted in 1962 that any group in this land was "oppressed." The word "oppression," now beginning to be used here and there, had an unfamiliar and an alien ring with reference to the United States.

The prevention of Negroes from voting in some sections of the South was one of the most brazen forms of discrimination. This received major attention during 1962. The Voter Education Project, established by the Southern Regional Council, with substantial financial backing from national philanthropic foundations, united leading civil rights organizations in a large effort to train Negroes in the complexities of registration in hostile communities and to encourage them to vote. The drive was attended by much white harassment, considerable police brutality, and occasional violence, including the burning of three Negro churches. The Department of Justice moved at the same time to protect the voting rights of Negroes; the total number of counties in which the department took action, ranging from inspection of records to lawsuits, increased from thirty at the beginning of the Kennedy Administration to a hundred and fifteen.[13] As a result of these activities, Negroes began to register and vote in many districts where the privilege had been denied them by intimidation and trickery. Promising to remove one obstacle to Negro voting, Congress on August 27 initiated the procedure for a constitutional amendment abolishing the poll tax; this fee of several dollars was still exacted in five Southern states as a prerequisite to voting, largely with a view to deterring Negroes from exercising the franchise.

Negroes now held a slightly larger percentage of all federal government jobs than the Negro percentage of the total population, though in the better-paid positions the Negro percentage was much smaller. President Kennedy had said on March 6, 1961: "I have dedicated my administration to the cause of equal opportunity in employment by the government or its contractors." The firms with government contracts of various kinds represented a vast segment of the nation's industry. The President's Committee on Equal Employment Opportunity, set up by President Kennedy and headed by Vice-President Lyndon Johnson, moved more vigorously in both these fields than any similar body had done before. The desegregation of the Armed Forces since President Truman's executive order of 1948 was the most successful exhibit of integration in the history of inter-racial relations; President Kennedy, in June 1962, appointed a Committee on Equal Opportunity in the Armed Forces to ferret out lingering vestiges of discrimination in that quarter and to investigate the hardships imposed upon Negro servicemen by the discriminatory practices of civilian communities near military posts.

The Department of Health, Education and Welfare had been strangely oblivious hitherto of the requirement that all segregation in public education should be ended. On March 30, 1962, that department gave an effective fillip to public-school desegregation in the South with the announcement that some federal financial assistance would be withheld from school districts which continued to practice segregation after September 1963. The schools affected were those receiving federal aid because they served large numbers of children of military or other federal government personnel; if necessary, the commissioner of education would be "authorized to make provision for the education of children on a nonsegregated basis on federal property or make other suitable arrangements."

An increasing volume of peripheral attacks was chipping at the structure of injustice to the Negro minority. Unprecedented concern was being displayed by the federal government; also by some state and city governments and by the press and the clergy. Yet "unprecedented" meant little in relation to the magnitude of the problem which was beginning to unfold.

Chapter 17

OLE MISS AND MISSISSIPPI

The last three states maintaining complete segregation in public education yielded at the state-supported college level in 1962–63—Mississippi in the fall of 1962, South Carolina in January, and Alabama in June, of 1963. Resistance at the University of Mississippi reached the proportions of an insurrection, which was suppressed by military force. Its grim reverberations had an undoubtedly sobering effect when the crisis came to the other two states. At Clemson College in South Carolina the critical aspect had virtually ended when the moment of desegregation arrived; Clemson accepted its first Negro student in an atmosphere of complete decorum. At the University of Alabama gestures of defiance on the part of the governor of that state caused widespread anxiety, police and military precautions were taken, and the outcome was awaited tensely by the nation; but the resistance at Tuscaloosa was limited to the governor's own brief melodrama and no violence or harassment was directed at the three Negro students who enrolled.

Both in its constitutional significance and in the magnitude of the upheaval the desegregation crisis at the University of Mississippi was the gravest that had occurred since the Brown decision. The convulsion was in no sense a race riot. The presence of a single Negro was the *casus belli,* and he was later to suffer ostracism and abuse. But the Negro was out of sight while the bloody battle raged. The enemy was the Government of the United States, and the targets of the mob's fury were its marshals and soldiers. The challenge to the Federal Union, the most serious since the Civil War, was met first with an inadequate force of federal deputy marshals and then with overwhelming military strength.

Though Mississippi furnished none of the major crises of desegregation, we have visited that state frequently in the pages of this book. We have examined race prejudice and oppression of the Negro, resentment of the Brown decision, unwillingness on the part of whites to discuss desegregation or to permit discussion of it, alienation from the mainstream of national life, and hostility toward the federal government. All these phenomena were more pronounced in Mississippi than in any other state. If there were fewer sensational explosions in Mississippi, it was attributable not to interracial amity, but rather to the ferocity with which "white supremacy" was maintained and to the submission of its intimidated Negro minority.

The most widely publicized incident in Mississippi since the "wolf-whistle murder" of Emmet Till was the lynching of another Negro, Mack Charles Parker, at Poplarville in April 1959. Parker, awaiting trial on a rape charge, was beaten and dragged from the county jail by fifteen or more masked men and killed. No one was punished for the deed. Earlier, in August 1955, Lamar Smith, a Negro who was reported to have urged Negroes to vote in a gubernatorial election, was fatally shot on the courthouse lawn in Brookhaven; a grand jury failed to indict the three men charged with the slaying. In September 1961 the press reported briefly the fatal shooting of the Negro Herbert Lee by a member of the state legislature. Lee had been active in a voter registration movement. A coroner's jury found that the act was committed to prevent a threatened attack and called it "justifiable homicide." Few doubted that other Negroes had been done to death by white men in Mississippi in obscure circumstances.

The Citizens' Council dominated the politics and, to a large extent, the business community of the state, as well as the lives of individual citizens. Judge Brady's *Black Monday* had ceased to be the Citizens' Council handbook and was in fact out of print. The increasingly status-seeking Council—and the state administration—adopted a more polished exposition of racism entitled *Race and Reason,* by Carleton Putnam, a Northern writer. Soon after Putnam's book appeared, the author was honored at a banquet under Citizens' Council auspices in Jackson, attended by the highest Mississippi dignitaries. The governor even issued a solemn proclamation which, after a series of whereases, said:

> Now, therefore, I, Ross R. Barnett, Governor of the State of Mississippi, do hereby proclaim that Thursday, October 26, 1961, is and shall be known as "Race and Reason Day," and hereby urge the people of Mississippi to observe this occasion by reading and discussing *Race and Reason,* calling the book to the attention of friends and relatives in the North, and by participating in appropri-

ate public functions, thereby expressing the appreciation of the people in our state for Mr. Carleton Putnam and for his splendid book *Race and Reason*.[1]

Ross Barnett had been elected governor in 1959, to succeed the relatively moderate J. P. Coleman. Unlike his predecessor, Barnett wooed the Citizens' Council and made it all but a part of his administration. The Council was in fact subsidized: the official State Sovereignty Commission contributed regularly to its "Radio and Television forum," and in 1962 it received over $100,000 of state funds through this arrangement.

A favorite Barnett saying might have been taken right out of a Citizens' Council pamphlet: "The good Lord was the original segregationist. He put the Negro in Africa—separated him from all other races." Another remark which the governor made repeatedly gave an insight into his thinking as to the efficacy of defiance in checkmating the federal government: "If the governors of Southern states had gone to Little Rock and congratulated Governor Orval Faubus when he called out the National Guard to prevent school integration, federal troops would never have been sent to that city." He promised again and again that "Ross Barnett will rot in jail before he will let one Negro ever darken the sacred threshold of our white schools." A bumbling, heavy-handed politician of sixty-two, Barnett was the butt of much ridicule—as when he had gold-plated bathroom fixtures installed in the Governor's Mansion at a reported cost of $10,000—but all his bloopers were forgotten when he stood in the breach to stop the federal advance.

By 1962 Mississippi was out of step even with most of the South, not only in industrial progress but in adjustment to the changing order in interracial relations. During the first few years after the Brown decision the attitude of that state was not strikingly different from that of the other ten Southern states. Mississippians still liked to identify themselves with "the embattled South" and constantly referred to their fight as "the Southern fight"; but in the matter of resistance to the desegregation rulings of federal courts the state's position now was more like that of a Casabianca on the deck of a burning ship whence all but Mississippi—and Alabama—had fled.

Confederate flags were to be seen almost everywhere in Mississippi; many were displayed on automobiles and in front of homes, shops, and local government offices. Confederate Army caps were worn by thousands of Mississippi youths, and full Confederate Army uniforms were often donned on festive occasions. Mississippi had given the Confederate States of America its president, Jefferson Davis. It had then been a proud and prosperous state, one of the richest.

A century later it was still a proud state, but it was the poorest in the Union. Its per-capital income in 1961 was $1229 when the national average was $2263. Negroes, formerly a majority, were now 42 per cent of its population of 2,178,141. The median annual family income of its whites was $4209 and of its Negroes, $1444. The population was predominantly rural; Jackson, the capital, had grown in twenty years from a city of 40,000 people to one of 150,000, but no other town in the state was as much as one-third that size. Jackson also represented an extraordinary concentration of the state's affluent citizens; in contrast to the general poverty in Mississippi, it had the distinction—which it shared with Houston, Texas—of having a larger percentage of families with incomes of $5000 or more than any other Southern city.

In spite of dramatic expansion of its public-school system during the 1950s, Mississippi had the third highest illiteracy rate in the nation, 4.9 per cent; 119,741 of its Negroes and 40,274 of its whites were considered functionally illiterate. Only the boldest Negroes in the most tolerant white communities dared to exercise the franchise. More than 95 per cent of the whites—but less than 2 per cent of the Negroes—over twenty years of age were registered voters.

Mississippi has produced its share of celebrities. Among the writers who still make the state their home are Hodding Carter and Eudora Welty. Until his death in July 1962, William Faulkner, a winner of the Nobel Prize, also resided there. An extraordinary number of native Mississippians left the state to achieve distinction—often with liberal identification—elsewhere. Conspicuous among these are Turner Catledge, managing editor of the *New York Times,* Mark F. Ethridge, publisher of the *Louisville Courier-Journal,* and Buford Ellington, the incumbent governor of Tennessee. Two other Mississippi exiles of renown are the crooner Elvis Presley and—a matter of embarrassment to white supremacists—the internationally acclaimed Negro opera-singer, Leontyne Price.

Many young men left Mississippi every year for more promising fields. Calculations made over a five-year period showed that 33 per cent of the graduates of the four white state institutions of higher

learning were leaving the state after graduation.[2] Among Mississippi
Negroes, teaching jobs in Negro schools were holding many college
graduates, but tens of thousands of others were emigrating every year.
The 990,282 Negro residents counted in the 1960 census were 69,687
less than in 1950; the total population of the state had declined by
773 persons.

Against these statistical generalizations it should be noted that
there were gleaming new buildings here and there in Mississippi and
evidences of industrial awakening. Indeed, along the Gulf Coast the
space age had intruded: nuclear submarines were being built for the
United States Navy at Pascagoula, and the National Aeronautics and
Space Administration had purchased a 13,000-acre site for testing
moon-rocket engines.

Nor was white Mississippi a complete monolith in its attitude
toward race-relations reform. The phenomenon was observable generally in the South that, when the preponderance of hostile elements
reaches a certain point, the minority favoring moderation and adjustment disappears from view. But it does not cease to exist. Traveling
in Mississippi in 1962, I was astonished at the number of prominent
individuals who, in the privacy of country homes or quiet offices, expressed apprehension over the anti-integration furor and the dangerous course upon which their state was set. These people were be-
numbed by the thought that any gesture of opposition would be futile,
and by fear of the consequences for themselves, their families, and
their businesses. Most of the Mississippi press followed the popular
anti-Negro, anti-integration, and anti-federal-government line. The
State Times in Jackson dissented cautiously—and found itself obliged
to cease publication at the end of 1961. Some smaller newspapers
counseled moderation with varying emphasis, notably the Hodding
Carters' *Delta Democrat-Times* in Greenville, the *Pascagoula Chronicle,* the *McComb Enterprise-Journal,* and the *Tupelo Times.* Mrs.
Hazel Brannon Smith suffered continual persecution as a result of her
bold voice of protest in the weekly *Lexington Advertiser.*

The University of Mississippi, established in 1844, occupies a group
of stately old buildings, and some of recent construction, on a campus
comprising one square mile of tree-shaded land near the town of
Oxford, 165 miles north of Jackson. (Oxford was the home, incidentally, of William Faulkner—an alumnus of the university—and the

town is recognizable in some of Faulkner's novels.) During the Civil War the ancient administration building, or the Lyceum—on whose floors a hundred wounded federal marshals were to lie on the morning of October 1, 1962—served at times as a hospital for both Confederate and Union soldiers. A cemetery along the campus's southern boundary held seven hundred Confederate dead. In 1854 Chancellor Frederick A. P. Barnard, in laying a broad plan before its board of trustees, had listed among the university's various purposes: "to determine the respectability of the state in the eyes of mankind." [3]

"Ole Miss," as it is called with affection by many, had been best known in recent years for the pulchritude of its women students and the prowess of its gridiron heroes. Its football team, nicknamed the "Rebels," has ranked annually among the nation's top teams; Ole Miss co-eds won the title of "Miss America" in both 1959 and 1960. The university's academic contribution, too, has not been without merit; although its record of freshman failures has been high, Ole Miss graduates often have done well.

In spite of the racist cloud which hung low over Mississippi and the unattractive pay—an annual average faculty salary of $6863—the university had drawn a number of professors of high caliber, and until the crisis of October 1962 most of them chose to stay with Ole Miss through the tribulations which beset it. In the wave of repression of liberal discussion, the university—a state institution with its appropriations controlled by politicians—walked a painful tightrope. Chancellor John D. Williams and more especially Dean Robert Farley of the law school battled frequently against fierce Citizens'-Council and political pressure to save liberal members of the faculty.

The students of Ole Miss, who numbered 4638, had lived in an atmosphere of intensified racist indoctrination and defiance of federal authority for eight years—most of them since their earliest teens. It would take little to set them on fire. Yet, under a clear policy of restraint on the part of state authorities and with the exercise of normal discipline, these volatile youths could have been held in check. When I visited Ole Miss in late 1961 and early 1962, few doubted that the next few months would bring a federal court order to enroll a Negro student. The prospect was seldom absent from the thoughts of administrators and professors; many plans and possibilities were privately explored. Their chief sources of uneasiness were not the Ole

Miss students, but the reckless bravado of the state's political leaders and the fear that throngs of extremists would invade the university.

The Negro around whom the battle of Ole Miss was fought was a quietly determined young man of twenty-nine, meticulous in his manners and his dress. Five days before the explosion the *Washington Post* said: "While the tumult rages all about him, while lawyers argue and judges rule, while governors fulminate and legislatures prate, one man in Mississippi—James Meredith, a central actor in the drama being played there—awaits his cue to walk upon the stage with silence and dignity and fortitude." He would play his part that way.

Meredith was born in Kosciusko, Mississippi, a town where he himself says the Negroes "might be a little more progressive than else-where in the state." After finishing high school, he served for nine years, becoming a staff sergeant, in the United States Air Force—which was by then racially integrated—and returned to Mississippi in 1960. Writing in the *Saturday Evening Post* of November 10, 1962, Meredith said: "I entered Jackson State College, a Negro school in Jackson, and quickly met other students who felt as I did—that Ne-groes in Mississippi did not have the rights of full citizens, including the right to the best education the state offered. Someone had to seek admission to the University of Mississippi, and I decided to do so. . . ." In January 1961 he applied for enrollment. When his ap-plication was rejected he sought the legal help of the NAACP, and in May a suit was filed in the federal district court.

In the sixteen months of litigation that followed, the state and the university used every conceivable argument and subterfuge. In bland contradiction of the screaming affirmations of Mississippi's immutable policy of segregation, they contended that racial segrega-tion did not in fact exist at Ole Miss. They held that the Negro ap-plicant was unqualified for reasons related to his character and in-telligence, which they assiduously assailed. However, the Fifth Circuit Court of Appeals on June 25 found that Meredith's application "was turned down solely because he was a Negro" and directed the lower court to order him enrolled.[4] After the Appeals court order had been repeatedly stayed and the stays had been repeatedly vacated, Federal District Judge S. C. Mize on September 13 finally enjoined the university from denying admission to the applicant or "discriminating against him in any way whatsoever because of his race."

Governor Barnett immediately invoked the battered doctrine of interposition. He directed Mississippi officials to "interpose the state sovereignty and themselves between the people of the state and any body politic seeking to usurp such power." The next two weeks were hectic with obstructionist maneuvers. A state court issued an injunction forbidding "any act intending to enroll" Meredith. The legislature enacted a law prohibiting the enrollment at a state university of any student under "a criminal charge of moral turpitude," and the necessary charge was furnished in a justice-of-the-peace hearing: Meredith was convicted of false voter registration. Federal court orders promptly frustrated these and other stratagems.

On September 24 the federal court of appeals ordered the enrollment of Meredith forthwith and instructed the university registrar to be available at the Jackson office of the board of trustees for the purpose. The same day, Governor Barnett issued a proclamation directing "that the arrest or attempts to arrest, or the fining or the attempts to fine, of any state official in the performance of his official duties, by any representative of the federal government, is illegal, and such representative or representatives of the federal government are to be summarily arrested and jailed. . . ."

At the early hour of 8:30 A.M. on September 25, the court of appeals issued an order restraining the State of Mississippi, its governor, and virtually all state and local officials and police from "interfering with or obstructing by any means or in any manner" Meredith's enrollment. Here Governor Barnett and Lieutenant Governor Paul B. Johnson, who now got into the act, carried their defiance physically to a point that drew convictions for contempt. As related in the court of appeals' judgment of September 28, the governor went to the college board office that same afternoon, "at a time when James H. Meredith was due to appear at the office to be enrolled, . . ." and "deliberately prevented him from entering. . . ." When Meredith tried to reach the registrar at his office in Oxford the next day, Lieutenant Governor Johnson blocked his entry to the university campus.

On September 28 and 29 the federal court of appeals ordered the governor to pay a fine of $10,000 per day, and the lieutenant governor a fine of $5000 per day, unless by the following Tuesday, October 2, they should demonstrate full compliance with federal court orders and notify all law-enforcement officers and other officials under them "to cease forthwith all resistance and interference."

Saturday, September 30, President Kennedy and his Attorney General each conferred repeatedly by telephone with Governor Barnett. The President dispatched a telegram asking the governor bluntly whether he would "continue to actively interfere" or whether his law-enforcement officers would co-operate "in maintaining law and order and preventing violence in connection with federal enforcement of the court orders." Barnett phoned the White House twice afterward but made no satisfactory reply.

Just after midnight President Kennedy issued the kind of proclamation that prepares for the use of military force in a domestic crisis. He noted that the governor and others were "willingly obstructing the enforcement of" federal court orders and commanded "all persons engaged in such obstruction of justice to cease and desist therefrom. . . ." At the same time he directed the Secretary of Defense "to take all appropriate steps" and authorized him to call the eleven thousand men of the Mississippi National Guard into "the active military service of the United States."

Between 4 P.M. and 5 P.M. Sunday a force of 320 United States marshals entered the university campus and took over the administration building. Shortly afterward a small party of marshals escorted Meredith on the campus and to quarters on Dormitory Row. Harassment by students sputtered quickly into a riot, and a battle raged all night between a frenzied mob and the Government of the United States.

The attackers used bricks, stones, clubs, bottles, iron bars, hunks of concrete from smashed benches, handmade gasoline bombs, and some firearms. The marshals relied mainly on tear gas. As the night wore on, the students in the mob of twenty-five hundred were outnumbered by self-appointed vigilantes from near and far; of two hundred rioters arrested, only twenty-four were from Ole Miss. The four hundred marshals were aided first by a handful of National Guardsmen and at last by a swelling tide of Regular Army troops. Shortly after 5 A.M. Monday morning, the military and the marshals swept forward together and drove the last two hundred rioters from the campus.

When day dawned, two onlookers had been killed, 375 persons had been injured, and the campus was strewn with wrecked motor vehicles, tear-gas canisters, fragments of thousands of bottles, and other debris. Of 166 marshals injured, 29 suffered gunshot wounds. The dead were a Frenchman, Paul Guihard, correspondent of the *Agence France Presse,* and Ray Gunter, an Oxford onlooker. Monday morning Chief United States Marshal James P. McShane escorted Meredith to the office of the university registrar and he was enrolled at 8:35 A.M.

President Kennedy clung long—too long, as it appears in retrospect —to the hope of winning a moral victory. At 10 P.M. (8 P.M. Mississippi time) he addressed Mississippi and the nation over television and radio. Rioting had already begun at Ole Miss, but Governor Barnett had issued a partial-surrender statement and the President was still seeking his co-operation. The nine-minute speech was a gently worded appeal to reason and patriotism. "The orders of the court," the President said, ". . . are beginning to be carried out. Mr. James Meredith is now in residence on the campus of the University of Mississippi." He appealed especially to the students (few of whom were listening to the broadcast). "The eyes of the nation and the world," he said, "are upon you and upon all of us, and the honor of your university and the state are in the balance." He explained carefully the constitutional situation which made his responsibility as President "inescapable," but it was evident that he still desired desperately to avoid the use of military force. It was around midnight when Regular Army units began to move from their concentration at Memphis and several hours later before they arrived in strength on the university campus.

The two hundred men of the Mississippi Highway Patrol assigned to the university were a highly uncertain element, and their performance became a subject of much controversy. Soon after tear gas came into play they withdrew from the campus; they were ordered back several hours later when Lieutenant Governor Johnson arrived on the scene. A National Guard captain said afterward that the Mississippi patrolmen "stood around their cars" and offered no help in clearing the way for his men. Attorney General Kennedy accused Barnett of going back on his word and withdrawing the state force— which the governor denied. A statement issued by Mississippi Senator James O. Eastland said the state troopers were "urging the students to withdraw" when, "without warning, the marshals fired tear-gas projectiles . . . at the students and Highway Patrolmen." Later in the week the Mississippi State Senate resolved that by "their faithful and courageous efforts to maintain peace and order, the Highway Patrol . . . reflected credit on themselves and on the State of Mississippi."

On the other hand, the manner in which the Mississippi National Guard answered the call of duty was a reassuring demonstration of discipline and loyalty in the Armed Forces of the United States. These part-time soldiers included a score of members of the Mississippi legislature and many segregationist leaders. Yet none faltered. The fifty-five men of the Oxford unit reached the Lyceum at 10:15 P.M. and were at the side of the federal marshals through the thick of the fighting. Their thirteen wounded included Captain Murray C. Falkner, a nephew of the famous novelist who spelled the name "Faulkner." About midnight two hundred members of other National Guard units made a heroic entry to the campus through a barrage of bricks, gunfire, and flaming gasoline. Approximately two thousand Guardsmen were deployed in the area by 10 A.M. Monday.

A pathetic leader of the mob was Edwin Walker, an embittered former major general in the United States Army (the commander, incidentally, of the federal troops in Little Rock five years before), who had resigned in anger after a rebuke for his attempt to indoctrinate troops under his command in Germany with ultra-rightist political propaganda. Early Monday afternoon Walker was arrested at a roadblock outside Oxford on charges of "rebellion, insurrection, and seditious conspiracy" and flown to a hospital for psychiatric observation. He was shortly released and declared capable of standing trial, but a federal grand jury failed to bring an indictment.

Governor Barnett's appeals for calm alternated with expressions of angry defiance. In his "surrender" statement at 9 P.M. he said: "Surrounded by armed forces . . . and physically overpowered, . . . we must preserve the peace and avoid bloodshed." But in another broadcast he said to federal officials: "Gentlemen, you are trampling on the sovereignty of this great state and depriving it of every vestige of honor and respect. . . . May God have mercy on your souls. Mississippi will continue to fight the Meredith case through the courts. . . . We will never surrender." Monday night he said: "The people of Mississippi are enraged, incensed—and rightly so"; and he called on federal authorities to "stop further violence by the immediate withdrawal of Meredith and the withdrawal of federal troops and marshals from our soil."

Governor Barnett's performance brought few cheers outside of Mississippi and neighboring Alabama. The reaction in the nation generally was one of anger and disgust. Press and politicians agreed that the administration had no choice but to suppress the revolt. Where there was criticism of the President it was generally to the effect of this comment in *Time* magazine of October 12: "President Kennedy could have learned one lesson from Eisenhower's performance in the Little Rock crisis: if forced to intervene, then intervene with sufficient force." The news from Mississippi was voluminously reported to excited readers in foreign countries, but the image abroad of oppression of Negroes in the United States was somewhat mitigated by this massive exertion of federal power to secure the rights of a single Negro citizen.

By nightfall Monday the federal military forces in the area had reached seven thousand, and the number was more than doubled the following day. At the peak the federal government had, counting Regular Army and Air Force and National Guard contingents, nearly thirty thousand troops committed. But withdrawal began almost at once. By the end of the month only five hundred soldiers were left, and a few weeks later, only three hundred. These were withdrawn in July, 1963.

Another Negro student, Cleve McDowell, was admitted to the University of Mississippi, under a federal court order, without incident on June 5, 1963. James Meredith graduated August 18, 1963, with a degree of bachelor of arts in political science. However, after a small pistol dropped from McDowell's pocket in class, he was expelled on September 24 for violating a regulation against carrying a concealed weapon on the campus, and Ole Miss was left again with an all-white enrollment.

Mississippi businessmen spoke out feebly, momentarily, and at a late hour. Monday morning, before order had been completely restored at Oxford, William H. Mounger, president of the Lamar Life Insurance Company, made a ringing appeal to his fellow-businessmen over Jackson television station WLBT-TV, which his company owned. He referred to "the conviction which many of us had that the events which were taking place would lead to violence," but he confessed that "none of us were willing to speak out and try to inform the people of Mississippi of the terrific tensions that resulted on the University of Mississippi campus last night." Accepting Mounger's challenge, a hundred and twenty-seven of Jackson's business and professional leaders met the following day and signed a statement calling for "law and order and not mob rule."

There were other manifestations of compunction and shock among Mississippians. Two Episcopal clergymen and several professors had made vain attempts in the heat of the melee to calm rioting students— who after all were only a minority of the students of the university. Miss Sidna Brower, the editor of the student newspaper, *The Mississippian,* writing in the sound of gunfire and exploding tear-gas shells for its Monday issue, told her fellow students they were bringing "dishonor and shame" to Ole Miss.

In a series of articles in the *Pascagoula Chronicle*—later published in a brochure—a member of the state legislature, Representative Karl Wiesenburg, recalled the falsehoods and folly which led to the night of horrors at Ole Miss and declared: "That innocent blood was shed was not the fault of the President, the federal courts, the Attorney General, or Chief Marshal James ·P. McShane. It was the price of defiance." The ten ministers of the Oxford-Ole Miss area issued a statement calling for "repentance for our collective and individual guilt in the formation of the atmosphere which produced the strife at the University of Mississippi and Oxford. . . ."

But sackcloth and ashes were rare in Mississippi, and the half-open period for self-criticism soon ended. In the systematic intellectual isolation of Mississippi, the roar of condemnation from the nation and the world was scarcely heard within its borders. Most white Mississippians accepted the official version of what happened at Ole Miss as expressed in Governor Barnett's broadcast of Monday night, October 1: "The unarmed Highway Patrolmen, with their backs to the federal marshals, were peacefully moving the students when a pop bottle thrown by one of the crowd shattered in the street. The marshals immediately fired point-blank into the backs of the state officers, who were only a few feet from them, and into the groups of young people. This was the direct cause of violence on the campus. Five unarmed Highway Patrolmen have been hospitalized from effects of tear gas fired by federal marshals. The federal marshals were inexperienced, nervous, and trigger happy. . . . In this matter the federal government has been the aggressor from the outset."

Substantially the same version was given, after a solemn "investigation," by a Mississippi grand jury, which charged Chief Marshal McShane with willfully "inciting a riot."

An Associated Press survey in August 1963 showed that fifty-four members of the university faculty listed in its 1962–63 catalogue were not returning for the 1963–64 term.

The Mississippi advisory committee of the Commission on Civil Rights reported in February 1963: "Terror hangs over the Negro in Mississippi." In the 1963 contest for a governor to succeed Ross Barnett the issue that overshadowed all others was the degree of attachment to the interracial status quo and of hostility to the federal government displayed by the three major candidates. The most bellicose candidate won. Lieutenant Governor Paul Burney Johnson, supported by Governor Barnett, Senator Eastland, and other extremists, defeated former Governor Coleman in the run-off Democratic primary by a vote of 261,065 to 196,651.

Mississippi remains in the most dangerous sense a "problem state." Whatever the advance in tolerance and understanding in the rest of the country, its penetration into Mississippi in the near future is likely to be precarious and ineffectual; whatever national legislation may be enacted to combat race discrimination will present enforcement problems of the gravest character in that state. The cloud that hangs over Mississippi is pregnant with storm.

Chapter 18

THE FUSE BURNS SHORT

There remained two states where, except for the brief and stormy adventure of Autherine Lucy in 1956, no Negro had been admitted with whites to a state institution of higher learning—South Carolina and Alabama. With Mississippi, these were also the three states which had yet to enroll the first Negro pupil with whites in a public elementary or secondary school.

The situation in South Carolina was less ominous than in the other two. A significant change in South Carolina's attitude toward desegregation had been discernible since early in 1962. It was not a sudden conviction that segregation was wrong, though condemnation of the system on moral grounds was heard increasingly among a few South Carolinians. Rather, a determination to resist at all costs had given way to a concensus that adjustment to the Supreme Court ruling was inevitable and that, when it could no longer be delayed, it should be effected with a minimum of disturbance. Traditions of gentility, perhaps somewhat more devoutly cherished in South Carolina and Virginia than elsewhere, militated against brawl and panic. When Charleston bowed painfully to a federal court order for the desegregation of its public golf courses in 1961, the "dignity of Charleston" precluded unseemly disorder.

Though many echoes of South Carolina resentment of the Brown decision have sounded in these pages, South Carolina has not produced any crisis of sufficient magnitude to draw our attention at length to developments in that state. There has been no breakthrough in the wall of public-school segregation to record; and, though demonstrations and some rioting attended the broad Negro protest movement, there have been no convulsions in South Carolina comparable to those that shook Montgomery, Tuscaloosa, Clinton, Little Rock, New Orleans, or Ole Miss.

South Carolina has a larger proportion of Negroes among its people than any other state except Mississippi—approximately 35 per cent of the total population. The attitude of paternalism toward Negroes—

though since the Brown decision it has yielded much to the harsher tenets of white supremacy—has nowhere been more deeply rooted than among the whites of this state. To most of them racial integration seemed a revolutionary and evil thing, and for eight years they offered uncompromising resistance.

The chorus of denunciations of the Brown decision reached a high pitch. In addition to Governor Byrnes, Senator Strom Thurmond, and voluble politicians at all levels, South Carolina furnished two of segregation's best-known literary defenders: Thomas R. Waring, the belligerent editor of the *Charleston News and Courier;* and William D. Workman, a columnist and author, who recently emerged as a Republican political leader.

There have been some voices on the other side. James McBryde Dabbs, the eloquent champion of racial integration who heads the Southern Regional Council, presides over his ancestral cotton plantation in the heart of South Carolina. Two editors of minor newspapers, J. E. Chaffin of the *Greenwood Index Journal* and, more emphatically, A. M. Secrest of the *Cheraw Chronicle,* have steered a moderate course without significant molestation. Most of the advocates of adjustment, however, have not been so fortunate. When in 1956 editor Jack O'Dowd of the *Florence Morning News* undertook to convince his readers that "the South cannot maintain its policies of racial segregation," [1] a storm of protest forced his resignation. In 1957 a dozen prominent citizens, led by five Protestant ministers, expressed concern over the cloud of racism and defiance which hung over the state in a brochure entitled *South Carolinians Speak.* They were subjected to a hail of criticism and abuse and the home of one of them was bombed. The latter outrage evoked condemnation from the South Carolina press; the *Spartanburg Herald-Journal* offered a reward of $2500 for apprehension of the perpetrator. The posture of unrelenting defiance continued to prevail through the term of Governor George Bell Timmerman, Jr., and into that of his successor, Governor Ernest F. Hollings.

Hollings in his inaugural address in January 1959 promised continued resistance to school desegregation, but, significantly, he took a strong stand for law and order. Midway in his term of office he began to exert a quiet influence looking toward a more realistic policy. The legislature ceased to grant funds to institutions "on a racially segregated basis only." In the 1962 appropriations bill earlier provisions for

the closing of schools or colleges to prevent desegregation were reversed by a clause which read: "No institution or activity for which
the legislature has herein provided shall be discontinued." Early in
1962, following some consultation among editors and with the governor, the press executed a concerted swing toward a more moderate
approach to the desegregation problem. In his farewell address to the
General Assembly in January 1963 Governor Hollings counseled:
"We of today must realize the lesson of one hundred years ago, and
move on for the good of South Carolina and the United States." [2]

The new governor was Donald S. Russell, a wealthy businessman,
a former president of the University of South Carolina, and a moderate. Two weeks after Governor Russell's inauguration, on January 28,
1963, a Negro entered a previously all-white institution of higher
learning for the first time since Reconstruction.

A suit in behalf of Harvey B. Gantt, the 19-year-old son of a Negro
employee at the Charleston Naval Yard, had been filed in federal court
six months earlier to restrain the state agricultural college of Clemson
from refusing admission to him and "other qualified Negro residents"
because of their race. Clemson has schools of architecture, arts and
sciences, engineering and textiles, as well as agriculture. Gantt had
dropped out during his junior year at Iowa University, where he had a
good record, and he now desired to resume his education in the field
of architecture at Clemson.

The legal fight ended in January. The Fourth Circuit Court of Appeals reversed a district court decision and directed that Clemson be
ordered to admit the Negro applicant and "others similarly situated,"
a request for stay was denied by Chief Justice Warren, and the order
was duly issued on January 22.[3] In the meantime the public had been
prepared by many voices for calm acceptance of the outcome. A
Columbia Record editorial of December 11 called on citizens for
"obedience to the law," on public officials for "responsible direction,"
and on the schools for "continued compliance with court directives
and provision for the protection of all individuals in their care." Governor Russell told Attorney General Kennedy that no federal marshals
were needed at Clemson, and none were sent.

The event proved sensational only in its felicity. When Gantt arrived
at the college to enroll, the hundred and sixty representatives of news
media outnumbered the students on hand. The latter were indifferent

or even friendly. News photos registered smiles all around—the broadest smile on the face of Harvey Gantt.

The South Carolina breakthrough having been accomplished at Clemson, public-school desegregation began and college desegregation was extended in September with tranquillity and ease. In the historic city of Charleston—in a district where Negro school children out-numbered whites three to one—eleven Negro pupils were admitted to four previously all-white high schools on September 3. The court order called for general desegregation in 1964. A week later three Negro students registered at the University of South Carolina at Columbia, and another Negro student—a young lady—joined Gantt at Clemson. State police patrolled the streets surrounding the university on the first day as a precautionary measure. Around the Charleston schools only two or three policemen were in evidence, mainly concerned with guarding street crossings!

The drama attending the admission of Negro students to the University of Alabama in June 1963 diverted attention only briefly from a historic nationwide upheaval. A few weeks earlier the flames from a series of massive Negro demonstrations in Birmingham and their suppression by the police with spectacular ferocity had lit the tinder of Negro discontent throughout the land. The magnitude and sweep of the onrush took almost everyone by surprise. But at the beginning of 1963 the situation still had the outward appearance of one that would await corrosive attack upon race prejudice and step-by-step adjustment over a period of years.

The fact that January 1, 1963, marked the one-hundredth anniversary of the issuance of the Emancipation Proclamation added some sentimental impetus to the Negro push for fulfillment of the promise of freedom. President and Mrs. Kennedy observed the centennial by entertaining four hundred prominent Negroes and a number of white champions of the Negro cause at an evening reception. The presence of so many Negroes in the White House was itself significant of the changing times. Complying with an earlier request of the President, the Commission on Civil Rights produced "a report on the civil rights progress of the nation during the past century" in book form, under the title—using the words of Lincoln—*Freedom to the Free*. In its concluding summary the report said: "As the century following emancipa-

tion draws to a close, more forces are working for the realization of
civil rights for all Americans than ever before in history. Government
is active in every branch and at every level, if not in every region.
Voluntary associations in the field have multiplied at such a rate that
it is difficult to catalogue them. . . . The final chapter in the struggle for equality has yet to be written."

On November 20, 1962, the President had issued a long-awaited
order prohibiting race discrimination in federally assisted housing.[4]
On February 28, 1963, he delivered his first message to Congress devoted exclusively to civil rights. In it he renewed an earlier proposal to
substitute a sixth-grade education for the literacy tests which in some
Southern states were freely manipulated to prevent Negroes from
voting; he noted that under existing law the government can initiate
suits to end discrimination in registering voters and proposed a measure authorizing federal referees to register Negro voters while suits
are pending in counties where fewer than 15 per cent of those eligible
are on the rolls; he recommended provision for technical and financial
assistance by the federal Office of Education to school districts facing
the problem of desegregation; and he asked that the life of the Commission on Civil Rights be extended at least four more years.

His recommendations contemplated some further gains for Negroes
but did not go as far as many liberals desired. They suggested a re-
luctance on the President's part to alienate support from what at the
time seemed more important legislative objectives.

A major battleground of the Negro protest movement in 1962 and
at the turn of the year had been the tightly segregated city of Albany
in south Georgia. That experience had been discouraging. The long
siege in the form of desperate but nonviolent demonstration, led for a
time by Martin Luther King, had resulted in more than eleven hundred
arrests and had failed to make any significant change in the regime of
discrimination there.[5]

Through the months of March attention focused on the town of
Greenwood, in LeFlore County, Mississippi, where white resentment
of the efforts of Negroes to register for voting was expressed in incessant harassment and police brutality. There was some shooting, in
which a Negro worker in the cause was wounded. The Voter Education Project on March 31 released a listing of sixty-four acts of vio-

lence and intimidation committed against Negroes in Mississippi since January 1961. The situation in LeFlore County was indefensible to begin with: 92.5 per cent of the 10,274 whites and only 1.9 per cent of 13,567 Negroes of voting age were registered; and widespread sympathy was aroused with the Negroes struggling for the right to vote there. When the Department of Justice moved to secure the release of jailed Negroes and stop intimidation, quiet was restored and a trickle of Negro registration proceeded.

William L. Moore, a white Baltimore mail-carrier and an eccentric idealist, set out in April from Chattanooga, Tennessee, to walk through Alabama and Mississippi with a message of brotherhood. On April 24 he was found murdered on a lonely Alabama road, his bullet-pierced body still holding signs, one of which read: "Equal Rights for All."

The state of Alabama was the chief stamping ground of the Ku Klux Klan. It operated more openly there than elsewhere; Ku Klux signs of welcome were posted on highways at the entrance to many towns along with the signs of churches and civic clubs. Though only a small fraction of the populace was actually identified with the organization, the Klan spirit characterized much of that state's re-action to the aspirations of Negroes for human dignity and citizenship. Citizens' Councils were also active in Alabama. The attitude of white Alabama, however, was not as monolithic as that of white Mississippi; in Alabama there were substantial elements favoring moderation and adjustment, and these became notably more articulate in 1962.

But Alabama's political leaders, supported by a majority of the electorate, were second to none in their posture of reckless resistance to change. The industrial city of Birmingham was under the control of rampant white-supremacy extremists. The situation in Birmingham was investigated in the spring of 1960 by Harrison E. Salisbury, a reporter for the *New York Times,* who was writing a series of articles on interracial relations in Southern cities. His findings appeared in a startling *Times* articles of April 12, 1960, under the headline "Fear and Hatred Grip Birmingham."

"Every channel of communication," Salisbury wrote, "every me-dium of mutual interest, every reasoned approach, every inch of middle ground, has been fragmented by the emotional dynamite of racism, reinforced by the whip, the razor, the gun, the bomb, the torch, the club, the knife, the mob, the police, and many branches of the state's apparatus."

The white leaders of Birmingham reacted to this disclosure with a roar of indignation. The three city commissioners filed a libel suit (ultimately unsuccessful) for $500,000 each against the *Times* and its reporter, and Salisbury was indicted by a grand jury on forty-two counts of criminal libel. The article amazed white Southerners; many liberals were incredulous. It was not a balanced survey of the whole city; as the *Times* stated later, it "did not stress the obvious fact that an overwhelming percentage of the citizens of that city lead happy and peaceful lives. . . ." Most Birmingham whites in their rigidly segregated world were unaware of the barbarities which were being committed. But Negroes and the few persecuted white workers for interracial justice in Birmingham recognized the picture that Salisbury had drawn. They sent out warnings from time to time during the next three years that the city was moving toward a convulsion of fearful proportions.

The *Times* article noted that some Negroes had nicknamed Birmingham "the Johannesburg of America." Indeed, nowhere was the oppression of Negro Americans more to be compared with the regime of apartheid in South Africa. That Birmingham was the largest American city still refusing to admit any Negro child to a school with whites was but one symptom of the infection. The Negro 34 per cent of the city's total population of 340,000 was crowded into ghettoes, outside of which it was practically impossible for Negroes to find homes. In the white business section where most of their income was spent, Negroes were denied employment except in menial capacities; they were barred from eating places; and lavatories, water fountains, and theaters were segregated or closed to them. There was no Negro on the city police force. Most galling of all for Negroes was the daily denial of human dignity and equal protection of the law: the arrogance of official Birmingham, the unwillingness of whites to listen to Negro complaints, the exposure of Negroes to harassment and violence from racist ruffians, and the harsh and insulting treatments of Negroes by the police.

The city was ruled by three commissioners, one of whom, Arthur J. Hanes, was also mayor. But the city was largely dominated, and its racist tone was set, by T. Eugene Connor, better known as "Bull

Connor," the coarse, bellowing 63-year-old veteran commissioner of public safety.

An explosion was feared by many in January 1962 when the commissioners closed all the city's parks, playgrounds, and golf courses rather than submit to a federal court ruling that they must be open to all citizens. This headstrong action precipitated a surprising movement among white businessmen for a more moderate interracial policy. By autumn the movement had grown into a formidable campaign against the Connor regime.

Birmingham voted in November to abandon the commission form of government and adopt the mayor-council plan. Connor ran for mayor, and in an election on April 2, 1963, he was defeated by a vote of 29,630 to 21,648. Chosen mayor was Albert Boutwell, a respected Birmingham lawyer and former lieutenant governor of Alabama. The *Birmingham News* announced the election results under the headline: NEW DAY DAWNS FOR BIRMINGHAM. However, legal difficulties prevented the new administration from taking over until May 23, which left Bull Connor in control during April and May.

The Negro direct-action campaign began, on a small scale at first, the day after the election. Martin Luther King, who had arrived the night before, joined the Reverend Fred L. Shuttlesworth, president of the Alabama Christian Movement for Human Rights, and became the central figure in the crusade. With a change of administrations imminent in Birmingham, many liberals thought the move untimely; some local Negro leaders held back; some white moderates were angered. Officials of the Department of Justice, among others, urged King to wait until conciliation had been tried in the new atmosphere. But King was never one to wait upon problematical differences in official attitudes. He favored headlong attack upon all racial wrongs— a spirit which was to characterize the larger Negro uprising. Sit-ins, picket lines, and parades, staged almost daily, grew into the largest and boldest Negro demonstrations yet seen. (A Negro boycott of white merchants was already in effect.) When one demonstration was beaten back by the police and many participants arrested, a bigger demonstration followed the next day. Negro students in their teens were brought into action until they predominated in the mass demonstrations.

During the first week of May a series of conferences took place between Negro leaders and a group of prominent white businessmen.

Assistant Attorney General Burke Marshall played an active mediatory role. The newly elected city officials kept in touch with the negotiations, but the group still in power would have nothing to do with them. "It breaks my heart," the outgoing mayor said, "to see some quisling whites negotiating with him [King] when we've got him on the run!" Nevertheless, an agreement was reached; it contemplated desegregation of some downtown lunch counters and public facilities "within ninety days," an upgrading of Negro employees, release of jailed demonstrators, and "public re-establishment" of interracial communication. For his part, King announced May 8 that demonstrations were being suspended.

The truce was short-lived. On Saturday night, May 11, following a meeting of the Ku Klux Klan near the city, two dynamite blasts demolished the home of the Reverend A. D. King, a younger brother of Dr. King. The minister, his wife, and their five children raced to safety before the second blast. The street quickly filled with angry Negroes. Within the hour two more bombs exploded, at the Gaston Motel, headquarters of the Negro movement. Thousands of Negroes surged through the streets, and despite the pleas of their leaders for nonviolence they were flinging bricks, brandishing knives, and pummeling policemen. A white man's store was set on fire; two Negro homes nearby went up in flames, then three more white men's buildings. Rioting continued until dawn Sunday, when two hundred and fifty Alabama state troopers came to the aid of the embattled city police. Fifty persons had been injured badly enough to require hospitalization. The next day three thousand federal troops were sent to positions near Birmingham, but returning calm made their presence unnecessary in the city.

By mid-May (the ninth anniversary of the Brown decision) three thousand Negro prisoners were crowding the Birmingham jails. The turmoil, copiously reported by news and camera men—most of all the use of police dogs and the playing of powerful fire hoses upon crowds of Negroes, including women and children—had shocked the world. One photographic gem, a white policeman clutching the shirt of a Negro youth with his right hand while his dog on the leash in his left hand lunged at the Negro's belly, became familiar to millions. A tenuous peace reigned in Birmingham when the new city administration took over on May 23, and within the next two months three municipal golf courses reopened desegregated and some lunch counters and public facilities began to be desegregated in accordance with the interracial agreement.

But the nationwide Negro protest had burst into flames. Demonstrations erupted in a hundred cities. A sign carried by Negro students in San Francisco said: "Birmingham is everywhere." Solidarity was expressed with the Negroes of Birmingham, while attention focused on local grievances. Los Angeles Negroes crowded Wrigley Field in a "Freedom Rally for Birmingham," but they called for an end to *de facto* school segregation and discrimination in housing, employment, and labor-union membership in Los Angeles; in St. Louis demonstrations protested segregation in school classrooms; in Nashville, where many race barriers had been dropped, mass demonstrations against continuing restaurant segregation led to clashes on the streets with whites; in Philadelphia fighting occurred between police and Negroes protesting exclusion from labor unions; in New York demonstrations in building-trade unions forced suspension of work on a city hospital; in Tallahassee, Florida, police arrested two hundred students protesting Negro exclusion from two theaters and broke up a crowd of demonstrators with tear gas; Cambridge, Maryland, and Danville, Virginia, were torn with interracial strife; in North Carolina, a state which had gone farther than most of the South in removing racial barriers, Negroes demonstrated against remaining discrimination in a dozen cities, and a riot in one of them, Lexington, resulted in the death of a white man.

An attempted Negro sit-in at a lunch counter in Jackson, Mississippi, furnished another inflammatory symbol for the Negro uprising —a picture of a white man kicking an injured Negro in the face as he lay on the floor, before a circle of complacent white onlookers.

Day after day, in city after city, demonstrations and incidents continued.

Chapter 19

THE REVOLUTION

The Supreme Court delivered its historic decision banning segregation in public schools on May 17, 1954; we are led instinctively to measure the distance traveled in the decade since that date. But in the context of the centuries-old "American dilemma," the end of the *ninth* year after the Brown decision would have been a fitting place at which to close this volume and begin another. The reverberating contention over school desegregation, the turbulent resistance, and the final resignation of most of the South to token or gradual adjustment to it in nine years were the prelude to a graver upheaval that enveloped the nation in the tenth year and whose end is not yet in sight.

Negro leaders called now for full and forthright compliance with the Brown decision in the South. But that demand was to a large extent submerged in a clamor for righting a variety of racial wrongs throughout the country. The pages of newspapers and magazines and the programs of electronic news media were filled mainly with reports of manifestations of Negro discontent, not without disorder and strife, from Washington to Boston to San Francisco and all across the land. Relatively little space and time were found for the South's public-school desegregation moves that so long had made the headlines.

The display of hostility by Governor George C. Wallace as Alabama yielded at last to the desegregation order at the university level diverted national attention from the broader Negro movement for only two or three days. When Wallace was inaugurated in January 1963 and Governor John Patterson retired, one segregationist firebrand succeeded another. In his campaign for election the new governor had pledged: "I shall refuse to abide by any such illegal court order [desegregation ruling] even to the point of standing at the schoolhouse door in person, if necessary. . . ." In the first Democratic primary two candidates campaigning as segregationists but known to be relatively moderate, State Senator Ryan de Graffenreid and former Governor Folsom, had each come within eight thousand votes of equaling

Wallace's vote; but in the run-off, Wallace's belligerence had triumphed over De Graffenreid's more sober approach by approximately 339,000 to 268,000 votes. In his inaugural address Wallace dared the federal government: "I draw the line in the dust and toss the gauntlet before the feet of tyranny and I say segregation now, segregation tomorrow, segregation forever. . . ."

Yet the awakening of moderate sentiment in Alabama was reflected in an inaugural statement of the new state attorney general, Richmond Flowers, who had been elected at the same time. Flowers warned that defiance of federal authority "can only bring disgrace to our state, military law upon our people. . . ."

On May 21 United States District Judge H. Hobart Grooms ordered the admission of three Negro applicants to the University of Alabama: Miss Vivian Malone of Mobile and James A. Hood of East Gadsden to the main campus at Tuscaloosa; Dave M. McGlathery to the University Center at Huntsville. The dates fixed were June 11 for the enrollment at Tuscaloosa and June 13 for that at Huntsville.

The university board of trustees had previously announced its intention to comply with the court's ruling, and sentiment in each of the two cities was predominantly opposed to unruly resistance. The element of anxious uncertainty was the governor. Wallace continued to breathe defiance, but he said repeatedly: "There will be no violence." Events were to prove, to the relief of many, that he meant it. Two days before the date set for the move at Tuscaloosa he sent five hundred members of the Alabama National Guard to stand by in that city, while a hundred and fifty state Highway Patrolmen and other state police were deployed on the university campus.

Several hundred Tuscaloosa businessmen had worked systematically to insure that there would be no violence when the university's moment came. They urged citizens to send letters, telegrams, and resolutions to Governor Wallace opposing any reckless gesture of resistance and drew businessmen from neighboring towns into the movement. The university administration took maximum precautions. The campus was closed to unauthorized visitors a week before the crucial day; a 10 P.M. curfew was imposed; even bottled drinks—which had been a favorite weapon at Ole Miss—were removed from dispensing machines. A majority of the students themselves supported the no-violence movement.

The national administration functioned smoothly in this crisis. The

Department of Justice dispatched a team of officials headed by Deputy Attorney General Nicholas De B. Katzenbach to Tuscaloosa before the crucial day. Two thousand Regular Army troops, sent to Alabama during the Birmingham riots, were on alert seventy miles away but were never called to the scene. Acting now for the first time in *advance* of a threatened explosion, President Kennedy, at 11:30 A.M. on June 11, issued a proclamation commanding the governor of Alabama and all others obstructing justice to "cease and desist" therefrom.

Wallace arrived on the campus at 11:52 A.M. and took his stand behind a specially constructed podium at the front door of Foster Auditorium, where the Negro students were to present themselves for registration. Miss Malone and Hood arrived at 12:40, accompanied by Katzenbach and two other Department of Justice officials. When the latter went up the steps, Governor Wallace stepped forward to the lectern and stopped them with his hand. Then the deputy attorney general, standing a few feet away, read the President's cease-and-desist proclamation. Governor Wallace replied with a "proclamation" of his own, denouncing "this unwelcome, unwanted, and unwarranted intrusion upon the campus of the University of Alabama. . . ."

When the governor finished, Katzenbach said: "I take it from that statement that you are going to stand in the doorway. . . ." Wallace replied: "I stand on my statement." Katzenbach returned to the car and escorted the Negro students to their dormitories.

At 1:35 P.M. the Alabama National Guard—of which, thanks to Governor Wallace, an adequate force was already in Tuscaloosa—was called into federal service.

When Miss Malone and Hood returned to the auditorium at 5:36 P.M. they were escorted by about one hundred of the now federalized National Guardsmen. "I am General Graham," their commander said to the governor, "and it is my sad duty to ask you to step aside, on order of the President of the United States."

With this the resistance charade ended. "We must have no violence," Wallace said. "The Guardsmen are our brothers. . . . God bless all the people of this state, white and black." He drove off with his motorcycle police escort. The Negro students entered the building and were duly registered.

Two days later Dave McGlathery was admitted to the University Center at Huntsville without incident.

On June 11, two hours after Governor Wallace had bowed to federal authority, President Kennedy addressed the nation over television and radio. He referred only briefly to the accomplished fact of desegregation at the University of Alabama. He seized this climactic moment of national anxiety to speak earnestly about the "fires of frustration and discord" which were "burning in every city."

"The Negro born in America today," the President said, ". . . has about one-half as much chance of completing high school as a white baby born in the same place on the same day; one-third as much chance of becoming a professional man; twice as much chance of becoming unemployed; about one-seventh as much chance of earning $10,000 per year; life expectancy which is seven years less; and the prospect of earning only half as much."

"The time has come," the President declared, "for this nation to fulfill its promises."

Calling upon all citizens to back legislation which he was preparing to send to Congress, he said, ". . . the events in Birmingham and elsewhere have so increased the cries for equality that no city or state or legislative body can prudently choose to ignore them."

The revolution still lacked a martyr. Early in the morning after the President's address, this need was filled. The field secretary of the National Association for the Advancement of Colored People in Mississippi, Medgar Evers, returning home from a rally in Jackson, was shot in the back by an ambushed assassin as he entered his driveway.

When the body arrived in Washington for burial in Arlington National Cemetery the slain Negro leader was given a funeral befitting one of the nation's honored dead. He had been a veteran of the Normandy invasion and the campaign in France in World War II. An estimated twenty-five thousand Negroes visited the church where the body lay in state, and the military ceremony of interment at Arlington was attended by a group of dignitaries which included a representative of the President, the Secretary of Interior, the Undersecretary of Commerce, an Assistant Secretary of State and half-a-dozen members of Congress.

The President now engaged in a systematic effort to enlist support for much more far-reaching civil-rights legislation than that contemplated in his message of February 28. He consulted members of Congress; large groups of businessmen, leaders of women's organizations, editors, labor leaders, clergymen, and some state governors were invited for successive talks at the White House. On June 19 his program was revealed in a somber 550-word message to the Congress. Pointing once more to the increasing efforts of Negroes to secure "the vindication of these rights through organized direct action, with all its potentially explosive consequences," he said: ". . . the result of continued federal legislative inaction will be continued, if not increased, racial strife—causing the leadership on both sides to pass from the hands of reasonable and responsible men to the purveyors of hate and violence, endangering domestic tranquillity, retarding our nation's economic and social progress, and weakening the respect with which the rest of the world regards us."

The key provisions of the administration's new omnibus civil-rights bill were:

A legal guarantee to all citizens of equal access to the services and facilities of hotels, restaurants, places of amusement, and retail establishments in interstate commerce;

Authority for the attorney general to bring suits against school segregation when requested to do so by persons affected who are unable to sue;

Permanent statutory basis for the elimination of discrimination in employment in all projects supported wholly or in part with federal funds, and a broad attack upon job discrimination elsewhere;

Creation of a Community Relations Service to act as a mediation agency in communities with racial tensions; and

Authority to deny federal financial assistance of any kind to any program or activity in which racial discrimination occurs.

Whatever the ultimate fate of the President's civil-rights program, the reaction to his proposals—which a few months earlier would have been considered incredibly radical—was indicative of the sweeping change which had taken place in American opinion. The bill was hotly denounced in the South, but even Southern politicians for the most part now conceded, as they had been unwilling to concede before, that the

Negroes had valid grievances. Senator Richard Russell of Georgia, the leader of the Southern bloc in Congress, said: "I believe the Negro has been imposed upon. He has been subjected to indignities. But we shouldn't upset the whole scheme of constitutional government and expect people to swallow laws governing their most intimate social relations. The tempo of change is the crux of the whole matter. . . ." The once small band of civil-rights champions in Congress had grown until it embraced nearly everybody outside the South; liberalism was uninhibited, suspicion of segregationist sentiments a source of embarrassment. Of the four most talked-of possible Republican candidates for President in 1964, Governor Nelson Rockefeller of New York—who considered himself more liberal than President Kennedy on the race question—declared it to be "imperative that . . . Congress act promptly to pass this long overdue legislation"; Governor George Romney of Michigan and Governor William W. Scranton of Pennsylvania agreed that legislation to guarantee racial equality was necessary; Senator Barry Goldwater of Arizona, the Republican possibility then leading in the public-opinion polls and the central magnet of conservatism in the nation, objected to features of the President's program but expressed sympathy with Negro demonstrations and conceded that race discrimination was "morally wrong."

The whole spectrum of attitudes had moved to the left: liberals now advocated sweeping reform at once; moderates moved into positions formerly held by liberals; and many conservatives edged over to what was once the middle of the road.

The race problem, which had long been regarded, with paradoxical detachment, as "the nation's greatest domestic problem," became at last the nation's preoccupation. It dominated public discussion not merely during the excitement of occasional crises but week after week and month after month. And in place of the timid circumlocution with which the subject had been approached by many in the past, such words as "wrongs," "revolt," and even "revolution" were freely used.

A strange organization known as the "Black Muslims" found no place in the Negro revolt except as an emotional outlet for those Negroes whose hatred of the white man precluded any constructive effort to improve their condition—and as a cogent reminder to whites that things might have been much worse. The Black Muslims were a group, or a sect, of Negro Americans, led by one "Elijah Muhammad" and his spokesman "Malcolm X," which claimed kinship with Islam but taught that every white man is a devil. It had grown since its formation in the 1930s to an estimated membership of a hundred thousand. It advocated, not integration, but the utmost separation of the races—to the point of demanding that a large area of the United States be set apart for Negroes only. In their religious eccentricity as well as in their separatist aims the Muslims seemed almost gratuitously to have alienated themselves from the Negro mainstream: the Negro movement was permeated with manifestations of Christian faith and led in large part by Christian clergymen. Nevertheless, crowds which thronged in Northern cities to hear Black Muslim speakers heap male-dictions upon the white man were an arresting indication of the bitterness in many Negro hearts.

The ultimate aim of Negroes generally was not to perpetuate a racial pressure group, but to disappear as a segregated group. As-similation was essentially the goal. That meant, not greater separation from, but rapprochement with white Americans—on equal terms. The civil-rights movement itself was becoming increasingly bi-racial.

A mammoth Negro demonstration, August 28, in Washington, D.C., called the "March on Washington," gave an illuminating revelation of the composition, as well as the spirit, of the Negro movement. Of the ten chairmen for this superlatively organized spectacle, four were prominent white men: Walter Reuther, powerful labor leader, presi-dent of the United Auto Workers and vice-president of the AFL-CIO; Mathew Ahmann, executive director of the National Catholic Con-ference for Interracial Justice; Rabbi Joachim Prinz of the American Jewish Congress; and the Reverend Dr. Eugene Carson Blake of the National Council of Churches. Of over two hundred thousand persons taking part in the demonstration, at least forty thousand were white.

The strong participation of religious groups in the march was in-dicative both of white sympathy with Negro aspirations and a new aggressiveness on the part of the clergy of all religious faiths in support of civil rights. Protestants, Catholics, and Jews were conspicuous in all phases of the demonstration. The House of Bishops of the Protes-tant Episcopal Church, in a large advertisement in the *Washington Post* on the morning of the march, said it welcomed and supported fully "the responsible discipleship which impels many of our bishops, clergy, and laity to take part in such an assembly. . . ." A pastoral letter drafted by the Roman Catholic Bishops of the United States warmly supporting the movement for interracial justice was read from thousands of Catholic pulpits on the Sunday before the march, and the invocation which opened the ceremonies of August 28 was offered by the Most Reverend Patrick J. O'Boyle, Catholic archbishop of Washington.

The "March on Washington" was a historic event. The vast crowd gathered first at the Washington Monument, then marched a mile, moving for more than two hours in parallel columns on Independence Avenue and Constitution Avenue to the Lincoln Memorial. They carried signs with a variety of civil rights slogans and sang patriotic and religious songs; most of all and unceasingly above the throng rose the strains of the movement's rallying anthem, now familiar to millions of Americans, "We Shall Overcome." At the Lincoln Memorial they heard a series of speeches, which concluded with a moving oration by Martin Luther King. "The whirlwinds of revolt," King warned, "will continue to shake the foundations of our nation until the bright day of justice emerges."

The march set new records in a number of respects. It was the biggest demonstration Washington had ever seen. It drew the largest concentration of news-media representatives from the nation and the world: 1655 police passes were issued to visiting employees of press, television, and radio in addition to the 1200 such cards already held by local residents. It was also one of the most orderly mass demonstrations ever.

For Washington it was one of the most law-abiding days on record, with or without a public demonstration; the only crime reported all day long was a single instance of pocket-picking away from the march. The unbroken peace was no doubt due in part to the elaborate police precautions taken: the Metropolitan Police Department had 5900 men at its disposal, including 2000 National Guardsmen and 2000 marshals provided by the demonstrating organizations. But the police at the march had practically nothing to do except in the way of friendly offices to weary or disabled marchers. The *London Daily Express* headlined its report of the event: "The Gentle Flood." Russell Baker, reporting for the *New York Times* wrote: "The sweetness and patience of the crowd may have set some sort of national highwater mark in mass decency." The promoters of the demonstration had prepared with greatest care to confound the many critics of the project who had predicted "a howling mob." From this point of view at least the "March on Washington" was a resounding triumph.

The official slogan was "Jobs and Freedom," and its advertised objective was to stimulate congressional action on the President's civil-rights program. Early in the planning stages, some Negro spokesmen had aroused fears of a riotous invasion of Capitol Hill, causing the plan to be frowned upon initially by other Negro leaders and many friendly white observers. But as the project grew it took on a very different character. On August 28 a small delegation from the March conferred in the morning with congressional leaders and in the afternoon with the President; both conferences were marked by courtesy and restraint.

Cynics said the next day that the "March on Washington" had accomplished nothing. Most observers agreed that few, if any, opponents of the civil-rights legislation in Congress had been won over by the demonstration. But its magnitude, its dignity, and its fervor had given vast new impetus to the Negro revolution. The nation was given impressive notice that Negro acquiescence in inferior status had ended. Above all, Negro Americans—those who were in Washington on that exhilarating day and millions of others who sat glued to television sets —experienced a spiritual rebirth. Negroes will never again rest until equal status is achieved.

The Negro movement made local gains in many places. Outside of Mississippi and Alabama, even the South was adapting with surprising equanimity. Figures compiled by the Department of Justice from mid-May to September 1963 indicated that theaters, restaurants, hotels, and lunch counters were being desegregated in about fifty more Southern and border-state cities each month. The march of public-school desegregation also quickened.

The Supreme Court manifested impatience with the slow pace of this process in two significant opinions. In a decision rendered May 27, 1963, in the case of *Watson v. Memphis,* the high tribunal said that its 1955 ruling "never contemplated that the concept of 'deliberate speed' would countenance indefinite delay in the elimination of race barriers in public schools." [1] In cases involving the desegregation plans of Davidson County and Knoxville, Tennessee, the Court ruled June 3 that the liberal transfer privileges that had attenuated school integration in a number of Southern cities "do not meet the requirements of

Brown." It said: "Now . . . eight years after this decree was ren-dered and over nine years after the first Brown decision, the context in which we must interpret and apply this language to plans for de-segregation has been significantly altered." [2]

During the 1963–1964 school term a total of approximately 30,800 Negro children attended school with whites in the South. In the border states, because of the residential pattern or Negro apathy and a few pockets of stubborn white resistance, there were still many segregated schools; but in these states and the District of Columbia 718, or 93 per cent, of the bi-racial districts were now desegregated and more than half the Negro pupils were now attending classes with white children. The number of school districts initiating desegregation in the fall of 1963 in each of twelve states was: Alabama, 4; Arkansas, 1; Florida, 6; Georgia, 3; Kentucky, 20; Louisiana, 1; Maryland, 1; North Caro-lina, 22; South Carolina, 1; Tennessee, 18; Texas, 67; and Virginia, 23. One hundred and sixty-six school districts had been desegregated for the first time, three and a half times the number initiating desegre-gation in 1962.

In 146 districts the action was taken voluntarily; only twenty districts moved in response to court orders. The threat of ultimate compulsion was always present, but in the ten-year period since the Brown decision an estimated 974 school districts had been desegre-gated without waiting for specific federal court action. School boards had proceeded under court orders in only 167 districts. The region has 3053 districts in which both whites and Negroes attend school.

In Texas the hampering requirement of prior referendum approval was removed on January 1, 1963, when State Attorney General Will Wilson ruled that the 1957 act of the legislature was unconstitutional. The 67 Texas districts desegregated in 1963 brought the total in that state to 244 out of 919 bi-racial districts. Elsewhere in the South some of the cities in which earlier evidence of public hostility had aroused the greatest apprehensions—such as Charleston, Savannah, and Jacksonville—accomplished the feat of enrolling Negroes in previously all-white schools without incident. Only in Alabama was serious trouble encountered.

Compared with previous years, the South's school desegregation performance in 1963–64 represented a leap forward. Five or six years earlier it would have been considered encouraging. But at this stage in history it was grievously inadequate. Ten years after the Supreme Court had declared the practice unlawful, 98.9 per cent of the South's Negro children were still segregated. Virtually all the Negro children who had reached the third grade at the time of the Brown decision had graduated or left school without ever emerging from the public-education ghetto. The long way from fulfillment of the bright promise of Brown was still fuel for the fires of Negro protest.

In Alabama, Governor Wallace indulged in ten days of pyrotechnics before yielding once more to federal authority. Twenty-four Negro children were under federal court orders to be admitted to previously all-white public schools in four cities; two in Mobile, thirteen in Tuskegee, five in Birmingham, and four in Huntsville. Local authorities were prepared to go ahead with desegregation in each city, and there was little evidence of impending disorder—except for the chronic tension in Birmingham—until the governor intervened. In what seemed to be a desire to create a spectacular crisis, he dispatched state troopers hither and yon to prevent desegregation plans from going forward, declaring: "We are going to show them they're not dealing with demoralized Cubans or regimented Balkans!" [3]

Wallace's maneuvers followed no consistent plan. He ringed the public school at Tuskegee with a hundred troopers on Monday, September 2, when school was scheduled to open, and forced it to remain closed—over the protests of the school board and the city's mayor. Tuesday, on the eve of school-opening in Birmingham, he sent in six hundred state troopers against the wishes of the city authorities. But on Wednesday he yielded to the pleas of local officials and kept his troopers in their hotel rooms while the schools opened and enrolled two Negro pupils with whites. Several small white mobs gave the police some trouble and half-a-dozen arrests were made before they were dispersed. That night a dynamite explosion damaged the home of a Negro leader, Arthur Shores, and injured his wife. Hundreds of Negroes swarmed into the streets, and in the ensuing battle with police one Negro was killed and twenty other persons were injured. The next day the schools to which Negroes had been assigned were closed.

State troopers also closed four schools in Huntsville, which the Negroes had not yet entered, over angry white protests; but the affected schools in Mobile were allowed to open Friday without the Negro pupils. It was announced that all schools would be allowed to reopen Monday, September 9. On Monday state troopers barred the

Negroes from the white schools in Mobile, Tuskegee and Birmingham, but they were allowed to enter and enroll in Huntsville. The same day five federal judges in Alabama's three judicial districts issued orders restraining Governor Wallace from further interference with school desegregation.

At this point Wallace decided to replace his troopers with members of the National Guard. Guardsmen surrounded the schools in three cities early Tuesday morning. But President Kennedy acted quickly; before the school bells rang, the Alabama National Guardsmen had been called into federal service and whisked back to their armories. Twenty Negro children entered white schools in Mobile, Tuskegee, and Birmingham. In little Tuskegee, under steady segregationist pressure moderate voices had been silenced and the attitude of whites had hardened during the week. Macon County, in which the town is located, has a population of about 22,000 Negroes and less than 5,000 whites. A few white children entered school at first along with the Negroes, but within a few days no whites were left in the school. They were signing up for a segregated private school which was being hastily organized. However, except for a week of abortive student boycotts, the immediate school crisis in Huntsville, Mobile, and Birmingham was over.

Wallace said: "I can't fight bayonets with my bare hands!" But it was the governor who sent the soldiers to the schools and the President who sent the soldiers home. If Wallace expected the kind of local acclaim that had greeted Faubus in 1957 and Barnett in 1962, he was sadly disappointed. His maladroit intervention against the wishes of city authorities drew criticism even from many of his former supporters. The *Montgomery Advertiser,* whose editor had enjoyed a close personal friendship with the governor, said: "The *Advertiser* must sorrowfully conclude that, in this instance, its friend has gone wild." The *Birmingham News* said: ". . . Birmingham was done a disservice by the governor." Still, letters applauding his performance poured in from many sections of the country. The governor's office at Montgomery boasted that its incoming mail was greater than that of the White House. Wallace had become the latest national symbol of anti-Kennedy racism, and a host of widely scattered extremists quickly welcomed him in that role. The Alabama governor even talked of running for President of the United States. Nearer home, Negrophobes were encouraged to acts of savagery.

Sunday morning, September 15, a dynamite bomb blasted a crowded Negro Baptist church in Birmingham. Four girls, aged ten to fourteen, were killed in their Sunday school classes, their bodies mutilated. Many other worshipers were cut and bruised by flying debris; a score required hospital treatment. In the two hours of rioting which followed before incensed Negroes were quelled by police or calmed by their own nonviolent leaders, a Negro youth was unintentionally shot by a policeman. During the excitement, but elsewhere in Birmingham, two young whites callously shot to death a 13-year-old Negro boy riding past on a bicycle.

The church-bombing could hardly have been better calculated to shock the nation and the world. In Birmingham the well-meaning new mayor wept when he heard the news. Some horrified white citizens gathered in churches to pray. But in that warped city many still missed the significance of the sickening outrage. Grieving for the murdered children, many Birminghamians still said the Negroes had "brought it on themselves." Rewards offered for the arrest of the perpetrators totaled over $76,000; $52,000 was offered by the city. Governor Wallace offered $5000, saying the tragedy had "saddened all Alabamians." But Martin Luther King wired the governor: ". . . The blood of four little children . . . is on your hands. Your irresponsible and misguided actions have created in Birmingham and Alabama the atmosphere that has induced continued violence and now murder."

The grisly fanatics who planted the bomb in the Birmingham church—and the innocent children whose lives were taken—may have done as much to advance the Negro cause as the "March on Washington." But even without that poignant stimulus, Negro leadership was committed to a fight, nonviolent but massive and unrelenting, to the end. Nonviolent action became an elaborate science. Earnest planners were multiplying and refining techniques that would have bewildered Mahatma Gandhi. Cadres of probably five thousand field workers from various Negro organizations were undergoing systematic training, and plans of attack in scores of cities, with timetables for coming months were on file.

Day after day the nonviolent offensive went on. Sit-ins took many forms for many purposes. They were also lie-ins, "study-ins" (Northern schools), "kneel-ins" (churches), "sleep-ins" (apartments), and "wade-ins" (beaches), as well as roadblocks, picket lines, parades, boycotts of discriminating establishments and the products of discriminating companies. "Jail-ins" were massive, for thousands of Negroes were arrested. Many submitted to arrest almost gleefully, others scuffled, and some fell limp so police would have to carry them away.

Negro demonstrations offended many. Cynical observers held that "pressure" harmed the Negro cause, that the proper way to achieve its goals was not in the streets, but in friendly talks around the council table. The critics of direct action were not all hostile to the movement, but they were seldom close students of the Negro's long struggle. Experience had taught Negro Americans that no significant advance was ever made without pressure; negotiation with whites around the council table all too often had ended with no appreciable change in the status quo. And even as criticism mounted, direct action was opening public facilities and bringing other concessions in hundreds of cities.

The usual demonstrations were not merely an exercise of the right of peaceful petition or a dramatization of grievances. They obstructed traffic, caused business to suffer, and invited clashes with unruly whites, taxing the police. They were frankly coercive. The granting of specified concessions was often the price of surcease from parades and picketing. The decorum and restraint that marked the "March on Washington" were far from characteristic of many lesser demonstrations. In much-publicized instances protesters lay on the pavement to block entry to segregated establishments or to impede construction work in which Negroes were denied employment. Militant Negro youths insulted some friendly leaders, both white and colored, whom they considered "too moderate"; they were sometimes most obstreperous where their grievances were minor or uncertain. Some Negroes marched merely to "get into the act." There was rivalry among Negro leaders and organizations and some angry friction. Was there ever a mass movement without undisciplined elements and a measure of human egotism and folly?

Among the nation's 170 million whites a mountain of prejudice still stood in the path of the Negro advance. A wave of sympathy for Negroes had been touched off by Bull Connor's firehose and police dogs. It deepened with the Birmingham church-bombing horror. But the feeling subsided when the realities of the Negro upsurge came nearer home. Many who deplored race discrimination from a distance were aroused to fierce resentment when a Negro family moved into their neighborhood. The old image of the Negro and the subconscious antipathy were still present among a majority of white Americans. The influence of these whites was felt in Congress, and the ignorant and unruly among them, as among the Negroes, were increasingly ready for interracial clashes. Negro leaders, while passionately urging non-violence, could not say how long demonstrators could be restrained. "Nonviolence" was not in the vocabulary of white hoodlums.

Stewart Alsop and Oliver Quayle reported in the *Saturday Evening Post* of September 7, 1963, the results of an informal poll of white attitudes in the East, the Middle West, and the West Coast. They showed a startling ambivalence. Many who condemned race discrimination in theory showed stubborn prejudice in their feeling about personal association with Negroes. Seventy-seven per cent of those interviewed thought a white man should have a legal right to refuse to sell a home to a Negro. "The danger," these writers said, "lies less in violent Negro action than in violent white reaction."

A formidable task confronted the clergy, the educators, the publicists, and all those who labored to hasten the "change in the hearts of men." Another task confronted the statesman. The decade had furnished abundant examples of the truth that law and compulsion can change not only practice, but, in turn, habits and attitudes. Under the discipline of the Armed Forces, recruits of prejudiced background were adapting themselves to racial integration quickly and cheerfully. In civilian life many whites who had inveighed vehemently against the lowering of race barriers were accepting the change with complacency after the fact.

The legislation which President Kennedy had tirelessly urged to advance the reform moved slowly through committees of Congress, stubbornly opposed by Southern members. The civil rights bill as it was approved by Judiciary Committee of the House of Representatives on October 29, 1963, embraced: provision for a fair employment practices commission, which was not included in the Administration's original draft; a ban on segregation in restaurants and other places of public accommodation; fresh steps against public school segregation; and half a dozen other provisions in support of equal rights for Negroes. It was stronger by far than any civil rights bill previously enacted by the Congress.

On November 22, 1963, the nation and the world were plunged

into mourning by the assassination of John Fitzgerald Kennedy. High among the virtues of the martyred President to which the world paid tribute was his dedication to the cause of human rights and interracial justice.

In Congress efforts were redoubled to secure passage of the civil rights bill "as a memorial to President Kennedy." Lyndon Baines Johnson, the new President, promptly announced his determination to carry forward the Kennedy programs, including emphatically the civil rights legislation. In his first address to Congress, November 27, President Johnson said his predecessor had vitalized by his drive and dedication "above all, the dream of equal rights for all Americans whatever their race or color." Now he said: "We have talked long enough in this country about equal rights. We have talked for a hundred years or more. It is time now to write the next chapter . . . in books of law."

The unrest will end sometime because it is inevitable that in America justice and humanity in time will prevail. The revolt will tend to diminish as Negroes find racial exclusions ended in one community after another. Individual integration in government and industry will both accomplish a prime objective and deplete the ranks of the militant intelligentsia. The latter trend is already visible. The captain in the Negroes' greatest legal battle—Thurgood Marshall—has moved to the detachment of a United States circuit judge. A former chairman of the board of the NAACP—Robert C. Weaver—is administrator of the national Housing and Home Finance Agency. Carl T. Rowan, as ambassador to Finland, has turned from literary assault upon racial injustice to national foreign policy. A hundred other Negroes hold important national, state, and city offices with responsibilities to all the people. Similarly, more and more talented Negroes will serve the public in managerial and executive positions in private life.

Shortcomings in training and experience will delay the full integration of the Negro in the national economy beyond the day when restrictions on account of race shall have been removed. The time when a Negro will be able to choose his home in accordance with his wishes and his means is probably even farther off. It is early to attempt to visualize the consummation of a movement that has a long, hazardous way still to go. What convulsions, what solutions, what miracles lie ahead no one can say.

Is there instruction for us in the experience of other times and places? We will look in vain in modern history for a prototype of the American Negro Revolution. In some respects it is unique. It bears most resemblance, perhaps, to the long struggle of the Irish people for dignity and freedom. There we saw rivalry of factions and leaders, moderates and extremists in all degrees, zealots both nonviolent and very violent. Britain waited tragically too long to face the problem with tolerance and understanding. Years and generations of "talk around the council table" brought no solution—until depredations, bombings, and assassinations were widespread. It is not an impulse of hysteria to find in the violence and terror in Ireland in the early 1920s a warning for the United States today. On the other hand, the aim of the Negro movement in America is in a sense the opposite of what the Irish were fighting for. The Irish wanted to get *out,* the Negro wants to get *in.* That is a thought full of counsel for the near term and of hope for the long future.

The Negro population has been in America as long as the white. Negroes joined the settlers at Jamestown before the *Mayflower* reached Plymouth Rock; Negro arrivals in the United States virtually ceased before the nineteenth-century flood of European immigration began. To the Negro American this is his country; he knows no other. What he was striving for in the tenth year after the Brown decision was to become at last a part of the American people.

APPENDIX

THE BROWN DECISION

(OLIVER BROWN ET AL. V. BOARD OF EDUCATION OF TOPEKA, SHAWNEE COUNTY, KANSAS, ET AL.)

May 17, 1954

These cases come to us from the States of Kansas, South Carolina, Virginia, and Delaware. They are premised on different facts and different local conditions, but a common legal question justifies their consideration together in this consolidated opinion.

In each of the cases, minors of the Negro race, through their legal representatives, seek the aid of the courts in obtaining admission to the public schools of their community on a non-segregated basis. In each instance, they have been denied admission to schools attended by white children under laws requiring or permitting segregation according to race. This segregation was alleged to deprive the plaintiffs of the equal protection of the laws under the Fourteenth Amendment. In each of the cases other than the Delaware case, a three-judge federal district court denied relief to the plaintiffs on the so-called "separate-but-equal" doctrine announced by this Court in *Plessy v. Ferguson,* 163 U.S. 537, 16 S.Ct. 1138, 41 L.Ed. 256. Under that doctrine, equality of treatment is accorded when the races are provided substantially equal facilities, even though these facilities be separate. In the Delaware case, the Supreme Court of Delaware adhered to that doctrine, but ordered that the plaintiffs be admitted to the white schools because of their superiority to the Negro schools.

The plaintiffs contend that segregated public schools are not "equal" and cannot be made "equal," and that hence they are deprived of the equal protection of the laws. Because of the obvious importance of the question presented the Court took jurisdiction. Argument was heard in the 1952 Term, and reargument was heard this Term on certain questions propounded by the Court.

Reargument was largely devoted to the circumstances surrounding the adoption of the Fourteenth Amendment in 1868. It covered exhaustively consideration of the Amendment in Congress, ratification by the states, then existing practices in racial segregation, and the views of proponents and opponents of the Amendment. This discussion and our own investigation convince us that, although these sources cast some light, it is not enough to resolve the problem with which we are faced. At best, they are inconclusive. The most avid proponents of the post-War Amendments undoubtedly intended them to remove all legal distinctions among "all per-

283

sons born or naturalized in the United States." Their opponents, just as certainly, were antagonistic to both the letter and the spirit of the Amendments and wished them to have the most limited effect. What others in Congress and the state legislatures had in mind cannot be determined with any degree of certainty.

An additional reason for the inconclusive nature of the Amendment's history, with respect to segregated schools, is the status of public education at that time. In the South, the movement toward free common schools, supported by general taxation, had not yet taken hold. Education of white children was largely in the hands of private groups. Education of Negroes was almost nonexistent, and practically all of the race were illiterate. In fact, any education of Negroes was forbidden by law in some states. Today, in contrast, many Negroes have achieved outstanding success in the arts and sciences as well as in the business and professional world. It is true that public school education at the time of the Amendment had advanced further in the North, but the effect of the Amendment on Northern states was generally ignored in the congressional debates. Even in the North, the conditions of public education did not approximate those existing today. The curriculum was usually rudimentary; ungraded schools were common in rural areas; the school term was but three months a year in many states; and compulsory school attendance was virtually unknown. As a consequence, it is not surprising that there should be so little in the history of the Fourteenth Amendment relating to its intended effect on public education.

In the first cases in this Court construing the Fourteenth Amendment, decided shortly after its adoption, the Court interpreted it as proscribing all state-imposed discriminations against the Negro race. The doctrine of "separate but equal" did not make its appearance in this Court until 1896 in the case of *Plessy v. Ferguson, supra,* involving not education but transportation. American courts have since labored with the doctrine for over half a century. In this Court, there have been six cases involving the "separate but equal" doctrine in the field of public education. In *Cumming v. Board of Education of Richmond County,* 175 U.S. 528, 20 S.Ct. 197, 44 L.Ed. 262, and *Gong Lum v. Rice,* 275 U.S. 78, 48 S.Ct. 91, 72 L.Ed. 172, the validity of the doctrine itself was not challenged. In more recent cases, all on the graduate-school level, inequality was found in that specific benefits enjoyed by white students were denied to Negro students of the same educational qualifications. *State of Missouri ex rel. Gaines v. Canada,* 305 U.S. 337, 59 S.Ct. 232, 83 L.Ed. 208; *Sipuel v. Board of Regents of University of Oklahoma,* 332 U.S. 631, 68 S.Ct. 299, 92 L.Ed. 247; *Sweatt v. Painter,* 339 U.S. 629, 70 S.Ct. 848, 94 L.Ed. 1114; *McLaurin v. Oklahoma State Regents,* 339 U.S. 637, 70 S.Ct. 851, 94 L.Ed. 1149. In none of these cases was it necessary to re-examine the doctrine to grant relief to the Negro plaintiff. And in *Sweatt v. Painter, supra,* the Court expressly reserved decision on the question whether *Plessy v. Ferguson* should be held inapplicable to public education.

In the instant cases, that question is directly presented. Here, unlike *Sweatt v. Painter,* there are findings below that the Negro and white schools involved have been equalized, or are being equalized, with respect to buildings, curricula, qualifications and salaries of teachers, and other "tangible" factors. Our decision, therefore, cannot turn on merely a comparison of these tangible factors in the Negro and white schools involved in each of the cases. We must look instead to the effect of segregation itself on public education.

In approaching this problem, we cannot turn the clock back to 1868 when the Amendment was adopted, or even to 1896 when *Plessy v. Ferguson* was written. We must consider public education in the light of its full development and its present place in American life throughout the Nation. Only in this way can it be determined if segregation in public schools deprives these plaintiffs of the equal protection of the laws.

Today, education is perhaps the most important function of state and local governments. Compulsory school attendance laws and the great expenditure for education both demonstrate our recognition of the importance of education to our democratic society. It is required in the performance of our most basic public responsibilities, even service in the armed forces. It is the very foundation of good citizenship. Today it is a principal instrument in awakening the child to cultural values, in preparing him for later professional training, and in helping him to adjust normally to his environment. In these days, it is doubtful that any child may reasonably be expected to succeed in life if he is denied the opportunity of an education. Such an opportunity, where the state has undertaken to provide it, is a right which must be made available to all on equal terms.

We come then to the question presented: Does segregation of children in public schools solely on the basis of race, even though the physical facilities and other "tangible" factors may be equal, deprive the children of the minority group of equal educational opportunities? We believe that it does.

In *Sweatt v. Painter, supra* [339 U.S. 629, 70 S.Ct. 850], in finding that a segregated law school for Negroes could not provide them equal educational opportunities, this Court relied in large part on "those qualities which are incapable of objective measurement but which make for greatness in a law school." In *McLaurin v. Oklahoma State Regents, supra* [339 U.S. 637, 70 S.Ct. 853], the Court, in requiring that a Negro admitted to a white graduate school be treated like all other students, again resorted to intangible considerations: ". . . his ability to study, to engage in discussions and exchange views with other students, and, in general, to learn his profession." Such considerations apply with added force to children in grade and high schools. To separate them from others of similar age and qualifications solely because of their race generates a feeling of inferiority as to their status in the community that may affect their hearts and minds in a way unlikely ever to be undone. The effect of this separation on their educational opportunities was well stated by a finding in the Kansas case by a court which nevertheless felt compelled to rule against the Negro plaintiffs:

> Segregation of white and colored children in public schools has a detrimental effect upon the colored children. The impact is greater when it has the sanction of the law; for the policy of separating the races is usually interpreted as denoting the inferiority of the Negro group. A sense of inferiority affects the motivation of the child to learn. Segregation with the sanction of law, therefore, has a tendency to [retard] the educational and mental development of Negro children and to deprive them of some of the benefits they would receive in a racial[ly] integrated school system.

Whatever may have been the extent of psychological knowledge at the time of *Plessy v. Ferguson,* this finding is amply supported by modern authority. Any language in *Plessy v. Ferguson* contrary to this finding is rejected.

We conclude that in the field of public education the doctrine of "separate but equal" has no place. Separate educational facilities are inherently unequal. Therefore, we hold that the plaintiffs and others similarly situated for whom the actions have been brought are, by reason of the segregation complained of, deprived of the equal protection of the laws guaranteed by the Fourteenth Amendment. This disposition makes unnecessary any discussion whether such segregation also violates the Due Process Clause of the Fourteenth Amendment.

Because these are class actions, because of the wide applicability of this decision, and because of the great variety of local conditions, the formulation of decrees in these cases presents problems of considerable complexity. On reargument, the consideration of appropriate relief was necessarily subordinated to the primary question—the constitutionality of segregation in public education. We have now announced that such segregation is a denial of the equal protection of the laws. In order that we may have the full assistance of the parties in formulating decrees, the cases will be restored to the docket, and the parties are requested to present further argument on Questions 4 and 5 previously propounded by the Court for the reargument this Term. The Attorney General of the United States is again invited to participate. The Attorneys General of the states requiring or permitting segregation in public education will also be permitted to appear as amici curiae upon request to do so by September 15, 1954, and submission of briefs by October 1, 1954.

It is so ordered.

May 31, 1955

These cases were decided on May 17, 1954. The opinions of that date declaring the fundamental principle that racial discrimination in public education is unconstitutional, are incorporated herein by reference. All provisions of federal, state, or local law requiring or permitting such discrimination must yield to this principle. There remains for consideration the manner in which relief is to be accorded.

Because these cases arose under different local conditions and their disposition will involve a variety of local problems, we requested further argument on the question of relief. In view of the nationwide importance of the decision, we invited the Attorney General of the United States and the Attorneys General of all states requiring or permitting racial discrimination in public education to present their views on that question. The parties, the United States, and the States of Florida, North Carolina, Arkansas, Oklahoma, Maryland, and Texas filed briefs and participated in the oral argument.

These presentations were informative and helpful to the Court in its consideration of the complexities arising from the transition to a system of public education freed of racial discrimination. The presentations also demonstrated that substantial steps to eliminate racial discrimination in public schools have already been taken, not only in some of the communities in which these cases arose, but in some of the states appearing as *amici curiae,* and in other states as well. Substantial progress has been made in the District of Columbia and in the communities in Kansas and Delaware involved in this litigation. The defendants in the cases coming to us from South Carolina and Virginia are awaiting the decision of this Court concerning relief.

Full implementation of these constitutional principles may require solution of varied local school problems. School authorities have the primary responsibility for elucidating, assessing, and solving these problems; courts will have to consider whether the action of school authorities constitutes good faith implementation of the governing constitutional principles. Because of their proximity to local conditions and the possible need for further hearings, the courts which originally heard these cases can best perform this judicial appraisal. Accordingly, we believe it appropriate to remand the cases to those courts.

In fashioning and effectuating the decrees, the courts will be guided by equitable principles. Traditionally, equity has been characterized by a practical flexibility in shaping its remedies and by a facility for adjusting and reconciling public and private needs. These cases call for the exercise of these traditional attributes of equity power. At stake is the personal interest of the plaintiffs in admission to public schools as soon as practicable on a nondiscriminatory basis. To effectuate this interest may call for elimination of a variety of obstacles in making the transition to school systems operated in accordance with the constitutional principles set forth in our May 17, 1954, decision. Courts of equity may properly take into account the public interest in the elimination of such obstacles in a systematic and effective manner. But it should go without saying that the vitality of these constitutional principles cannot be allowed to yield simply because of disagreement with them.

While giving weight to these public and private considerations, the courts will require that the defendants make a prompt and reasonable start toward full compliance with our May 17, 1954, ruling. Once such a start has been made, the courts may find that additional time is necessary to carry out the ruling in an effective manner. The burden rests upon the defendants to establish that such time is necessary in the public interest and is consistent with good faith compliance at the earliest practicable date. To that end, the courts may consider problems related to administration, arising from the physical condition of the school plant, the school transportation system, personnel, revision of school districts and attendance areas into compact units to achieve a system of determining admission to the public schools on a nonracial basis, and revision of local laws and regulations which may be necessary in solving the foregoing problems. They will also consider the adequacy of any plans the defendants may propose to meet these problems and to effectuate a transition to a racially nondiscriminatory school system. During this period of transition, the courts will retain jurisdiction of these cases.

The judgments below, except that in the Delaware case, are accordingly reversed and the cases are remanded to the district courts to take such proceedings and enter such orders and decrees consistent with this opinion as are necessary and proper to admit to public schools on a racially nondiscriminatory basis with all deliberate speed the parties to these cases. The judgment in the Delaware case—ordering the immediate admission of the plantiffs to schools previously attended only by white children—is affirmed on the basis of the principles stated in our May 17, 1954, opinion, but the case is remanded to the Supreme Court of Delaware for such further proceedings as that court may deem necessary in light of this opinion.

It is so ordered.

BIBLIOGRAPHY

A mass of periodical literature was consulted in the preparation of this book, but a file of the *Southern School News* was a constant companion. This monthly journal, promoted by a group of Southern newspaper editors and educators and financed by the Ford Foundation, began in September 1954 "to tell the story, factually and objectively, of what happens in education as a result of the Supreme Court's May 17 opinion that segregation in the public schools is unconstitutional." It has since been an inestimable boon to officials, educators, writers, and all concerned with that problem in the South.

The *Race Relations Law Reporter,* a magazine, also financed by the Ford Foundation, was drawn upon heavily. Edited by the Vanderbilt University School of Law, the aim of this magazine is to give "a complete, impartial presentation of basic materials, including court cases, legislation, orders, regulations," in the race relations field. Although it did not begin publication until February 1956, it covered in its first issue the period from May 1954 through December 1955 and included the Supreme Court decisions of May 17, 1954, and May 31, 1955, in the School Segregation Cases, with the Court's extensive footnotes. The *Race Relations Law Reporter* is now published quarterly, together with the *Southern School News,* by the Southern Education Reporting Service at (P.O. Box 6156, Acklen Station) Nashville, Tennessee.

The United States Commission on Civil Rights has assembled a mass of authoritative data and, beginning with its Report for 1959, has furnished a series of illuminating reports in paperbound volumes.

A major purpose of the Southern Regional Council is the collection and dissemination of information on race relations in the South. In addition to its monthly magazine, *The New South,* it has published many pamphlets and reports which may be had by addressing the Southern Regional Council, 5 Forsyth St., Atlanta 3, Georgia.

The following books will be helpful to the student of the race problem, as they were to the author of this book:

Allport, Gordon W. *The Nature of Prejudice.* Boston: Beacon Press, 1954.

Ashmore, Harry S. *An Epitaph for Dixie.* New York: Norton, 1958
——. *The Negro and the Schools.* Chapel Hill: University of North Carolina Press, 1954.

Baldwin, James. *Nobody Knows My Name.* New York: Dial Press, 1961.
——. *The Fire Next Time.* New York: Dial Press, 1963.

Bardolph, Richard. *The Negro Vanguard.* New York: Rinehart & Co., 1959.

Bates, Daisy. *The Long Shadow of Little Rock.* New York: David McKay Co., 1962.

Boyle, Sarah Patton. *The Desegregated Heart.* New York: William Morrow & Co., 1962.

Brady, Tom P. *Black Monday.* Winona, Miss.: Association of Citizens' Councils, 1955.

290   BIBLIOGRAPHY

Cable, George Washington. *The Negro Question*. New York: Doubleday, 1958.

Carmichael, Omer, and James, Weldon. *The Louisville Story*. New York: Simon & Schuster, 1957.

Carter, Hodding, III. *The South Strikes Back*. New York: Doubleday, 1959.

Cash, W. J. *The Mind of the South*. New York: Knopf, 1941.

Cook, James Graham. *The Segregationists*. New York: Appleton-Century-Crofts, 1962.

Dabbs, James McBride. *The Southern Heritage*. New York: Knopf, 1958.

Dixon, Thomas. *The Clansman*. New York: Doubleday, Page & Co., 1905.

Du Bois, W. E. B. *The Souls of Black Folk*. Chicago: McClung & Co., 1903.

Dykeman, Wilma, and Stokely, James. *Neither Black Nor White*. New York: Rinehart & Co., 1957.

———. *Seeds of Southern Change*. Chicago: University of Chicago Press, 1962.

East, P. D. *The Magnolia Jungle*. New York: Simon & Schuster, 1960.

Furnas, J. C. *Goodbye to Uncle Tom*. New York: William Sloane Associates, 1956.

Griffin, John Howard. *Black Like Me*. New York: New American Library (Signet Book), 1962.

Handlin, Oscar. *Race and Nationality in American Life*. New York: Doubleday, 1957.

Hays, Brooks. *A Southern Moderate Speaks*. Chapel Hill: University of North Carolina Press, 1959.

Hughes, Langston. *Fight for Freedom—The Story of the NAACP*. New York: Berkley Publishing Corp., 1962.

Key, V. O., Jr. *Southern Politics*. New York: Knopf, 1949.

Kilpatrick, James Jackson. *The Sovereign States*. Chicago: Henry Regnery Co., 1957.

King, Martin Luther. *Stride Toward Freedom*. New York: Harper & Bros., 1958.

Lincoln, Eric. *The Black Muslims in America*. Boston: Beacon Press, 1961.

Lomax, Louis E. *The Negro Revolt*. New York: Harper & Bros., 1962.

Martin, John Bartlow. *The Deep South Says NEVER*. Ballantine Books, Inc., 1957.

McGill, Ralph. *The South and the Southerners*. Boston: Little, Brown, 1963.

Muse, Benjamin. *Virginia's Massive Resistance*. Bloomfield: University of Indiana Press, 1961.

Olmsted, Frederick Law. *The Cotton Kingdom*. New York: Knopf, 1953.

President's Committee on Civil Rights. *To Secure These Rights*. New York: Simon & Schuster, 1947.

Peltason, Jack W. *58 Lonely Men*. New York: Harcourt, Brace & World, 1961.

Peters, William. *The Southern Temper*. New York: Doubleday, 1959.

Putnam, Carleton. *Race and Reason*. Washington: Public Affairs Press, 1961.

Rice, Arnold S. *The Ku Klux Klan*. Washington: Public Affairs Press, 1962.

Rose, Arnold. *The Negro in America*, condensation of Gunnar Myrdal's *The American Dilemma*. Boston: Beacon Press, 1956.

Rowan, Carl T. *Go South to Sorrow*. New York: Random House, 1957.

Saloman, Leon I. (ed.) *The Supreme Court*. New York: H. W. Wilson Co., 1961.

Shoemaker, Don (ed.). *With All Deliberate Speed*. New York: Harper & Bros., 1957.

Spurlock, Clark. *Education and the Supreme Court*. Urbana: University of Illinois Press, 1955.

Talmadge, Herman E. *You and Segregation*. Birmingham, Ala.: Vulcan Press, 1955.

Torrence, Rexford G. *The Story of John Hope*. New York: Macmillan Co., 1948.

Wakefield, Dan. *Revolt in the South*. New York: Grove Press, 1960.

Warren, Robert Penn. *Segregation*. New York: Random House, 1959.

White, Theodore H. *The Making of the President 1960*. New York: Atheneum, 1961.

Woodward, C. Vann. *Origins of the New South*. Baton Rouge: Louisiana State University Press, 1951.

————. *The Strange Career of Jim Crow*. New York: Oxford University Press, 1955.

Workman, William D., Jr. *The Case for the South*. New York: Devin-Adair, 1960.

White, Francis Walter. *How Far the Promised Land?* New York: Viking Press, 1955.

REFERENCE NOTES

Chapter 1
1. Harry S. Ashmore, *The Negro and the Schools* (Chapel Hill: University of North Carolina Press, 1954), p. 139.
2. C. Vann Woodward, *The Strange Career of Jim Crow* (New York: Oxford University Press, 1955), p. ix.
3. Ashmore, *op. cit.*, p. 15.
4. J. L. Blair Buck, *The Development of Public Schools in Virginia* (Richmond: State Board of Education, 1952), pp. 231–32.
5. Ashmore, *op. cit.*, pp. 60–65.
6. Langston Hughes, *Fight for Freedom* (New York: Berkley Publishing Corporation, 1962), p. 138.
7. *Southern School News,* October 1954, p. 16.
8. Edmund Cahn, *New York University Law Review* (1955), p. 150 and p. 159.
9. *Richmond Times-Dispatch,* December 11, 1952.
10. Ashmore, *op. cit.*, p. 106.

Chapter 2
1. *New York Times,* May 18, 1954.
2. *Time,* May 24, 1954.
3. *Atlanta Daily World,* May 21, 1954.
4. *Atlanta Journal,* May 18, 1954.
5. *Birmingham Post-Herald,* May 19, 1954.
6. *Atlanta Daily World,* June 25, 1954.
7. *Richmond Times-Dispatch,* May 18, 1954.
8. *Id.*
9. *Richmond News Leader,* May 18, 1954.
10. *New York Times,* May 18, 1954.
11. *Southern School News,* September 3, 1954, p. 12.
12. *Ibid.,* p. 13.
13. *Ibid.,* October 1, 1954, p. 1.
14. *Ibid.,* p. 6.
15. *Ibid.,* September 3, 1954, p. 13.
16. *Ibid.,* June 8, 1955, p. 3.

Chapter 4
1. *Variety,* January 8, 1958.
2. Thomas Dixon, *The Clansman* (New York: Doubleday, Page & Co., 1905), p. 291.
3. *Ibid.,* advertising, back page.
4. Thomas Dixon, *The Leopard's Spots* (New York: Doubleday, Page & Co., 1902), p. 244.
5. Thomas P. Brady, *Black Monday* (Winona, Miss.: Association of Citizens' Councils, 1955).

6. *Southern School News,* March 1957, p. 7.
7. *Ibid.,* April 1957, p. 13.
8. Arnold S. Rice, *The Ku Klux Klan in American Politics* (Washington: Public Affairs Press, 1962), p. 118.
9. *Birmingham Post-Herald,* February 18, 1956.
10. Atlanta: Southern Regional Council *et al., Intimidation, Reprisal and Violence,* p. 10.
11. *Southern School News,* March 1956, p. 10.
12. *Chattanooga Times,* April 8, 1956.
13. *Ibid.,* February 10, 1956, editorial.
14. *Ibid.,* March 2, 1956.

Chapter 5

1. *Southern School News,* April 1955, p. 13, and August 1956, p. 9.
2. *Ibid.,* February 1956, p. 8.
3. *Ibid.,* June 1956, p. 9.
4. *Ibid.,* April 1955, p. 2.
5. Hodding Carter III, *The South Strikes Back* (New York: Doubleday, 1959), p. 67.
6. *Southern School News,* April 1956.
7. Don Shoemaker, ed., *With All Deliberate Speed* (New York: Harper & Bros., 1957), pp. 135–36.
8. *Ibid.,* p. 139.
9. *Chattanooga Times,* January 10, 1957.
10. *Southern School News,* September 1955, p. 6.
11. Benjamin Muse, *Virginia's Massive Resistance* (Bloomfield: University of Indiana Press, 1961) p. 21.

Chapter 6

1. *New York Times,* March 21, 1956.
2. *Delta Democrat Times,* March 15, 1956.
3. *Atlanta Constitution,* March 1, 1956.
4. *New York Times,* May 24, 1956.
5. Theodore R. McKeldin, "The Role of Public Officials," *Notre Dame Lawyer,* Vol. xxxiv, No. 5, Symposium 1959, p. 611.
6. J. W. Peltason, *58 Lonely Men* (New York: Harcourt, Brace & World, Inc., 1961), p. 5.
7. *Southern School News,* July 1955, p. 16.
8. *Race Relations Law Reporter,* Volume 1 (1956), p. 73.
9. *Ibid.,* p. 43 and p. 299.

Chapter 7

1. *Southern School News,* October 1956, p. 14.
2. *Race Relations Law Reporter,* Volume 1 (1956), p. 885.
3. *Southern School News,* September 1956, p. 3.
4. Wilma Dykeman and James Stokely in *The New York Times Magazine,* September 16, 1956, p. 76.
5. *Chattanooga Times,* September 6, 1956.
6. *Time,* December 24, 1956, p. 15.
7. *Southern School News,* April 1959, p. 9.
8. *Ibid.,* October 1960, p. 5.

Chapter 8

1. *Washington Evening Star,* September 25, 1956.
2. *Southern School News,* October 1956, p. 6.
3. Muse, *op. cit.,* p. 128.
4. Carl F. Hansen, *Miracle of Social Adjustment* (1957) and *Addendum* (1960) (New York: Anti-Defamation League of B'nai B'rith).
5. *Washington Evening Star,* June 4, 1961.
6. *Southern School News,* January 1963, p. 13.
7. *Interracial Review,* February 1963.
8. *Southern School News,* December 1962, p. 15.
9. *The Washington Post and Times-Herald,* January 9, 1963.
10. *Ibid.,* January 13, 1963.
11. *Ibid.,* January 10, 1963.

Chapter 9

1. *Southern School News,* August 1957, p. 3.
2. *Charlotte Observer,* September 5, 1957.
3. *Southern School News,* February 1957, p. 8.
4. *Ibid.,* March 1957, p. 7.
5. *Atlanta Constitution,* Septemebr 11, 1957.

Chapter 10

1. Brooks Hays, *A Southern Moderate Speaks* (Chapel Hill: University of North Carolina Press, 1959), p. 160.
2. *Race Relations Law Reporter,* Vol. 2 (1957), pp. 931–1934. The texts of all opinions of state and federal courts, as well as the proclamation and executive order of the President, are given in pages 931–1965 of this issue. For convenience numbered references are also made to the October 1957 issue of *Southern School News.*
3. *New York Times,* September 28, 1957.
4. *Southern School News,* October 1957, p. 1.
5. *Id.*
6. *Id.*
7. *Ibid.,* p. 2.
8. *Id.*
9. *Southern School News,* October 1957, p. 2.
10. *Id.*
11. *Id.*
12. *Id.*
13. *Id.*
14. *Ibid.,* p. 3.
15. *Id.*
16. *Id.*
17. *Id.*
18. *Arkansas Gazette,* September 24, 1957.
19. *Chattanooga Times,* October 2, 1957.
20. *Id.*

Chapter 11

1. *Southern School News,* September 1956, p. 8.
2. D. C. Somervell abridgement of Toynbee's *A Study of History,* pp. 315–316.

3. Statement released by Senator Harry F. Byrd, December 18, 1955.
4. Muse, *op. cit.*, p. 42.
5. *Southern School News*, October 1958, p. 3.
6. The texts of the school-board resolution and agreement of lease and the Court's temporary restraining order are given in *Race Relations Law Reporter*, Vol. 3 (1958) pp. 887–93.
7. *Ibid.*, p. 1143.
8. *Ibid.*, p. 855.

Chapter 12

1. Resolution of the American Council of Churches, representing fifteen fundamentalist Protestant groups, Greenville, S.C., May 2, 1958.
2. *Race Relations Law Reporter*, Vol. 3 (1958), p. 283.
3. Report of the Commission on Civil Rights, *Freedom to the Free*, February 12, 1963, p. 169.
4. *New South*, December 1958, p. 9.
5. *Southern School News*, November 1958, p. 5.
6. *Ibid.*, July 1957, p. 4.
7. *Ibid.*, April 1958.
8. *Ibid.*, March 1960.
9. "Are Southern Ministers Failing the South?" *Saturday Evening Post*, May 13, 1961.
10. *Presbyterian Outlook*, October 28, 1957, p. 8.
11. *Richmond Times-Dispatch*, April 8, 1956.
12. *New Leader*, April 23, 1956, p. 15.
13. *Jackson Daily News*, November 15, 1955.
14. *Chattanooga Times*, May 3, 1955.
15. *Columbia State*, March 25, 1956.
16. *Southern School News*, June 1957, p. 6.
17. *Ibid.*, November 1959, p. 8.
18. Anonymous leaflet.

Chapter 13

1. The episode is related in detail in Benjamin Muse's *Virginia's Massive Resistance*.
2. The documentary story of the collapse of "massive resistance" in Virginia, including the texts of pertinent court opinions and the governor's address and legislative enactments, is given in the *Race Relations Law Reporter*, Vol. 3 (1958), pp. 1155–59 and Vol. 4 (1959), pp. 29–78 and 183–93.
3. Virginius Dabney, in *U.S. News and World Report*, January 18, 1960.
4. *Race Relations Law Reporter*, Vol. 4 (1959), p. 301.
5. *Ibid.*, Vol. 8 (1963), p. 94.
6. *Ibid.*, Vol. 4 (1959), p. 553.
7. *Ibid.*, p. 543.

Chapter 14

1. *Richmond Times-Dispatch*, August 22, 1955.
2. *Southern School News*, August 1956, p. 7.
3. *Ibid.*, November 1955. Greene was quoted frequently in the *Southern School News* during the 1955–59 period.

4. *New York Times,* March 2, 1960.

5. In *Bailey v. Patterson, Race Relations Law Reporter,* Vol. 7 (1962), p. 15.

6. Claude Sitton in the *New York Times Magazine,* January 22, 1961, p. 70.

Chapter 15

1. *Southern School News,* October 1959, p. 1; *ibid.,* December 1961, p. 1; *ibid.,* November 1962, p. 6.

2. James Graham Cook, *The Segregationists* (New York: Appleton-Century-Crofts, 1962).

3. *Southern School News,* October 1961, p. 9.

4. Peltason, *op. cit.,* pp. 116–22.

5. *Race Relations Law Reporter,* Vol. 1 (1956), p. 306.

6. United States Commission on Civil Rights, *The New Orleans School Crisis,* p. 34.

7. *Race Relations Law Reporter,* Vol. 5 (1960), p. 655.

8. *Ibid.,* p. 661.

9. *Ibid.,* p. 666.

10. *Ibid.,* p. 1017.

Chapter 16

1. J. Kenneth Morland, *Token Desegregation* (Atlanta: Southern Regional Council; New York: Anti-Defamation League of B'nai B'rith, 1963), pamphlet.

2. *Race Relations Law Reporter,* Vol. 7 (1962), p. 43.

3. *Ibid.,* p. 700.

4. *Ibid.,* p. 669.

5. *Ibid.,* p. 675.

6. Mainly from state-by-state reports in the *Statistical Summary,* November 1962, of the Southern Education Reporting Service, Nashville, Tenn.

7. 1961 United States Commission on Civil Rights Report, *Education,* pp. 99–100.

8. NAACP memorandum, June 1962: "NAACP Public School Desegregation Front in the North and West."

9. *U.S. News and World Report,* July 8, 1963, p. 47.

10. *Race Relations Law Reporter,* Vol. 8 (1963), p. 63.

11. *Ibid.,* Vol. 6 (1961), pp. 90, 418, 700, 968.

12. *Ibid.,* Vol. 7 (1962), p. 361.

13. Attorney General's report to the President, January 24, 1963.

Chapter 17

1. Carleton Putnam, *Race and Reason* (Washington: Public Affairs Press, 1961). For the governor's proclamation and Putnam address, see Citizens' Council magazine, *The Citizen,* November 1961.

2. *Southern School News,* September 1960, p. 14.

3. *Bulletin of the University of Mississippi,* 1961.

4. *Race Relations Law Reporter,* Vol. 7 (1962), pp. 739–65, gives a summary of litigation in the Meredith case and text of pertinent court opinions, acts of the Mississippi legislature, proclamations of the governor, resolutions of the Board of Trustees of State Institutions of Higher Learning, and the President's proclamation and executive order.

Chapter 18
1. *Southern School News,* March 1956, p. 9.
2. *Ibid.,* February 1963, p. 8.
3. *Ibid.,* p. 9.
4. *Race Relations Law Reporter,* Vol. 7 (1962), p. 1019.
5. Howard Zinn, *Albany* (Atlanta: Southern Regional Council, 1962), pamphlet.

Chapter 19
1. *Race Relations Law Reporter,* Vol. 8 (1963), p. 380.
2. *Goss v. Knoxville School Board, Race Relations Law Reporter,* Vol. 8 (1963), p. 377.
3. *Southern School News,* September 1963, p. 2.

INDEX

Aaron, John, 157
Action Patterns in School Desegregation (Phi Delta Kappa), 36
Adams, Sherman, 123–24, 132, 133
Agitators, itinerant, role of in racial disturbances, 43–47, 60, 85, 92–93, 96, 102, 213, 250
Ahmann, Mathew, 272
Alabama, 46, 61, 62, 67, 71, 72, 81, 148, 204, 206, 207, 208, 210, 215, 223, 228, 229, 230–31, 253, 258, 261, 274–78
Alabama Christian Movement for Human Rights, 263
Albany, Ga., 260
Alexandria, Va., 181, 184
Alford, Dale, 159, 193
All in One Lifetime (Byrnes), 22
Allen, Jo Ann, 94
Almond, J. Lindsay, 13, 21, 150, 152, 153, 165, 180–81, 182–84, 185, 186, 189
Al-Shara (Beirut), 135
Alsop, Stewart, 280
American Association of University Women, 179
American Dilemma, An (Myrdal), 12
American Friends Service Committee, 49, 50, 163
American Jewish Committee, 49, 163
Amsterdam News, 19
Anderson County, Tenn., 84, 93
Anniston, Ala., 207
Anti-Defamation League of B'nai B'rith, 34, 46*n*, 49, 163, 172
Arkansas, 23, 24, 25, 27, 46, 275. *See also* Little Rock
Arkansas Gazette, 123
Arlington County, Va., 148, 151, 178, 184, 234
Armed forces, desegregation of, 3, 241
Ashmore, Harry S., 3, 123, 137

"Association for the Advancement of White People," 44
Association of Citizens' Councils. *See* Citizens' Councils of America, Inc.
Athens, Ga., 229
Atlanta, Ga., 84, 157, 211, 214, 216–217, 223, 224, 225, 229
Atlanta Constitution, 17, 216
Atlanta Daily World, 19
Atlanta Journal, 42
Atwell, William H., 215
Austin, Tex., 87

Baker, Russell, 273
Baltimore, Md., 23, 32, 33
Baltimore Sun, 18
Barnett, Ross R., 243–44, 249–55
Bass, Harry, 125
Bass, William A., 117
Baton Rouge, La., 219
Beamer, George N., 238
Bearden, Ark., 84, 85
Beaumont, Tex., 88
Bell v. School City of Gary (Ind.), 237
Besser, Robert, 172
Bethune, Mary McLeod, 20
Big Spring, Tex., 84
Bingham, Leroy W., 237
Birmingham, Ala., 207, 211, 259–65, 276, 277–78, 279
Birmingham News, 263, 277
Birmingham Post-Herald, 17
Birth of a Nation, 41
Black, Hugo, 11, 220
"Black Belt," as stronghold of resistance to integration, 66
Black Monday (Brady), 42, 43, 47, 82, 243
"Black Muslims," 271–72
Blair, Ezell, 204
Blake, Eugene Carson, 272
Blossom, Virgil T., 137, 194